Rudi (and me)
by Carl Hultberg

2013

Preface / Dedication

My field has been recycling. Starting out in the 1980s with my involvement with the New York Greens. But of course I am also Rudi Blesh's grandson, and for years I lived in the grand old apartment at 38 East 4th Street where so much Jazz, Art and Ragtime history took place. So, after Rudi's passing, in my grandfather's honor, I ran the Rudi Blesh Ragtime Society, producing cassettes and later CDs from his records (and others I acquired) for use on various radio shows, music research projects, presentations, and of course given away as gifts. All gifts really, from the wonderful musical legacy I had been handed down.

But I also hid from that family identity and tried to create my own personal narrative, out from the old man's shadow so to speak. After all, it was my grandfather... how great could it really be? You know, the usual family thing. Mostly I took the long way getting here, and it took a long time... but I guess I had to find out the family story for myself, in a tale that now includes me.

I left New York City in 2005 and settled into a wonderful hermit's life of genteel poverty here in New Hampshire. My local job now, in addition to writing poetry, is helping to run the town's transfer station/recycling operation. My partner in ecological non-crime at the dump is longtimer Jim Larkin. After listening to me go on and on about my grandfather for probably about two years he finally laid it down. Why don't you write a book about it?

Rudi always looked out for the downchild. The forgotten people who created the scene but were still somehow left out of the history books. The Bunk Johnsons, the Scott Joplins, Joe Lambs, Buster Keatons... People like Bert Williams, Ben Harney, Eubie Blake, Bertha Chippie Hill, Jacqueline Lamba, Huddie Ledbetter, Montana Taylor, Dan Burley and all his Skiffle Boys. Donald Lambert and Donald Ashwander. Pops Foster and the Baby...

Suddenly I realized my grandfather Rudi was also in danger of being left out of the big story, the history of music and art he did so much to preserve. So here it is. Thank you Rudi for having such a great story and culturally vital existence for me to draw upon and also thank you to Jim Larkin for telling me what to do.

Introduction

Rudi Blesh has been described as America's Historian of the Lively Arts. And certainly the Jazz band concert or dance, Ragtime piano music, the pratfalls of Buster Keaton--even the splashes of paint on the canvases of the Abstract Expressionist painters are all considerably "lively", as in: re-affirming of Life. This Life of ours that constantly needs reaffirming, upending occasionally, even seasonally like a field needs turning. History books that need rewriting, cultural heroes brought back from obscurity to well deserved fame... our myth needs constant retuning to remain true. That which was hidden, those passed over by forces of ambition and greed need to be re-exposed, so our culture can grow on a solid base of common understanding.

We can't afford to get it wrong you know.

But what can we do when we have it wrong? Right the wrongs, bring the unsung originators to light. Give due to the underdog, genius of the species, the true creators forbidden by race or class, or just too sensitive and poetic to promote themselves. This was the role of my grandfather Rudi Blesh. His was a mixture of brash boldness and aesthetic understanding that put him in a unique place to be especially effective in promoting this fullness of American culture. To make waves, change popular opinion, and inevitably along the way make enemies in the hyper-opinionated, super competitive fields of the Art World, Jazz, Ragtime, Film criticism--then to be misunderstood to a certain degree, shunned, be written out of the established histories, even in the fields he pretty much created, and ultimately, be (almost) forgotten.

Knowing the back story, the true myth, that which reinforces our understanding of the actual origins of our lively popular culture is second nature today. Nowadays we all know that Rock and Roll came from the Boogie Woogie/Blues which came from Africa. But at one point not that long ago (1940s) these understandings were underground, the secret knowledge of certain hipster historians who dared to venture outside the parameters of existing academic knowledge. In other words, into the Black community, that great rich source of so much of our USA popular culture. This deep dark secret was like a stain, a blot on the myth of White supremacy, even like a hint of Black blood in the family. You only have to look now at the horror at which a substantial portion of the American population feels at having a "Black" president in the

White House to get a sense of the breach of proprieties potential "Black" origins had for such sacred USA cultural items like "Swing" "Hot" "Jazz" "Boogie Woogie", and before that "Ragtime".

There were some who had always bucked that trend. As early as the 1930s Benny Goodman, Jimmy Rodgers, John Hammond, the pioneering Jazz critics, Black historians like folklorist Zora Neale Thurston, the well known father/son team of John and Alan Lomax were standing up for Black origins and performers in American music. Still, they were the fringe, usually eccentrics supported by a manic obsession, the Smithsonian or their own personal fame or wealth. Not the mainstream by any means.

Later, after the twin 1940s Trad Jazz/Folk Music revivals had played out, the traditionalist mission kept on growing, but it was by then mostly undergound. Pete Seeger pretty much single handedly kept Folk Music alive and Harry Smith, a somewhat deranged alcoholic my father once knew living at the Chelsea Hotel created his hugely influential Anthology of Folk Music on Folkways Records in 1952. After that it was all Beat Group / Skifflers out of England, with their purist approach to the Blues and classic Rock and Roll that led the way into the renaissance that was the 1960s. But of course, by coincidence (or not) that purist approach and even Skiffle itself all seem to have come from none other than Rudi Blesh. As ever, this is the art of cultural self-discovery, often totally unconcious it would seem.

And so what exactly was "Art"? Coming from an aesthetic background in furniture and interior design my grandfather had well defined and long held opinions on styles, periods, elements that enhanced function or were in different ways pleasing to the senses. Likewise in pictorial art and sculpture, well established fields of study and criticism, and then also of course in Music where he had a well developed understanding of the so called "Classical" elements, composers and styles. So when Rudi's interest suddenly returned to the world of Jazz in that second hand record shop in San Francisco in 1935, why shouldn't he have turned his fully developed aesthetic sensibilities onto it's various styles and performers? And why shouldn't he get his young friend Doug MacAgy in 1943 to showcase New Orleans Jazz cornet originator Bunk Johnson at the San Francisco Museum of Art as "Performance Art"? Oh the audacity of it all!

Similarly, Buster Keaton was held in derision by some in Hollywood mostly likely for his allegiance with Fatty Arbuckle, another travesty of justice. And I suppose you could also say the Abstract Expressionists were still the underdogs in 1956 when Rudi wrote <u>Modern Art USA</u>. But of course those (art) clowns mostly all became fabulously wealthy through subsequent corporate sponsorship, big multi-nationals desperately trying to be "hip", formerly the province solely of Negroes, Beatniks and of course Jazz Critics. Ah, the ironies!

Finally of course, Ragtime the original illegitimate child of American Music. Long forgotten by 1949, still for Rudi and Hansi a story untold full of unsung American heroes, Black and White pioneers in their own field of endeavor, struggling to get this incredibly beautiful Afro-American music out of it's disreputable places of origins into the conservatories where it belonged. When Rudi encountered the ghosts of Scott Joplin, Tom Turpin, Louis Chauvin, Ben Harney, Bert Williams... when Rudi and Hansi rediscovered great living Ragtime geniuses Joseph Lamb and Eubie Blake, music history was rewritten for the benefit of all Americans. These once lost underdogs were uncovered and Ragtime music started to be written again. A musical miracle.

And so just as Rudi Blesh wrote about those artistic outsiders on the verge of cultural extinction, that mission he and Hansi had - so it has befallen his poor inept grandson to try to reclaim Rudi's own mostly forgotten legacy from the ashes, the siftings left by the ruthless commercially driven forces of history. Time to try to remember the thousands of things my grandfather said to me when I wasn't listening, preoccupied with my own mostly futile attempts to be successful on my own. Those things Rudi said to me probably knowing that there would be no one else who would ever get around to writing them down, even now thirty years later.

But of course as quick and nimble as he was, Rudi was usually too early with the story everyone wanted to hear. So maybe it is time <u>now</u> after all, for the Rudi Blesh story. Time also hopefully for readers to listen to my own story, intertwined as well.

Time to reaffirm Life. One's ancestors, the people from the people who put us here. Time also perhaps to go against the grain one more time in the best interests of Jazz/Art scholarship. Time to stand in front of the train again I'm afraid. The axe, please...

Table of Contents:

Pre-history

As far as I know Rudolph Pickett Blesh was born in Guthrie, Oklahoma Indian Territory on January 21, 1899. He was the second child of Abraham and Belle Blesh.

Abraham Lincoln Blesh had been born on the day the President was assassinated in 1865. His story goes back to the time when he had been a carpenter working on a big hotel job in Colorado in the 1880s. When the scaffolding collapsed Abe broke most of the bones in his body. While convalescing at a hospital in Chicago he noticed the similarities between carpentry and surgery and decided to become a physician, enrolling at Northwestern University. At this point he met and married Belle Pickett, then a nurse I believe and the family was begun with Rudi's older sister Theo. After gaining his medical degree, Dr. Blesh set up practice in what was then the heart of the Prairie, the wild frontier - the Oklahoma Territory. A period photograph shows his medical business in Guthrie before the turn of the century on a dirt street with a plank sidewalk and hitching posts out front for the horses. A sign points to the second floor showing where the doctor's office was - above the apothecary that was run by his father in law.

Belle's story is also interesting. Her family had originally been from Pennsylvania but I believe she was raised in Kansas. It appears that at some point her mother sought and gained a divorce from her husband William, Belle's father on the grounds of mistreatment, probably before Abe, Belle and father Bill moved to the Territory. This would have been highly unusual in the 19th Century, even impossible in some states. Still, it was a sign of a definite hard independent streak in that side of the family. Also interesting is the fact that daughter Belle seems to have chosen to live take her father with them, not her mother. Rudi told me when I was a kid that he was descended from General George Pickett on his mother's side, but geneological research done by my mother and the curt reply I got from the Pickett Society in Virginia seems to have disproved this. Rudi wasn't one to exaggerate, so I'd put this story up to his maternal grandfather the druggist Bill Pickett (the one who was sued for divorce).

Rudi told me the first thing he remembered hearing his father saying about him was: "Looks like we'll have to break him", as in breaking a horse. It seems that Rudi was prone to tantrums as an infant when he didn't get his way. His technique was to bang his forehead on the floor. That independent streak again. Attending elementary school in Guthrie Rudi told his class another family story that proved to not be true. This time it was the legend that his father's grandfather in Switzerland had invented ice cream by rolling a strawberry down a snowy mountain slope. My mother's research has uncovered photos of Rudi's Swiss grand-parents, the Bloesch's, elfin folks with ears that resemble his. Rudi did well in school as a youngster, making the finals in the state spelling bee championship. My grandfather told me he threw the contest to his girl competitor because she was so pretty. Sounds like Rudi.

Growing up in the "Territo" must have been amazing. This was the real Wild West. Oklahoma had been promised to the Indians, in perpetuity, in particular to the Cherokee Nation that had been forceably moved from their original Smokey Mountain holdings before the Civil War. Like many others, this proved to be a shallow promise as White settlers put on pressure to push the Native Americans out once more. In 1889 the US Government staged a land race to set up claims with the "legal" settlers waiting on the Kansas border until dawn to rush in and stake out land. To their surprise they found that other White folks had snuck in the night before to take the best holdings. So today they call Oklahoma "The Sooner State" to celebrate the people who cheated the people who were cheating the Indians. That's called heritage.

The folks who didn't cheat, or perhaps just the people who promoted the original land grab were known as "the Boomers". And boom Oklahoma did. They say the new towns of Guthrie and Oklahoma City where Dr. Blesh had his practice sprang up overnight. Literally from zero to ten thousand inhabitants in a single day. Not sure if Dr. Blesh was a Boomer in the sense that he favored the annexation of Indian territory to begin with, but he and Belle were definitely Boomers coming in with the rest of the crowd during the big land rush in 1889. Just a physician out to make a name for himself in the new territory.

This was Western history and Rudi got to experience a lot of it first hand. Once when the family lived in Guthrie, Rudi said he'd been forced to hide under the family porch when a shoot out occurred after a jail break. One of Rudi's first jobs in Guthrie was delivering by bicycle big balls of opium carefully wrapped in newspaper from his grandfather's apothocary to the local houses of ill repute. Outside Rudi's elementary school the Mexican hot tamale stand also sold reefers for small change. It was 1910 and

2

Coca Cola still packed the punch of pure cocaine. Rudi said on the Fourth of July the Oklahomans dug a mile long trench, filled it with gasoline and lit it. That's America. California was a far off place with a fantastic reputation. Once a relative sent back a souvenir to the Blesh family, a head of lettuce. Not knowing what it was or what to do with it, Rudi said they grated it and ate it with cream and sugar like a breakfast cereal. What else would you do with an unknown substance? Another time Rudi's father took him to a county fair where they had a poor pathetic Native American folded up in a dog cage hung with a sign: "Bad Indian". Abe instructed: "That is man's inhumanity to man, son."

Doctor Blesh started in Guthrie and then in 1907, moved his practice to Oklahoma City. Rudi said his father administered medicine to Whites, Blacks, Indians and Mexicans alike. Once when on his rounds out in the prairie the doctor's buckboard was caught in a freak storm that dumped a few feet of snow. Unable to do anything else, Abe killed his horse, gutted it and climbed into the carcass as the snow piled up. When he awoke the doctor found he was sharing his shelter with dozens of sleeping rattlesnakes. All in a day's work.

Rudi's dad may have been open minded about the folks he helped heal, and another time outraged at the treatment of a fellow human being even if he was an "Indian", but in other ways Abe was probably more conventional in his attitudes. Rudi said that his father's comment on seeing a Black person with red hair was classic: "must have been a rabbi in the woodpile"... Funny? Perhaps, but not particularly politically correct maybe not even at the time. There were also Black people living within the Blesh household, Auntie and Uncle Dave, freed slaves. She helped keep the house and Dave took care of Dr. Blesh's fast horses, the ambulance of the day. Only played church music, though.

In 1910 Rudi experienced a culture shock that surely affected him his whole life. His father took the family with him while he studied surgery with Doktor Adolf Lorenz in Vienna, Austria. They spent the next two years there, with Rudi and his sister Theo attending the local German language school. Rudi said his Austrian classmates were somehow convinced he was from Japan. Oklahoma was surely somewhere near Yokohama. He also said at lunch time the girls would come out and pee in the gutter. The things a twelve year old might notice. While at the Lorenz's family house outside the city Rudi played with their young son

Konrad who grew up to be a world famous zoolologist and writer. Of course they played cowboys and indians, just like in Oklahoma.

Vienna during its golden age couldn't have been more different than Guthrie, another extreme. From subsistance and rugged individualism to the height of artistic decadence. (Though Rudi said there was Ragtime in Vienna as well.) In the evenings Rudi got to chaparone his older sister Theo, the violin pupil to classical concerts. He said as a ten year old he stood through the entire production of Wagner's Ring Cycle for a Crown (20 cents). Rudi also took an interest in collecting stamps, and autographs, and so with his father's help was able to get many valuable distinguished signatures. From Classical Music composers like Gustav Mahler, for example and opera stars. Also Marconi - the inventor of the radio and Louis Bleriot - the man who had just flown solo across the English Channel in an early monoplane. Celebrities.

Back in the US when he turned twelve, Rudi was given a gun by his dad, a 22 caliber rifle, for his birthday. My grandfather told me the first thing he did was to go out and shoot a little bird, upon the sight of which he burst into tears and threw the rifle away. He then went on to create a pet cemetery with his friends, hand painting wooden markers and performing funerals for cats, birds, dogs, rabbits, guinea pigs, etc.. His father must have been wondering what kind of kid Rudi was. An early animal activist?

Rudi's mother was strict. But even so her oldest son got into trouble. One day she caught him singing an off color song: "How long will eight inches of Snow last in May...", these being the names of the two stage characters. "Oh you've been to the Lyric Theatre" Belle surmised, twisting him by the ear. Another time she heard an invective that followed a minor mishap. "What was that I heard you say?" "I GOT DOWN those stairs, Mom..." Before dinner time Mrs. Blesh would often ask her son Rudolph to go out into the yard in Guthrie and get her a roasting hen. Rudi told me he would do it, but that he couldn't bring himself to wring their necks, he left that for mom to do right before she chopped off their heads. "That's the Way To Spell C-H-I-C-K-E-N," as the old "coon" song goes. Rudi revered his mother Belle.

"My mother had been a music teacher, but she also loved to paint. She had dual talents in painting and music, and also was a great lover of poetry and, a habitual joiner of the types of women's clubs they had in those days." (John Hasse interviews - 1978)

4

Rudi played the cello throughout his childhood, all the Blesh kids had to learn an instrument. He told John Hasse he realized later that it corresponded to the trombone in Jazz - one of his favorite instruments. He also told Hasse he heard Ragtime as a child and was even involved in some sort of Minstrel type production at the Guthrie Opry House, as the pesky kid (who stuttered) in the midst of a production of (Coon Song) Rufus Rastus Johnson Brown.

"You couldn't be brought up in Oklahoma without trains coming through and the tramps sitting on them singing White and Black country music that was all around --- cowboy music." (ibid)

Rudi got his first real job at a local Oklahoma City department store when he was about thirteen, after a period of volunteering to open the door for ladies for tips as a child. He graduated to stockboy then to the window dressing department where he developed his fine calligraphy manufacturing hand made price signs in different styles. He once got in trouble for hanging a prominent sign in the window advertising "Ladies' Dresses Half Off!" for a laugh. At age 15 Rudi got his first car, a model T. A picture from the time shows him in a snappy suit leaning on the fender, one lucky American teen living the dream in 1914.

At high school Rudi seems to have been particularly fortunate to have had one teacher who really inspired him in the field of Art. It seems hard to believe now, but way out in wild and wooly Oklahoma there was actually a lady educator who was following (and teaching about) the still developing world of European Impressionism, the Fauves, the beginnings of early Modern Art. Of course Rudi was her star pupil.

When it came time to go to college Rudi lucked out being too young for the first military draft in 1917. If he'd been just a little older, our story might be ending right about now. Instead of going to war - after a discussion with a local football star Rudi opted to attend Dartmouth College, somewhere back East in a state called New Hampshire. Dartmouth had been a school set up in the eighteenth century to help educate the Indians, and there are still grants and scholarships for Native Americans to attend.

Rudi had Indian friends, but I doubt that had any bearing on my grandfather's decision. I once thought that Rudi might have had some native blood, specifically through his mother, back when I still believed she was George Pickett's niece. General George is best known for losing the Civil War for the South at Gettysburg, but before the war he'd been operating out in the US Northwest Territories as a US Army officer, perhaps covertly trying to create a war with Britain over San Juan Island as a (Southern) secret agent. The theory being that if the US was at war with England, England would side with the South in a secession. My romantic theory was that Rudi's mother Belle was descended from an early marriage Pickett had been involved in at that time with an "Indian Princess" (probably a slave girl). Adding this to the fact that Abraham Blesh had chosen the Oklahoma Indian Territory to start his practice and the fact that Rudi decided on Dartmouth, I figured there had to be a thread. Unstated of course, since there was no honor attached to being Native at that time. Anyway, to put it to rest, none of the above seems to be true. I now believe that Rudi Blesh was not even remotely an Indian.

At Dartmouth Rudi seems to have fit right in. Even though he was a Literature major and Art was not really on the curriculuum at that time, Rudi appears to have set himself up as the class artist, creating the kind of John Held Jr. style bobbin head cartoons for the school paper that would later become so popular in the 1920s. Dartmouth had some things going on. For one thing, snow and the brand new American sport of skiing. It was actually a Dartmouth undergrad, an exchange student from Scandanavia who'd been the first to introduced skiing to the USA a few years earlier, going to a local Hanover New Hampshire barrel maker to have a set of skis made custom. So in 1918 it wasn't uncommon to see Dartmouth guys risking their lives out "ski-yorring" - getting pulled by draft horses mostly out of control around the tree lined campus. I can assure you Rudi was not one of them. Rudi also told me the chambermaids in the dormitories doubled in much older trades. How convenient.

Rudi was well known on campus for his growing collection of "Jass" recordings, 78s of the earliest young (White) bands just starting to come out of New Orleans at that time. This frenetic frantic music was like anarchist Ragtime, a blast, a real teenage rebellion. Oddly enough, Rudi first heard this wonderful music (the "Original Dixieland One Step") in a record store in Franklin, New Hampshire. Go figure. As Rudi told John Hasse:

"We went into this record store and the guy said, 'Have you heard this?' … It struck everybody as something new under the sun. …it made Ragtime seem old fashioned."

That year (1917) Rudi organized a trip to New York City for him and a few of his Dartmouth buddies to see the band that recorded the "Original Dixieland One Step" - The Original Dixieland Jazz Band at Reisenweber's supper club on Columbus Circle (59th Street). The ODJB were hardly older than the Dartmouth kids, but at this point they basically had the world at their feet. The Beatles in other words. Experiencing the Original Dixieland Jazz Band live first hand was an experience that would have lasting repercussions for the young Rudi Blesh. There were other repercussions on the trip home. Getting off the train in Tilton, New Hampshire, the boys decided to take in a local bar. No one seems to remember who said what about or to some local guy's girlfriend but the upshot of it all was that the Dartmouth boys spent the night in the Tilton jail before heading back up to Hanover the next day. That demon Jazz!

Oddly enough, the route they would have take from Tilton to Andover, through Potter Place up to Hanover was the same as young Daniel Webster would have walked going from his home in neighboring Franklin to attend Dartmouth in the early 1800s. Franklin was where Rudi and his Dartmouth buddies bought their first Jazz records. Again oddly enough, this journey would have taken both Rudi and Daniel Webster right by the place where I presently live in Danbury, New Hampshire and right through the town where my mother (Rudi's daughter) presently lives in Lebanon, NH. Some places just seem to resonate.

During his Junior year at Dartmouth, something momentous happened to Rudi. His parents separated with his mother filing for divorce two years later. A family tradition it would seem. At the time though it was still highly unusual for women to stand up for their rights and make moves to dissolve their marriages. Rudi was shattered and he rushed home to be with his mother.

It seems Abe had always had a thing about nurses (hadn't Belle been one?). Belle had warned him and as Rudi said: "denied him the bedroom", which of course only made things worse. Dr. Blesh left the family on a bitter note, never really seeing his kids again. In a document I uncovered it was stated specifically that they were to receive exactly one dollar from his estate. Probably a legal move, but still a cold gesture. Dr. Blesh went on to found the

Southwest Medical Conference and become one of the nation's leading brain surgeons and pediatric specialists. Rudi told me his dad once had one of the richest men in Oklahoma City on the operating table with a ruptured organ: "So tell me Mr. So and So, before I start to operate to save your life how much you are going to donate to the children's hospital that will be named in your honor?" Rudi said his father was no fan of modern medicine, calling the doctor's pledge: "the Hypocritic Oath". Abe Blesh's philosophy can perhaps best be defined by the adage he passed down to his son: "As the Old Indian once said: It goes along like that for a while ...then it gets worse." A pioneer in modern medicine who now leaves the story.

Back in Oklahoma Rudi returned to work at the local department store. His mother took in roomers, a familiar practice back then to make ends meet. One of these young men who stayed with the family was named Chester Gould, later well known as the creator of the comic strip Dick Tracy. Rudi said at the time however (1919) it was Rudi who was the cartoonist and young Gould was the far better horseshoe player. Years later (1966) when Rudi was about to go on The Today Show he thought he recognised one of the fellow interviewees. "Say you look familiar..." Chet Gould.

Rudi and his younger brother Kelly took a summer job in 1920 that required them to do some dredging work with a small boat on a local canal. Rudi told me there was an accident while they were handling equipment and Kelly had been gravely injured, so badly that Rudi's little brother died as a result of those injuries a few years later. I know my grandfather blamed himself for whatever happened. After the departure of his father, this - yet another family tragedy. These first entries onto the pages in one person's secret diary of disaster, what would someday grow into my grandfather's legacy of not only empathy for others, but also personal sadness and inevitably a predisposition for depression. This heaviness, a counterbalance perhaps to Rudi's unstoppable aesthetic enthusiasm - certainly contributed in the long run to Rudi having an open imagination, a prediliction for the Blues and a receptivity to all forms of art from the downtrodden.

But the twenty one year old Rudi could have had no way of knowing all this then. Still grieving for his injured brother, my grandfather's biggest hope at that point was to find a way to return to school somewhere to finish his college studies.

The Designer

In 1922 Belle made an important life decision, relocating as a single mother to Berkeley, California. Rudi, Kelly, Theo of course went along, and my grandfather enrolled at the University of California where he earned a degree (with honors) in design and architecture, two subjects that hadn't been offered at Dartmouth College at that time. (Despite having dropped out, Dartmouth has long kept Rudi in their Alumni listings, a fine gesture).

So just as the 1920s were getting going young Rudolph Pickett Blesh, hot out of design school and living with his mother in a fashionable California neighborhood, with his hundreds of hard to find Jazz records was ready to face the future. Vo dee oh doe! It must have been a solid swinging time to be young talented and artistically hip. Following European Modern Art trends, studying Oriental design, subversive Mexican muralists. Rudi told me he and his friends read F. Scott Fitzgerald's novels "as they came out." The social narrative behind the Jazz. Another author Rudi was very much influenced by was George Santayana, especially his essay on Aesthetics. Also: silent movie absurdism, Charlie Chaplin, Buster Keaton, Harold Lloyd. And a novel: Green Mansions, A Romance of the Tropics by William Henry Hudson about a woman from a mythical former race in South America.

But suddenly in 1923 there was the Berkeley fire. Rudi said there was no fire in their neighborhood and that he was out with his mother in the yard gathering up the laundry so that ashes from the distant fires wouldn't soil them when their house erupted into flames. They lost everything, including the autograph collection and all of Rudi's records, everything except for the clothes they had just taken off the line. Ironically this burn out would spell the end of (Hot) Jazz in my grandfather's life for about twelve years.

As a young architect in the San Francisco area Rudi had taken what work that came his way. Not finding work as a draftsman he went to work in a design house in Sacramento for a while until he broke out on his own doing period design work and with the help of local craftsmen made fine reproductions of antique furniture. He also did important design work for the on going gallery scene at the then still preserved San Francisco Palace of Fine Arts, a remnant (from 1915) of one of the great world Arts expositions that had once brought with them so much new culture.

In 1925 Rudi got married, to a kind of - what they used to call - flapper girl named Editha Tuttle. By his own admission the marriage was rocky, Rudi said they moved constantly, his wife being unsatisfied with any location: Sausalito, Marin County. Sounds pretty nice to me, especially back in the 1920s. But no. One good thing did come out of the marriage however, my future mother Hilary was born in 1929. Actually Editha Hilary, for her mother had named her after herself. After the couple brought the baby home the man who ran the Chinese laundry downstairs asked Rudi if it was a boy. When Rudi said no, the neighbor replied, "Go tell your wife to go back and bring you a boy".

In Berkeley Rudi's mother Belle was written up in the local papers for her amazing flower garden. Asked the secret of her success she replied simply that she talked to the plants. This was the period when people like Luther Burbank and Paramahansa Yogananda were having some widespread West Coast influence, hybrid seeds of what California culture was to become.

At some point my grandfather was involved in a dispute with the City of San Francisco regarding the operation of their trolley cars. Seems Rudi's car was hit by one of them and his claim was that they were speeding. Not satisfied with the original ruling against his case, Rudi used cameras and time motion recording equipment to prove the trolleys were going faster than they claimed and got a settlement in a higher court. Don't mess.

Rudi also appeared in some local advertising at that time as a model for a photographer friend, beginning to put himself in the public eye. In addition to furniture design, Rudi was fast moving up in the San Francisco Art scene. In 1928 he suddenly had an option to buy into the city's most prestigious design house and gallery, the Vicery Atkins and Torrey salon. This is where Mexican muralist Diego Rivera had his first US showing. It was also the gallery of the famous American Art photographer Edward Weston at one point. Rudi remembered a young Ansel Adams there as well, but only as a character who played the piano with an orange. Rudi knew asking his mother for a loan to buy into the gallery would mean mortgaging her home but by then it was 1929 and things were going great guns. What could possibly go wrong?

After the crash, Rudi came sailing downward. A friend stopped him on the street and asked what he was doing. Selling toilet paper dispensors to businesses was Rudi's reply. The friend then suggested that Rudi get in touch with the folks at Gumps, then and still today San Francisco's premiere importers of antiquities and fine collectables from Asia - items made of jade, bronze and fine silk. They hired Rudi on the spot putting him to work redesigning their entire store using his own notions and modern interpretations of Chinese/Japanese style. The original establishment was probably a gorgeous Art Nouveau but Rudi took on the job, working out with up to date materials and exotic lush Orientalist themes, creating a beautiful place to shop in the early 1930s. On visits with her father my mother remembers being considered almost part of the Gump family at that point.

In her own account, my mom grew up wild in the streets of San Francisco. One story has her as the lookout for a local gang. No one at home? She remembers being on a class field trip the day in 1937 when the San Francisco Bay Bridge was opened. A photo shows Rudi out on the bridge the same day lighting a cigarette celebrating with his friends. It seems already he and his daughter were inhabiting separate worlds. Rudi was involved with his art and design career and Editha seems to have been one of the original hippies, always looking for something new. By 1938 the couple had divorced and Editha, then with custody of young Hilary was getting more and more off the wall. They lived a dreary transient existence going from rooming house to rooming house. Twice Editha sent my mother to summer camp and forgot to pick her up. She tried to coerce her into becoming a nudist. At some point my mother left (ran away?) and went to live with maternal relatives. A picture at the time shows her leaning over a rake, an agricultural worker? Rudi may have thought the Editha was holding it down, but the truth of the matter is that in the breakup of this marriage, the real victim was my mother Hilary.

In 1938 Japan invaded China and suddenly it looked like Gump's whole international import business was through. It was Rudi who gave the firm the idea of sending him down to Mexico to purchase antiquities and manufacture copies for sale. So Rudi got to spend the last years of the depression and the beginning of World War II in Mexico City having a ball with a few friends. And as it had been at Dartmouth, the cleaning girls did double duty. I don't know what contact if any my grandfather had with the members of the art elite in and out of Mexico at that time: Diego Rivera, Frida Kahlo, Tina Modotti, etc. perhaps none. I vaguely remember a story of Rudi or perhaps it was my uncle Paul Hultberg (later) going to visit Ms. Kahlo at her father's house that was all brightly painted, but of course she wasn't there. I do remember hearing one story from Rudi about the Mexico adventure, about the cab drivers. Asked why they always sped up when they got to crowded intersections, the cabbie replied: "Of course I go faster there Senor, it's much more dangerous!"

Back in San Francisco in 1941 Rudi returned to work at Gumps, and also as an interiorist and a furniture designer, by now having switched from antiques reproduction to "Modern" design. Among his commissions was a small pocket library with an stainless steel sliding ladder for a millionaire. Another fancy apartment was furnished in chrome, glass and leather (all new materials at the time) with a view of the newly built Bay Bridge for the mistress of a big time local gangster. His modern designs for furniture and interiors were featured in at least one national design magazine.

From Interiors August 1942:

"Rudi Blesh, native of Oklahoma, disliked the way in which modern designers were 'catalogued,' but he was clearly one of the Californians."

From Interiors September 1942:

"Rudi Blesh is one of the leaders of the California group, and despite the fact that his professional name sounds very Bauhaus indeed, he is as American as corn pudding..."

"If the oriental influence that is becoming a hallmark of California modernism seems a little overstressed in Mr. Blesh's work, that is perfectly all right with his present employer [Gumps]."

"Mr. Blesh has a private phobia about the word 'modern.'

'Catalog minds have been at work on it, and it is now as honeycombed with categories as period design is. Let's just do our designing with reference only to practical and aesthetic requirements and call it nothing.'"

Still, it seemed that the life of a successful designer, even in sunny California, had it's limitations. By the early 1940s my grandfather was starting to branch out into other fields.

The Jazz Critic

For starters, by 1942 Rudi was becoming a radio personality in San Francisco. He told me that one of the reasons he went on the air was to cure his tendency to stutter. One of his interviews was with an U.S. Navy submarine captain on leave at that point during the war. While asking the naval officer about water use on the subs and the fact that the men on board were allowed to grow beards, Rudi was challenged to grow one himself. And this is exactly what my grandfather did, sprouting his trademark goatee, and probably influencing generations of beatniks in the process.

In 1935 Rudi had also begun to rekindled his interest in Hot Jazz, dormant since he'd lost his record collection in the ashes of the Berkeley fire. Just as it had been in Franklin, New Hampshire back in the teens, the record that caught his ear in a San Francisco second hand shop and got things going again was the "Original Dixieland One Step". Price of re-admission: the usual 25 cents.

The hot local Trad unit in San Francisco in the early 1940s was Lou Watters and the Yerba Buena Jazz Band, performing nightly at the Dawn Club on Annie Street. These (White) cats, including ace trombonist Turk Murphy were the real thing, according to emerging amateur Jazz Critic Rudi Blesh. In addition, during intermissions, Lu Watters' piano player, Wally Rose would come out and play old Ragtime standards unheard since before the First World War. Seeds for future developments for sure.

It may sound strange that San Francisco would be a hotbed of Jazz but by some theories Jazz may have even originated there independently, concurrent with the New Orleans pioneers. The word "Jazz" was first recorded in the San Francisco press, used originally to describe sports stars around the turn of the century. At the 1893 Chicago World's Fair Ragtimers had been astounded to see Little Egypt perform. As much as it was her scantily clad belly dance it was also the Egyptian musicians who accompanied her to great effect. The freedom in their playing, the wild bent notes, trancelike improvisational element, the soulful wailing. Riffs. This type of show was recreated at the 1915 San Francisco Exposition and had a huge effect on certain local musicians, leading to the release of On the Streets of Cairo and Cairo, the first recordings by the Art Hickman Orchestra in 1919. It's easy to see: Ragtime + Middle Eastern Music = Jazz. Klezmer is really the same sort of thing, some kind of Jewish first cousin. This of course is another theory, more recent and certainly not Rudi's.

As the originating Jazz Critic in the city of San Francisco Rudi was in a position to have great influence. For one, with his friend Douglas MacAgy, he was the first to bring a Jazz band into the San Francisco Museum, as ...Fine Art! That's Art with a capital A. David Beasley, in his book <u>Douglas MacAgy and the Foundations of Modern Art Curatorship</u> claims that "Performance Art" really started then in 1943 with these Jazz shows, and with the circus performers brought in for an earlier Alexander Calder show of mobiles. If that is so, it was all downhill from there. Starting inspiration for both shows would have been Rudi's good friend Clay Spohn, an early San Francisco abstract expressionist free spirit known for collecting "found objects" for his "Museum of Unknown and Little Known Objects. Big influence all around. For Rudi it began with a series of lectures at the San Francisco Museum in 1943 and a pamphlet entitled: "This is Jazz". The first lecture drew 75 people, the second, 750. Rudi played records on stage and had folks clip cash contributions to their programs to raise money to bring Jazz man Bunk Johnson to San Francisco.

The wave was starting.

By now Rudi had become the first Jazz Critic at the San Francisco Chronicle. Also in that year (1943) my grandfather did what can be considered his first nationally recognized Jazz accomplishment, bringing the elder Bunk Johnson, Louis Armstrong's trumpet teacher to San Francisco in conjunction with New Orleans Jazz fan Bill Russell. Although Bunk, long in retirement, needed new teeth and a little time to redevelop his embouchure, the shows at the museum and the concerts that ensued in San Francisco were a big deal, even being broadcast to the troops overseas, a precursor of things to come. The Trad Jazz Revival starts here in San Francisco with Rudi emerging as it's champion.

from "This is Jazz" (1943):

"We have defined Hot Jazz as a music of the American Negroes, going back to African origins, with rhythmic, melodic, tonal, and harmonic characteristics racial and unique in character. Developing in the South and particularly in New Orleans, from and with the *true* (not the *concert*) spirituals, the work songs, hollers, stomps and the blues, it came to involve use of European instruments, brass band instrumentation, and some European musical elements chiefly band marching tunes and French dance music, especially the Quadrille. To what slight extent Spanish and West Indian rhythmic and musical elements entered in would be difficult to say. Ragtime piano music--also originally an American Negro music--entered in. The music resulting was the original Hot Jazz."

All in all 1943 was a big year for Rudi. For one, he fell in love.

Rudi had remarried in 1939 to a woman named Barbara, but that was a somewhat mysterious and short lived relationship. He told me she had connections through her family with organized crime syndicates and that once they had attended a party at a fancy restaurant in Chicago where there were naked girls swimming in big aquariums. A period picture shows the couple at a restaurant (a different one, no nude swimmers), looking miserable.

Not so with his new relationship. Rudi met Harriet Janis through his friend Douglas MacAgy in San Francisco while she was on the West Coast chaperoning her son Conrad, a teenage film star in Hollywood. A stage mother in other words. But of course there was more. A woman of exquisite artistic taste and boundless personal energy, she fell for Rudi as he was peaking on his own artistic curve (Fine Art + Hot Jazz). Soulmates it would seem. But of course there was more. She was also Sidney Janis's wife.

Over the years I heard things, though certainly not from Rudi, about Sidney Janis. That he'd been a New York clothing retailer manufacturer who'd invented the two pocket short sleeve shirt and made a fortune. And perhaps it was Sidney's financial success and his wife's wonderful aesthetic sense, together - that created the Sidney Janis Gallery in New York City in the early 1940s. There they followed in the footsteps of Peggy Guggenheim and a few others to present what was becoming Modern Art in the USA. Another Sidney Janis tale has him in rural New York State, first purchasing pictures from Primitivist painter Grandma Moses at a yard sale in the early 1940s. In the story Sidney challenges the aged artist about the price on one of her paintings. Her reply: "A dollar fifty is too much?" "Make it a dollar" was his alleged answer. (He'd thought the price was $150.) Yet another story has Grandma missing from the family dinner. Going out into the barn the family finds her sawing one of her paintings in two because she'd promised her "New York dealer" ten and she only had nine.

The wisdom of Solomon. I don't know how much creedence to give these type of stories no doubt tinged with anti-semitic envy. Still I would guess that in this marriage, to a certain degree, Sidney was the money and Harriet, or Hansi as she was known was the taste. The books that came out under Sidney Janis's name, They Taught Themselves (1942) about the Primitives and Surrealist and Abstract Art in America (1944) may very well have been written by Harriet Janis and left uncredited. It must have been tremendously exciting for Hansi to be with Rudi, her artistic equal, who was more than willing to give Hansi her due for her contributions to anything they might create together.

As if all this wasn't enough, in 1943 an old friend of Alfred Frankenstein, Rudi's boss at the San Francisco Chronicle, suddenly showed up wanting to get educated about Jazz. That would have been Virgil Thompson, really America's top music critic at that time. As hard as it might be to imagine now, old time Traditional Hot Jazz (as opposed to schmaltzy Swing Bands) and even the Blues were virtually unknown entities, even to the music experts back in the early 1940s. Thompson was blown away by Bunk Johnson, who was still playing around San Francisco, and also by Rudi's records and enthusiasm. Virgil Thompson then went back to New York City and wrote a rave article about the San Francisco Hot Jazz scene for the New York Herald Tribune.

He also invited Rudi to come to New York and bring his records.

This was fateful stuff. I'm not sure what records Rudi brought with him to New York (Bunk, Bessie, Jelly, ODJB?), but at the ensuing listening session at the Chelsea Hotel among those in attendance were Avant Garde composer Edgar Varese and Herbert Weinstock, music editor for the Alfred Knopf publishing house, as well as Virgil Thompson, music editor of the New York Herald Tribune. Things must have gone well because at the end of the evening Rudi Blesh had a contract to write a book and after that was done, a promise of a new job as the first Jazz Critic at the Herald Tribune. A new life in other words.

But first he had the book to write. As big as Jazz is now it's hard to imagine that in the 1940s most people thought Swing was Jazz and that was it. The idea that Jazz was a music that evolved out of Field Hollers, Spirituals, French Quadrilles, Marching Band Music, Ragtime, Country Blues was mostly unknown. The idea that popular syncopated music in America had it's origins in

16

Africa back then was still a serious affront to the mainstream dominant White culture. So you see there was much that had to be written - and a bit of an axe to grind as well. Grrr....

Mainstream Jazz at that point (1943) meant commercialized Swing bands, huge mechanized units playing sometimes exciting but often blandly similar sounding, highly arranged show pieces for dancers, borrowing riffs and ideas from the much more vital, much more exciting, much more Black small combo Traditional Jazz. Guess which style Rudi favored? Blues and even much of Country and Western Music were all considered to be part of Jazz at that point, basically inferior types of rural Folk music played by uneducated musicians for hicks. Then as now, people were confused about Popular Music. "But I thought this was Jazz..." "Not so," Rudi instructed in the 1943 pamphlet from his San Francisco lecture series: "This is Jazz".

Hot on the trail of the Jazz story in 1943/1944 Rudi (and Hansi) traveled to Louisiana and Chicago and back to NYC to interview key figures still alive from the development of early Jazz. The Keppard brothers in New Orleans, Lil Hardin Armstrong, Louis' first wife (and main motivator) in Chicago, Lovey Austin, Kenneth Lloyd Bright in Harlem and others. Hansi took pictures of the old places like Preservation Hall where the music had started. Then it was off to the Library of Congress where Rudi was fortunate enough to meet someone who sent him back to Chicago to discuss the origins of Jazz with Melville Herscovitts, one of the most preeminent anthropologists of the day. Dr. Hershovitts had never heard real Jazz and Rudi had never heard authentic West African drum music. To say there were similarities would seem obvious now but at the time it was a revelation.

When it was finished, Rudi's book: Shining Trumpets held up an uncompromising position for Jazz, advocating for a "socialization of music" to prevent commercial forces from debasing the sacred Folk elements ad infinitum. Radical stuff.

All kinds of good ideas went into Shining Trumpets. The journey of Jazz from Africa to the American South was sourced from the excellent research done with Hershovitts and others. The story of Jazz through New Orleans up to Chicago was well documented, mostly from the sources--the originals. Then there was this Swing thing, the commercialized mostly White Pop music that Rudi truly hated. And it showed. The axe.

In Rudi's mind perhaps the spectre of Frederick Ramsey loomed large. The American author had created his book, JAZZMEN with Charles Edward Smith in collaboration with other emerging Jazz critics in 1938 and already it was developing into the original USA book (Bible) of Jazz. Rudi's much autographed copy bought new was worn from constant study. Still, most Jazz critics from this period were from Europe. From Belgium came Robert Goffin fleeing the Nazis. Goffin was a trial lawyer but he'd written and published Jazz poetry since the 1920s. His Jazz From the Congo to the Metropolitan (1942) forwarded the theory that Jazz was a combination of French musical forms and African rhythms. From France, Charles Delaunay with his Hot Jazz Discography was also extremely influential in Hot Jazz circles at that time. Rudi's French language copy is copyright 1938. The same only more so for The Real Jazz (1942) by Hugues Panassie and earlier in French, Panassie's Le Jazz Hot (1934). In The Real Jazz (edited by C. E. Smith), and especially in Delaunay's Discography and world, Swing was not tolerated. It simply was not Jazz.

from The Real Jazz by Hugues Panassie:

"But there have never been any large white orchestras comparable to these Negro groups. The oldest, like those of Jean Goldkette and Ben Pollack, had several good soloists but turned towards commercial executions rather than real jazz.

However since 1935 and especially 1936, with the arrival of the 'swing fad' a number of white orchestras have grown up. These groups have freed themselves to a great extent from commercial concessions. The principal are Benny Goodman's, Tommy Dorsey's, Bob Crosby's and Artie Shaw's. These orchestras play with a good sense of ensemble work; they are polished and precise, and in fact hold to a minute exactness. But they have never had the *abandon* of the Negro orchestras. Consequently they play with a stiffness which prevents them from swinging. Moreover the majority of their soloists are not suffieciently fine musicians. Ironically enough practically all their arrangements are written by Negroes."

Rudi picked up on this and tried to take it even further, chewing out everything and everyone associated with Swing, even legitimate geniuses like Duke Ellington and Billie Holiday. Whatever points Rudi Blesh scored in Shining Trumpets with the

18

hardcore Jazz snob set were lost on the general public trying to wade throught the polemics. Brilliant in parts and difficult, opinionated and divisive in others, at least <u>Shining Trumpets</u> was done. Now he could get on with the rest of his new life.

from <u>Shining Trumpets</u> (1946):

"Music is the most highly developed and universally practiced of the arts in West African culture. On the plastic side, this culture produced the superb wood sculptures of Gabon and the bronze ones of Benin, work that, early in this century, decisively altered the course of European painting and sculpture, and provided space concepts utilized in modern architecture. The music, as it survived and developed in Afro-American music, is exerting an equal effect upon our composers. Particularly in Jazz, it has developed into an art of prime importance in itself, unassailable as a whole into our music."

"Buddy Bolden's Ragtime Band of 1893, generally considered the first jazz band, undoubtedly represents the transition from the archaic street jazz to a more developed, classic stage. Bolden's was well developed technically and had a much wider reperatory than march tunes..."

Then quoting New Orleans informant Wallace Collins: "Bolden, he says was the first to bring the rags in band form, and the blues as well. These were two revolutionary advances from archaic jazz.

To 'rag' a tune, Collins says, 'He'd take one note and put two or three to it. He began to teach them -- not by the music -- just by the head. After he'd get it down right, he'd teach the others their part. They had lots of band fellows who could play like that after Bolden gave them the idea.

'Any Rags' was one of the tunes. You know they had an old blind man who came around with a wagon to pick up junk. He'd go around singing -- he wasn't singing -- he was talking but he was really singing:

> Any rags, Any rags, Any rags
> Ain't you got anything today?

Bolden picked it up and made a rag out of it.'"

"...when those *possessed* in ritual *speak with tongues,* we have a supernal language. These strange, often guttural, sounds are unforgettable when once heard. Thousands of miles from Africa, one can recognize the same cryptic tones and phrases in Louis Armstrong's jazz playing and singing and in the rapt, unconscious responses of his devotees when both are *sent out of this world.*"

By this time of course Rudi had moved to New York City. Both to start at his new job at the editorial desk of a major world newspaper and to be near the woman he loved. Fortunately his sister Theo's daughter Malada (Mraz) was living in the City at that time, working as a dancer with the Ballet Russe. Sharing an apartment with your ballerina niece couldn't have been the easiest but for now Rudi made do. This would certainly define the dividing line in this artistic family at any rate, the European classicists (his sister Theo's girls) and himself the Art/Jazz rebel. In 1944 Rudi found the ground floor apartment on the first floor of the old merchant house at 38 East 4th Street, the place where he lived for over forty years.

In New York City Rudi took on this newly invented role in America: the professional Jazz Critic. Previously Jazz Critics had been underground, or from Europe, but now Rudi was in the mainstream, set to challenge them all in the field of artistic purity. Look out world. For as artistically cultured as Rudi had been growing up, his aesthetic was by now totally reversed. For the ultimate Jazz snob of 1940-1948, sometimes it seemed if it wasn't Black, illiterate, impoverished and/or seriously alcoholic... what you call that Jazz? Of course almost all the Jazz stars Rudi Blesh met disproved that stereotype, still.[1]

Starting with the Bunk Johnson shows, then riding the crest of the 1940s Traditional Jazz revival (concurrent with the first big USA Folk Music revival) by 1946 my grandfather had the job at the local edition of the Herald Tribune, a king sized apartment in the ground floor of an 1850s merchant house off the Bowery, and soon, with Hansi, a Trad Jazz record label and also his first book in print. Someone had told Rudi that if you didn't do it by the time you were 45, it didn't get done. So, he got right to it.

[1] - RB Review of "A Night in New Orleans", NY Herald Tribune Wed. January 2, 1946: "Also participating ...Josh White, the balladist ... the artful and sophisticated pseudo-folk musician... [one of] the only false notes in the program". Josh White too polished, not funky enough?

Circle Sound

The record company Rudi and Hansi started together in 1946 was called Circle, and it got its start when New Orleans drummer Baby Dodds moved in with Rudi at 38 East 4th Street. After playing all night at clubs, Baby would get up and begin practicing on his kit around noon, sometimes with his teenage fan club outside on the sidewalk listening through the window. Hansi was fascinated with the solos so she suggested they start their own label to release them. Baby Dodds of course had been Louis Armstrong's original drummer in the early river boat orchestra days, the teens, really one of the originators of Jazz drumming. From the start Circle Records specialized in the classic Jazz - Boogie Woogie and Stride piano still being practiced by the surviving veterans. Luckey Roberts, James P. Johnson, Willie the Lion Smith. Rudi also coaxed Hubert Blake out of retirement in 1949. Eubie was in his mid fifties and would keep on playing Ragtime Piano for another forty odd years. Tony Parenti from New Orleans. Kid Ory in L.A.. Lou Watters in San Francisco. Circle bought Solo Art records and released their 1930s recordings of Jimmy Yancy, Albert Ammons and others. Acting on a tip from "The Baby" Rudi and Hansi went to Cleveland and found primitive Boogie player Montana Taylor and got him playing again so he could record along with Chippie Hill and Cow Cow Davenport. Circle went on for a number of years weaving it's way in and out of the narrative.

The name for the new record company came from Rudi's new friend Marcel Duchamp. As Rudi told John Hasse:

"Then we were over at the Stuyvesant Casino, after we had made the recordings [Baby Dodds drum solos], and I know we were sitting with a friend of ours--Marcel Duchamp, who loved the music--and we said we here hung up on getting a name for our record company. 'Well' he says, 'it's easy.' He says, 'What shape is the record?' We said, 'Round.' He says, "and you people are not squares, why don't you call it 'Circle'.

Marcel Duchamp's studio at that time was nearby off Union Square. At one point the originating Surrealist borrowed one of Rudi's records to exhibit as one of his "Readymade" factory produced items. The title on the 1943 George Brunis disk: That Da Da Strain, another one of those great artistic coincidences (or was it?). When Duchamp moved out of his studio he gave Rudi an enormous antique desk that had also once also been the possession of Max Ernst and Dorothea Tanning. From the same sources (Duchamp/Ernst/Tanning) also came antique Kachina dolls from the Hopi Tribes. These priceless museum pieces had been pilphered by the director of the Museum of the American Indian in Harlem to impress the famous Surrealists. When Marcel got too many to keep around, he gave a few to Rudi. In 1946 Rudi hired the son of Max Ernst, Jimmy as Circle's art director. Jimmy Ernst did most of the covers for the Circle record albums. Max Ernst had nothing to do with either his son Jimmy or Rudi however.

Life at the 38 East 4th Street pad must have been a scene. Jazz musicians came and went. Some even lived there. Cornetist Wild Bill Davison loved to follow fires. Whenever the Great Jones Street fire department bell would ring right behind the apartment Wild Bill would grab Rudi's antique fireman's helmet to run and see if he could jump on the truck. Rudi also said Davison was a bit of a clepto. One day the doorbell rang and a hand (Wild Bill) was thrust in holding two Burmese kittens. These are for you Rudi as the great Jazz man beat a hasty retreat down the hall and out. These cats became Rudi and Hansi's precious apartment pets. Up the avenue from the East 4th Street apartment was Wanamakers, a serious 1940s department store that spanned two buildings in Cooper Square with an enclosed bridge across 8th Street. Rudi said the guy who ran the record department was Maurice Waller, the young son of the recently deceased Fats Waller. Now that was the connection for hot disks for sure. At parties there was seems to have been some degree of madcap experimentation, although it was probably just alcohol that was consumed. Certainly the mix of people: writers, intellectuals, Surrealist and Abstract Expressionist artists, Jazz musicians was pretty unique at the time. Dada meets Dixieland. Wordplay was especially important and it probably wasn't unusual for Rudi to answer a simple question like say... about the weather around Christmas time with a carefully prepared statement like "Rudolph the Red knows rain, dear..." Devastating.

Rudi told me at parties in the 1940s they used to fool around with phono needles. Back then in the 78 rpm days the most common needles were made of steel. These did a number on the old shellac records, especially when they got dull. Some old Victrolas even had needle sharpeners built in. If you were an aficionado you went for cactus quills or bamboo needles, pricey since they were pretty much single use items. Sometimes at parties Rudi and his pals went a few steps further clenching the cactus or bamboo right in between their teeth and bending over the record player. In this manner they were able to "hear" the music right though their jaws into their skulls. We tried lots of things later in the 1960s but I don't think I would have tried that experiment. Brain Jelly. Another glimpse of the party in progress comes from an old photograph. Guests posing in front of Rudi's new Picasso painting, one of the partiers' eyeglasses mounted on the side of her head to imitate the portrait. Rudi was an early Picasso adopter. He bought his original before the artist was known in 1946 for $1500 and made a killing when he sold it a few years later for $5000. What a businessman.

Actually Rudi had decided to try his hand at Modern Art as well. Starting at the very top his first show was at Peggy Guggenheim's Art of This Century gallery. It seems a joint show between Robert deNiro Sr. and wife Virginia Admiral had fallen through, along with their marriage. So Rudi got a show with Ms. Admiral. As an artist my grandfather was a bit tightly wound. His years of design and illustration work showed in his overwrought dreamscape semi-abstractions, they resembled portraits of sculptures but without the compelling vision of Giorgio de Chirico or Salvador Dali, for example. A strange vertical painting of Rudi's resembles to some a sailboat though to me it's obviously a self portrait, the sail being Rudi's beard and the mast his swizzel stick dipped in his drink. A solitary tear runs down the stick into the drink. Deep. Rudi also screwed up when he mixed sizing into his paints resulting in cracked surfaces where the splits closely resemble motifs in the paintings. Really deep. Decrackage? I'm not sure how much evidence remains of the art work of Virginia Admiral. She is best known today as the mother of the actor Robert deNiro Jr. Probably one the better moves Rudi made at this time was to abandon painting for his career as a music critic, writer, record producer and radio personality.

At one point later, in the early 1950s Rudi got an offer from Esquire Magazine to go down and cover the Mardi Gras in New Orleans. He and Langston Hughes were to write about Jazz and the night life, parades and all and their photographer companion on the trip was to be none other than the infamous Lisette Model. The petite Ms. Model had already made a name for herself as a photographer, specifically for her sarcastic style. Rudi told me took a look at her photos and turned the job down. A few years later a few of Lisette Model's satirical pictures of fat women and ugly men were featured in the photo documentary book and exhibition <u>The Family of Man</u>. Rudi much preferred the lonely flattened cityscapes created by Lisette's husband Evsa Model, purchasing two of Model's paintings which are still in our family.

But by now a runaway remnant from the past had appeared in NYC and had moved in with Rudi at 38 East 4th Street off the Bowery. It was Hilary, Rudi's daughter, almost 16 and ready to resume some sort of life with her father. Rudi and Hansi looked at each other. Where will she stay? The front room of the apartment was promised to Circle's drummer, Baby Dodds, brought up from New Orleans by Rudi to find work playing during the Trad Jazz revival. Somehow accomodations were made for my mom on a couch and soon she was back in class attending Elizabeth Irwin High School in Greenwich Village.

There had been plenty of adjustments to be made all around. Rudi and Hansi were a couple, but of course she was still married to Sidney Janis, a major player in the Art world. And Hansi wasn't ready to leave Sidney. She had her sons Conrad and Carroll to think about and of course, the power of the Sidney Janis gallery to consider in the bargain. Perhaps with no real family money of her own, the present arrangement would have to do (Sidney during the week/winters, Rudi on the weekends/ summers). Perhaps also, like some other wealthy philanderers Sidney was willing to tolerate his wife's discreet lover in return for his own freedom to stray. My grandfather's copy of Sidney's book <u>They Taught Themselves</u> is inscribed by the author: "To Rudi Blesh, an old friend of the family."

But Hansi's family came through anyway. The money for the struggling record company experiment (Circle) came mostly from Hansi's brother Eugene Grossman, a successful New York City antiques dealer who lived with his family in the Dakota Apartments. Gene or Botsy as he was known was a terrific mensch, a good sport and he sunk untold amounts of cash into Rudi and Hansi's recording projects. The family connection.

Running an independent record company in the 1940s sounds exciting but the pitfalls were everywhere. From the crummy post-war shellac that made records crack in two to the musician's strike and union work rules. Some independents made it fantastically big, like Rudi's buddies the Ertegan brothers with their Atlantic Records. Circle recorded some of the same people but with Rudi and Hansi's purist approach, they were not the beneficiaries of any major hits. Historians nowadays like to refer to Circle as a "boutique label", I guess because Rudi and Hansi put historical context before commercial success. Nowadays they call that historic, classic, vintage, archival, authentic, Americana, folklore. But at Circle it was a "boutique" as if it was some sort of frivolity. Was Commodore a boutique label? I know there was pressure on Rudi to make some sort of commercial success out of Circle so I don't think it was really a hobby or rich person's self indulgent diversion. Think of all the historical labels that came after Circle. Just part of a tradition of traditionalism really. Still unbroken.

One Circle release series was historic and sold well as a limited edition item, but still managed to lose money. Code named the "Delta Project" Rudi and Hansi worked hard to release all of the Library of Congress recordings made by Jelly Roll Morton in 1938. Rediscovered back then when the Ertegan brothers were still teenagers attached to the Turkish embassy in Washington DC, Jelly Roll Morton could claim with some authority to being the one who had basically adapted Ragtime into band Jazz. The Library of Congress recordings, made by the young Alan Lomax were long and convoluted, especially after Ferdinand (Jelly Roll) had drunk some of the whiskey Alan brought along. Therein lay the problem. In talking about the days when Black itinerant piano players performed in bordellos Jelly often got right to the point. Somehow it fell to Hansi to organize and expurgate this material, about 100 disks of it, and so it got an explosive WW2 code name. The finished product: The Saga of Mr. Jelly Lord streamed across dozens of 12 inch 78 rpm records in twelve separate album sets. From the 1947 Circle Records flyer:

"imagine if Beethoven had recorded" "a living history of jazz"

"now they will be issued The enterprise and prestige of CIRCLE SOUND, Inc., documentors of pure Afro-American music, have secured the rights to release this American documentary."

"reserve your set now Two albums will be issued every three months between August-September 1947."

The cost was high, sales were good, but the big 12" records often got delivered broken (bad shellac), the transcriptions were somewhat botched (turntable speed problems at the Library of Congress? - *2)... the upshot was, many people who bought the

25

Saga of Mr. Jelly Lord series wanted their money back. There was also a persistant annoying tick that runs through a good portion of Jelly Roll Morton's narrations, singing and piano playing. Some people wrongly attributed this sonic defect to Circle but the fact is it was in the original masters as well. Some have said it was Alan Lomax, tapping a pencil nervously on the microphone stand or Jelly Roll himself tapping the microphone stand with his patent leather shoe. Both men were recording professionals so to say that either of them was negligent would take a stretch of the imagination. My own theory is that Jelly Roll Morton spiked the recordings intentionally so that Lomax (or someone else) couldn't profit from them commercially. Alan Lomax no doubt told him the disks would only be used by the Library of Congress but why should Jelly believe this White man? He might give the recordings to one of his friends later on to sell for profit. In other words even though Circle paid royalties to the Morton estate, maybe Jelly saw Rudi coming. Rudi said he had just missed meeting Jelly Roll Morton in Los Angeles in 1941. Rudi had gone down from San Francisco to interview him for The Chronicle, but the great Jazzman had just died the day before.

Another day at the NYC Circle offices in 1946 Jimmy Ernst, Rudi's art director came in with some exciting news. Someone had found Bessie Smith's long lost movie, The St. Louis Blues, in South America and there would be a showing in NYC. Rudi got on the phone and quickly secured the rights to the soundtrack. So it was that then, nine years after she had died in Mississippi, Bessie Smith released her only recordings not made for the Columbia Record Corporation. The only recording she ever made of W.C. Handy's original Blues song St Louis Blues came out on Circle. A musical seance. The original Blues man Mr. Handy came to a cinema showing of the film in NYC (though he was blind) and wrote Rudi a letter of acknowledgement for the release.

When Rudi rediscovered and secured a single recording date with famed 1920s Blues singer Hociel Thomas in San Francisco in 1946, he took his teenage daughter Hilary along as well. Hociel Thomas had been a child star with her family act and a Black recording star of some reknown in the Bessie Smith era. So at this point Hilary got to see her father in action as a producer, the whole process. Ms. Thomas was somewhat disgruntled, perhaps about payments from Circle but things progressed okay once Rudi purchased some alcohol. Right after the sides were made however things got rough and my mother had to be ushered out of the studio by trumpet player Mutt Carey. Hociel Thomas had gone after Rudi with a knife.

Rudi scored a big rediscovery for Circle when he found Bertha "Chippie" Hill, another Blues belting gal who'd sung alongside Ma Rainey and worked with Louis Armstrong back in the 1920s. Again a tip from Baby Dodds who told Rudi and Hansi Chippie was working as a waitress in Chicago. Re-recording her signature tunes How Long, and Look Down That Lonesome Road, Circle might have had a hit of some sort. Rudi also wanted to get Ms. Hill under exclusive contract so between recordings, potential copyrights and personal performances Circle Records could possibly be on the road to profitability. This was not to be however. After appearing with Kid Ory at Carnegie Hall and Art Hodes in Chicago, Bertha Hill returned to NYC in 1950 but was run down and killed by a taxicab in Harlem before getting a chance to go back to work with Circle. The world got to hear her just this one last time and then no more. How long.

Rudi also said at one point he'd had a chance to sign Mahalia Jackson, then still solely a church singer, to an exclusive contract but was beaten out by John Hammond from Columbia Records by only a few minutes. Hard to believe, Mahalia was already selling lots of records on the Apollo label at that point. Another time Rudi witnessed the pitfalls of commercial recording for sanctified singers previously only known for singing in church. Rudi said he watched in humiliation and horror as one of his artists (Berenice Phillips perhaps, or a singer associated with Mary Lou Williams) was forced to crawl on her knees down the aisle to the altar of her church in Harlem to beg forgiveness for having recorded a secular song ("the devil's music") - for Circle, of course.

Traveling around the country in 1946 Rudi recorded his old pals the Yerba Buena Band in San Francisco and the hot Kid Ory Band in Hollywood. In Chicago he and Hansi captured the last recordings of primitive Boogie Woogie pianist Montana Taylor and of course, Chippie Hill. Circle goes national. In 1949, in conjunction with their new research, Rudi and Hansi recorded turn of the century survivors Charles Thompson in St Louis and Eubie Blake in New York. They also made acetates of rare player piano rolls for research purposes and release. In the early 1950s Circle shifted to New Orleans where they recorded the cream of the local Dixieland units: George Lewis, Original Zenith Brass Band, Paul Barbarin, Armand Hug, Sharkey Bonano, Lizzie Miles.

They even gave a young Pete Fountain his first recording opportunity, playing with The Basin Street Six. Hot!

In 1951 Rudi gave the just out of retirement Eubie Blake some exposure with Circle's Jamming at Rudi's albums just out on 10" revolutionary unbreakable vinyl records. These hot party records were recorded right there at 38 East 4th Street apartment at night, even with the enthusiastic approval of the downstairs landlord and the neighbors. Also present at one of these sessions, members of the Duke Ellington Band. I guess it was okay to be a Swing musician at a late night "Jam Session".

Rudi told me that in addition to the South Side Shake record selling in the UK (for some odd reason) another good selling record Circle had was Nick's Creole Serenaders' Mo Pas Lemme Ca, the flip side of which was a jam which someone in the band gave another Creole name "Salee Dame, Bon Jour". After wondering why the record was selling so well in Quebec of all places, Rudi and Hansi did a little research and found the title meant Dirty Woman, Good Morning. Circle's entry into the Party Record industry. Thank you Albert Nicholas.

At one of the Jamming At Rudi's sessions Circle's young recording engineer (possibly Peter Bartok, son of Bela) asked Eubie Blake what the title of the last tune was, and he wrote down what he heard: Make Believe Rag. You see Scott Joplin wasn't well known back then. Also at one of those 38 E 4th sessions in 1951 the recordings had to be stopped at one point because a one year old baby was crying. Fortunately, the wife of veteran originating Jazz bassist Pops Foster was on hand to quiet me down. As Rudi told me later: "with her ample bosom". Smothered.

As the 1950s dawned record companies were faced with a range of choices as new formats. There were RCA's small 7 inch 45 rpm records to hold one, maybe two songs per side. These were small and convenient, eventually capturing the teen singles market. There were Columbia records 12 inch 33 rpm LPs which were designed to hold entire movements of long Classical symphonies. And then there were the 10 inch 33 rpm midsized (almost) LPs which seemed ideal for Jazz. As an added benefit the 10 inchers were the same size as the 78s they were replacing on the shelves. To Rudi the answer seemed obvious.

Guess which format didn't survive.

28

List of releases. (Circle recording dates in Appendix #4)

78 rpm albums (1946-1950):

Marching Jazz - Original Zenith Brass Band	S1
Montana Taylor Barrel House Blues	S2
South Side Shake - Dan Burley and his Skiffle Boys	S3
Deep Woods Blues - Chippie Hill, Hociel Thomas, Montana Taylor	S4
Chippie Hill	S5
Bessie Smith The Saint Louis Blues	S6
This is Jazz Vol. 1	S7
The Ragtime Band - Tony Parenti's Ragtimers	S8
Bill Davison Showcase	S9
Kid Rena's Delta Jazz Band	S10
This Is Jazz Vol. 2 (12 inch)	S11
Lucky Roberts Ragtime King	S12
Jazz ala Creole (Nick's Creole Serenaders)	S13
Claude Luter Vive le Jazz Hot	S14
This Is Jazz Vol. 3 (12 inch)	S15
Climbin' and Screamin' Solo Art Piano Jazz Vol. 1, Pete Johnson, Albert Ammons, Art Hodes, Clarence Lofton, Jimmy Yancey	S16
Session With Baby Dodds	S17
Claude Bolling Jazz Band	S18
This Is Jazz Vol. 4 (12 inch)	S19
Ralph Sutton St. Louis Piano	S20
Parenti's Rag Pickers	S21
?	S22/S23
Bob Wilbur Jazz Band Vol. 1	S24
Sidney Bechet's Circle Seven	S25
Eclipse Alley Five New Orleans Jazz	S26
Bechet - Wilber	S27

Jelly Roll Morton The Saga of Mr. Jelly Lord Vol 1-12
(12 inch) limited edition

later 78 rpm releases:

The 6 & 7/8 Band	CD301
Pianola Ragtime	CD302

33 rpm 10 inch LPs (1950-1952):

This is Jazz	L402
Dixieland From New Orleans - Basin Street Six	L403
Conrad Janis and his Tailgate Jazz Band	L404
Wild Bill Davison Showcase	L405
Bob Wilber and His Jazz Band	L406
Jammin' at Rudi's Vol. 1	L407
Paul Barbarin and his Jazz Band	L408
Kid Rena's Delta Jazzband	L409
Jammin' at Rudi's Vol. 2	L410
Armand Hug New Orleans	L411
Mary Lou Williams Trio	L412
Ralph Sutton at the Piano	L413
? ? ? ?	L414-L420
George Lewis and his New Orleans ALL STARS	L421
? Lizzie Miles?	L422
Muggsy Spannier Broadcasts	L423
Henry Cowell	?

33 rpm 12 inch LPs (1952-1962):

The Saga of Mr. Jelly Lord Vol. 1-12	L12001-L12012
Paul Hindemith	
Ferrucio Busoni Sonata for Piano, Indian Diary book 1	
	Composer's Workshop L51-104
Giant Stride Donald Lambert at the Piano Solo Art	
	BJ18001

note: the Claude Luter and Claude Bolling sides were exchanges from French label Vogue which released Circle material in France.

*2 - Here is how Rudi described the remastering process performed at the Library of Congress in 1947:

"So then we went over to have them play it at the Library of Congress... John Steel--was in charge of the recording process there. ...he worked out a special way of handling these discs, very, very carefully to play them. The tempo of the recording machine that Allan Lomax rented to record Jelly ran at a defective speed. This all had to be overcome. ...instead of recording at 78, it was something like 75 or so, ...it threw the pitch off. And we did all that. Also, the machine had a lot of difference in the amount of highs in the outer grooves, [compared] to the center... [Steel corrected all this.]" (source: John Hasse interviews)

In 1947, Rudi went back on the radio, this time on the East Coast after submitting an idea for live Trad Jazz to a national amateur hour show and ending up with one of the biggest shows on the radio airwaves at that time, again called "This Is Jazz".

The list of Jazz stars appearing on Rudi's weekly radio show was impressive, the best players from New Orleans and elsewhere. Even more amazing was the fact that Rudi crammed the show with information, a Trad Jazz tutorial really, all going out live on the air. The show started as a submission to the weekly talent hunt "For Your Approval" but once Trad Jazz clicked with the national audience (international also, on Voice of America and over Armed Forces Radio thousands of troops overseas heard it on shortwave) there was no getting This is Jazz off the air. Despite that fact the show could find no sponsors. The reason was simple. It was 1947 and Rudi refused to honor the color line. He went ahead and mixed Black and White performers in most of the shows just like most of these musicians were playing together in the cool New York City clubs at the time. Racial integration was the key element and really implicit in all the activities of the twin 1940s Folk and Trad Jazz revivals. But this was national, the people at WOR network explained to Rudi, think of the tortured sensibilities of people down South. Or in Queens for that matter. Throughout the 1940s people of color were forbidden access to elevators, other ammenities.. in New York City!

So it must have been really offensive for people of prejudice to have to watch mixed race performances on the radio. Rules were rules. All Rudi had to do was to do some careful editing and his show could be earning money for everybody. Rudi told me that eventually he just stayed in the control room and when would be sponsors came pleading he said he gave them the finger through the glass. That sounds about right.

Going out live over the airwaves with a strictly arranged yet somehow spontaneous Jazz show was a challenge that Rudi was uniquely equipped to handle. Despite all the potential for chaos the show went off weekly without a hitch. Rudi told me the only time things almost went off the rails was when Louis Armstrong appeared. The interplay between Satchmo and George Brunis went something like this: Louis: "What makes my wife so crazy about you?" "...it must be my glorified frankfurter" was what came through of Brunis' reply. Luckily in the midst of the post-war euphoria this too passed without a fuss. The few complaints that came in the midst of sacks of positive fan mail were from Jazz purists disagreeing with Rudi's interpretations, and also one, according to Circle's Robert Allen Aurthur, from a Christian lady objecting to the desecration of When the Saints Go Marching in. Well you can't please everyone, can you?

At this point Rudi had reached the pinnacle of purist Jazz success in America, a growing but still mostly unknown field for both the intelligentia and the general population. With his trademark goatee, tweed jackets, loud shirts and ties my grandfather was set to influence Jazz fashion and style, perhaps even for generations. A big sensation, Rudi's This is Jazz radio show ran through for 35 weeks in 1947. With no sponsor it survived on fan mail alone.

Some have said the show was perfection, a Trad Jazz lover's dream come true, but of course there were problems. From the start there had been grumbling from some of the musicians about the choice of numbers performed and the lack of input from the players. Not everyone in the band was as excited about "Classic" Jazz as Rudi was. George Brunis left in a huff for some reason. Muggsy Spannier walked also, though he denied there had been any conflict. But when Albert Nicholas, The Stompers all star clarinetist quit he made a lot of noise, to Downbeat magazine to be specific. Calling Rudi a "dictator" Nicholas decried the aesthetic interference from the show's host. He went on in some detail, also exposing efforts Rudi had made to get musicians on the show to sign exclusive contracts with Circle with Rudi in the management role. Most of these machinations backfired because my grandfather really didn't know anything about the music management business. Undoubtedly eager to help these artists avoid the pitfalls of the music industry he had none the less neglected to register with the musicians union as a manager. All the contracts he had in hand then became null and void and Rudi's reputation was tarnished from the bad publicity. Splat!

But I'm sure it wasn't greed. No doubt all of this was the result of pressure Rudi felt, perhaps from the Janis family, to make Circle profitable. The trouble of course was that while Rudi Blesh might very well have been the consumate Jazz music connoisseur in 1947, he certainly wasn't a tough minded NYC manager. Not much of a businessman really either, for that matter.

(Listing of This Is Jazz dates and performers in Appendix #3.)

Quotes from Jazzology Records CD reissue notes:

from This is Jazz A remembrance by Steve Steinberg:

"There was a reason why broadcasters were willing to take an
interest in jazz at that time. Even in the bleak cultural landscape
of commercial radio, there was an awareness that something
special was going on in the music world. That "something" was
the New Orleans Jazz Revival, and although this was hardly a bell
ringer in commercial terms - it was scarcely noticed in New
Orleans itself - the music was getting some real attention in the
popular media. When the Bunk Johnson Band with Jim
Robinson, George Lewis, Baby Dodds and other New Orleans
greats came to New York's Stuyvesant Casino in 1945, they were
written up in "Time" and other national magazines. This was also
a time when Bunk's band was recorded not only by specialty jazz
labels but by Columbia, Victor and Decca, the top three record
labels of the day."

"I was 14 years old when these broadcasts were first heard. but I
remember them vividly, for I was not only a listener, but a regular
member of the studio audience. Rudi Blesh seemed perhaps a bit
stiff to the raucous band of teenagers I hung around with back
then, but we had no problem with his taste in music. ...For our
crowd, the musicians at these sessions at the WOR Studios were
not only great jazz artists, they were heroes, to be treated to all the
unmitigated adoration that teenagers glory in bestowing upon
their idols. Sinatra, Presley, and Jimmy Dean may have been
bigger draws in their time, but take it from me, they never had
more devoted fans."

from This is Jazz by Bob Aurthur (RA Aurthur worked at Circle
and helped produce This is Jazz for the radio):

"There was once a time when on Thursday afternoons, at about
two o'clock, I would walk around to Rudi Blesh's on Manhattan's
East Fourth Street to see what was happening. The Circle record
company was then housed in Rudi's apartment, and the place was
one of the most fantastic shambles in all history. On seeing the
place for the first time, visitors would register emotion raging
from simple surprise (they were the hardy ones) to outright
hysteria. A huge joint to begin with, the apartment was jammed

to the ceiling with records, boxes, files, cartons, cardboard squares, newspapers, and cats. On the walls was a fine representative collection of modern painting with the work of Picasco (sic), Brauner, Ernst Pere et fils, Blesh himself, and many others. Somewhere in the middle of the apartment lived Rudi's lovely young daughter, Hilary (now married and living in San Francisco--she has escaped, lucky girl), always under the constant threat from Daddy of having to sleep suspended from the ceiling in a hammock so that growing Circle could utilize the floor space. Interspersed among everything else were hundreds of objects of art, Americana, and trivia. (And who can tell the difference?) Somewhere, too, wild-eyed with beard awry, could be found Blesh--doing business. Outside, Bowery bums chorused their pleas for booze, and inside, Hansi Janis, Circle's special moving force, sounded her plea for sanity, each as futile as the other. Hansi has since learned better."

"The program never seemed like a real radio show. It was too easy and too good. Nothing important ever went wrong and everyone had a wonderful time. Maybe that's why THIS IS JAZZ is not longer on the air and never got a sponsor. You know you can't have a radio program without ad men, their dripping commercials and their ulcers. The musicians worked hard because they liked what they were doing, and that too, is unusual in radio. The program didn't knock anyone or hurt anyone, nor did it give away any money. It just dispensed pure pleasure in large portions, something new and different in these times. Radio couldn't stand it."

-both sets of quotes taken from: "This is Jazz" Volume Four The Historic Broadcasts - Jazzology, notes to CD set JCD103/32

NYC Clubs/Artists in late 1940s:

Harlem: Connees (closed 1933) Cotton Club (closed in 1940)

52nd Street: numerous shoebox clubs in old townhouses, sites of old speakeasies hidden in residential neighborhoods during the 1920s. Jimmy Ryan's. Much of the heyday of 1930s-1940s Swing (and later Bop) Jazz played out here (or nearby): Billy Holiday, Stuff Smith and many others made their names here mingling with up and coming stars like Frank Sinatra. Like most Prohibition era carryovers (like Harlem Jazz, like Skiffle) the Jazz street struggled when liquor was available everywhere. In the

1950s 52nd Street was mixing strippers with Jazz, not a good sign. Now mostly under a huge skyscraper, the CBS Building perhaps?

West Village: Tradland - Nicks, Eddie Condon's. Nicks came first, really the original NYC Jazz "club" opened in 1922 by Nicolas Rongetti. Part of the wonderful Italian American largesse that made the Village Art scene happen to begin with. Acceptance. Finally closed in 1963 after it had moved to Christopher Street.

From the Village Voice August 15, 1963:

"Nick was devoted to Dixie, and the musicians he and "Mrs. Nick" featured over the years compose an impressive roster. Some of them were George Wettling, Max Kaminsky, Vic Dickinson, Pee Wee Russell, Jack Teagarden, Wild Bill Davison, Sidney Bechet, Ray MacKinley, Meade (Lux) Lewis, Bobby Hackett, Bill Butterfield, Miff Mole, Edmond Hall, Bud Freeman, Muggsy Spanier, Phil Napoleon, and Peanuts Hucko. Another was Eddie Condon, who has had his own Dixie emporiums since."

(Eddie Condon started at Nick's but soon had his own place on West Third Street. Moved uptown to 52nd Street. Big presence.)

Cafe Society. Started by Jazz Svengali John Hammond in 1938, this experimental leftist cabaret mixed races, social sets, gay and straight - while also introducing Billie Holiday and Boogie Woogie (Rock and Roll) to the intellectual set. Not bad for starters. Basically Spirituals to Swing in a small setting with alcohol. Some said it was a Communist front (it was) - so shut down by 1947.

East Village Tradland 2 (Second Avenue): Stuyvesant Casino (East 9 St), Central Plaza (East 6 St)

sample bills:

Stuyvesant Casino, Oct 8, 1947: Wild Bill Davison, Edmond Hall, Mill Mole, James P. Johnson and Chippie Hill...

Stuyvesant Casino, Oct 15 1947: Sidney Bechet, Benny Morton, James P. Johnson, Baby Dodds, Champion Jack Dupree...

Stuyvesant Casino Jan 7 1947: Georg Brunis, Tony Parenti, Bobby Hackett, Art Hodes...

Central Plaza, Feb 18, 1947: Sidney Bechet, Wild Bill Davison, Bobby Hackett, Joe Marsala, James P. Johnson...

again, from This is Jazz A remembrance by Steve Steinberg:

"On Saturday evenings, assuming there was money for it, we would head for the Central Plaza or the Stuyvesant Casino on the Lower East Side, where a whole series of groups were playing in the aftermath of Bunk's 1945 gig. these were places where nobody checked our ID's, beer was sold by the pitcher, and set ups of ice and ginger ale were provided for those who wanted to bring in their own bottle."

The Traditional Jazz scene flourished in New York City in the mid 1940s with Rudi Blesh on the radio, in the newspaper, Jazz mags, putting out records, booking bands. Teenagers went nuts hanging around with the New Orleans greats (like Baby Dodds living at 38 E 4th) and the best Trad players came to the Village from all over the USA. It was an on-going Black/White Jam session, possessed of a definite sense of delirium, a bit of everyone's shared post-war joy. It was pretty obvious, pure African American Jazz had just whipped the evil Nazis, who hated all such things. In the Village race mixing went on unchecked, pot got smoked, intellectuals held forth, short haired artist girls in slacks "hung out" - all this leading directly to the beatnik/hippie Village Scene of the 1950s-1960s. Then suddenly Trad went away, along with the Blues, flipped out - replaced by urgent arty Modern Jazz and eventually, the inevitable pulsating gyrating Rock and Roll.

But first, there was Skiffle...

Skiffle

What does it mean? A Folk word related perhaps to scuffle, part of the American Negro vernacular from the early 20th century, possibly earlier. The man who introduced the word Skiffle to my grandfather Rudi Blesh in 1946 was Dan Burley, editor of the Amsterdam News, Harlem's main newspaper. A few years later, Burley would also be instrumental in helping Rudi locate Lottie Joplin, Scott Joplin's widow, in Harlem a few years later. The papers my grandfather and Hansi scooped up from the trash in Mrs. Joplin's basement (including Treemonisha, Scott's opera) became the basis for the 1970s Ragtime revival.

Wanting to make a record in 1946 with friend Dan Burley, Rudi chose the theme: a Chicago rent party from the earlier heyday of the Boogie Woogie. South Side Shake would reflect the styles Burley had heard in the 1920-1930s when even stars like Fats Waller could make more money (and have much more fun) playing at parties than recording tunes they would probably never receive royalties for. These piano "cutting contests" were vestiges of the earlier Ragtime competitions originating in the 19th century. As a young man growing up in Chicago, Burley had lived a double life, A student in Journalism at Wendell Phillips High School by day and lowdown Boogie Woogie piano player alongside who knows what by night. When he hit New York City Dan became the Theatre/Sports Reporter at the Amsterdam News in 1938 and Chief Editor a few years later. His main claim to fame seems to have been his infamous "Dan Burley's Original Handbook of Harlem Jive" an Uptown souvenir from the early 1940s you wouldn't want to be caught without.

Of course Burley didn't invent Jive, it had been around since the Ragtime entertainers like Bert Williams first broke out of the minstrel show and presented Black culture to the public at large before World War One. It was the language spoken by Jazz musicians to avoid arrest for illegal drugs. It was also what every young White hipster wanted to get in on in the 1940s and of course the essence of what would become Rock and Roll. So for the White jivers Dan Burley was the man. But also within the Black community Burley commanded great respect, even being consulted by Langston Hughes for one of his poems regarding the "dozens aspect" (pre-curser to Rap). Dan Burley was also the one who introduced Lionel Hampton to the Boogie Woogie. So you could say that Burley is the Godfather of Rap and Rock and Roll, both again presented for kids like me, the teenage general public in the 1950s by Bo Diddley.

But back to Skiffle. Oddly it does not even appear in Burley's Dictionary of Jive, although the word Scuffle is listed. Perhaps because Skiffle was already archaic in 1946, the precursor to Boogie Woogie in the hipster lexicon. Dan had already appeared "With His Skiffle Boys" on a recording made with Leonard Feather a few months earlier, but for the 1946 Circle session Rudi chose Brownie McGhee and his younger brother "Sticks" as the guitar rhythm section. The goal of Skiffle was to make good party music without so called "professional" musicians (horn players). So the fact that a piano and two surging lead/rhythm guitars could make acceptable popular music was a novelty, primitive, a revelation, both an insight into Jazz's originating process and a vision of the stripped down R&B combos of the future.

original 1946 liner notes by Rudi Blesh:

south side shake

party music

From 1910 to about 1933, Chicago, at the confluence of rivers and railroads to the south, became the center of a great northward industrial migration of the Negroes and thereby a meeting place for barrel-house and boogie-woogie players. The great South Side institution of "rent party" (locally known as "skiffle," "shake," or "percolator") run by the landlady, paid the rent by the proceeds from the sale of homecooked food and nefarious, bootleg liquor, and was the scene of gambling, dancing, brawls and "good time," These social affairs of a submerged, underprivileged, and partly expatriate dark population were the haven of those piano blues players who, making the rounds of the innumerable "skiffles," subsisted on the free food and drink the large tips from those who emerged as winners in the crap game.

At their height in the 1920's, these parties kept together the bodies and souls of several hundred players. Native Chicagoans, like Dan Burley, rubbed elbows with players form other sections, some of whom were well known through their records, like Montana Taylor (Circle Album S-2: Barrel House Blues by Montana Taylor,) while others, like "The Toothpick," "Tippling

38

Tom," "Detroit Red," and the 375 pound James Hemingway, have disappeared, surviving only as legends.

The Depression seriously curtailed the "skiffle" institution, to which, previously, Prohibition raids had been, more or less, only a perpetual annoyance (Dan Burley says, " Real playing--the 'arm breakers'--began about midnight when the crap game broke up, and went on until five or six, whenever the 'wagon' came." The legalizing of liquor effected what the depression and the Prohibition raid could not, the end of the "skiffle." The hundreds of fine players scattered and went into other forms of employment, and a wonderful folk art all but disappeared. Recorded to a degree on the race lists of the 1920's it seemed to be a lost art. It remained for CIRCLE to begin in 1946--as part of its program of recording the best in Afro-American music and jazz-- to rediscover the great barrel house pianists like Dan Burley and Montana Taylor, and to record their mature art.

the artists

Dan Burley is widely known as the dynamic managing editor of Harlem's Amsterdam News. Only his intimates have known, however, that the selfsame Dan was once a leading party piano player of the Chicago South Side.

Born in Kentucky and taken to Chicago in 1917, as a boy of ten, Dan Burley grew up in the midst of the "skiffle" blues. By fifteen, playing at the parties alongside the "professors," he was holding his own and evolving his own style. More articulate--and with a keener intellectual interest than his self-taught contemporaries, Dan learned to distinguish the individual styles of the players and the sectional styles they represented. Master of more than two dozen different basses, Dan can demonstrate "Arkansaw" or "Memphis" piano, the turpentine camp boogie fo eastern Texas, the "Forty-four" piano of northern Louisiana, and the "deep woods blues" of Florida. All of these rich influences color his playing on these records.

George "Pops" Foster is not only grand-daddy of all the New Orleans bass players but a player unmatched in jazz circles today. It was forty years ago that Pops' bow broke at a dance and, throwing it away, he began to slap his bass. On the riverboats in 1917, and in Chicago by 1920, Pops Foster's solid rhythm has propelled many of the great jazz bands. In the "skiffle" days, however, he was to be found, as often as not, at some landlady's, backing up the boogie player.

Brownie and Globe Trotter McGhee, two brothers from Tennessee, are famed blues artists, the former as a singer, both as masters of the exciting, rhythmic blues guitar style. They team together perfectly in the real "skiffle" spirit.

These four artists form a group characteristic of the rent party. Their fast blues rock with excitement, while their slow blues sing with the "low down" sadness of real "bottom music," These disks are important documents of American music, and they are great fun to hear. So We say, Put on a record and come to the party, There's "good time" here!

(end of quoted section)

The operative words in Rudi's South Side Shake notes seem to have been "the real 'skiffle' spirit". Lonnie Donegan, the guitarist for The Chris Barber Band, was one of the first if not the first true Skiffle believers to use the word appropriately in Great Britain. As Lonnie told Tony Palmer in All You Need is Love (1976): "The name 'Skiffle' came from Chicago, It was music people would play for rent parties. Impoverished neighbors would get together and hold a party. They'd have a whoop-up with home-made wine and then play bits of music with a broomstick or a washboard- anything that was handy. Then they'd pass the hat around to collect for the rent." These ideas came from Rudi's notes on the South Side Shake album, and/or from Rudi's radio show, This is Jazz which was broadcast to servicemen like Donegan serving in Europe on the Armed Forces Radio Network. This is Jazz on March 15, 1947 had featured Dan Burley in a raucous band arrangement of South Side Shake, including a spoken Skiffle intro by Rudi. Inspired by that same message, various Skiffle groups were organized in England by 1949 and in 1954 UK originating Skiffler Lonnie Donegan set off a Folk boom like no other while singing Leadbelly songs during his intermission show with Trad Jazzmen Ken Colyer and Chris Barber. What "Folk" or "Jug Band" meant in America was called Skiffle in the UK. Rudi told me that South Side Shake had been a strong seller in England of all places, on the Vogue label I believe. I don't think he had an inkling of what had actually transpired. Unbeknownst to Rudi, Skiffle became huge in Great Britain.

Because all the great original Rock and Roll revivalists from the UK in the 1960s were Skifflers to start and that would include Lennon McCartney Harrison Starr, Stones, Animals, Kinks, Faces, Clapton, Fleetwood Mac, Who, Moody Blues, BeeGees, Hollies, Searchers, Hermits, Syd Barrett, Bowie, Zeppelin, etc.. And of course Skiffle (and Blues) had come out of Traditional Jazz. As Jagger once said of Rolling Stones founder Brian Jones in derision: "He was a reformed traddie, and, although he despised them, he was really one of them."

Well it hadn't always been a put down like that. Back in 1962 when schoolboys Mick and Keith had seen Brian "Elmo Lewis" Jones perform on Blues slide guitar they thought maybe he really was Elmore James. Before they became rich effete art poseurs all the Stones had once had "the real 'skiffle' spirit". The day Paul McCartney met the somewhat inebriated fifteen year old John Lennon performing at the Church Fete he could see young Lennon had "the real 'skiffle' spirit". In Bill Wyman's Blues Odyssey book, his tribute to the Blues artists who created the music the Rolling Stones did so well, the Stones bassist takes a whole page to pay tribute to Rudi Blesh, not specifically for Skiffle but for his other contributions including writing first about Robert Johnson.

What a Traddie.

But back in 1946 the difference between Rudi and Hansi's Circle label and Atlantic Records, for example, each just one of the many small independents, was commercial ambition. Perhaps at the Skiffle sessions Sticks McGhee had auditioned a song he'd heard in the Army: "Drinking Wine... (maternal profanity)" for Circle and of course Rudi would have rejected it. At Atlantic Ahmet Ertegan heard that same song, had Brownie switch a few lyrics, changed the title to "Drinkin' Wine Spo Dee-O-Dee" and Atlantic had their first major "race record" hit.

By coincidence (or not) later in the 1960s-1970s the owner and founder of Atlantic Records Ahmet Ertegan became the mentor of the Rolling Stones and Led Zeppelin, the latter group soon thereafter caught plagiarizing Blues artists. Ertegan had also been instrumental in the breakup of Cream, meddling with the group and even later publicly belittling Jack Bruce and Ginger Baker, calling them Eric Clapton's "rhythm section."

Whatever happened to "the real 'skiffle' spirit"?

But back at Circle Records in the late 1940s Rudi and Hansi with their traditionalism were aimed backwards, not forwards into Rhythm and Blues like Atlantic. Halfway through the growing Trad Jazz revival a strange thing happened. A new ultra arty type of Jazz started coming into vogue. Originally thought up as a form of musical shorthand by Jazz pioneers like Lester Young (saxophone) Charlie Christian (guitar) Thelonius Monk (piano) and also probably Mary Lou Williams (piano) Bop caught on with Jazz musicians sick to death of Swing, and then suddenly as a craze it was starting to have a big effect on the young intellectual set. This was really ironic because if there was anything that Rudi had been pushing for all along it was the recognition of the Art in Jazz. So here comes this new type of Art Jazz that wants to have nothing to do with Trad, Blues or Swing. From his position as one of the heads of the NYC Jazz critic fraternity Rudi came down hard on Bop. "Morning After Music" he called it, a thinly veiled reference to the drug influences allegedly fueling the creative storm. Moldy Fig was the name the Bopsters pinned back on Rudi and the other Traddies and that one stuck. There was bad blood flowing and Rudi wasn't one to back down from the fight.

This was in direct contrast with the scene in Europe and England where Trad and Bop more or less coexisted, especially in the beginning. This was the reason South Side Shake, the Skiffle record was successful in England. There the scene was less commercialized and the audience was much more inclusive and naturally hip. Or maybe in the UK, Trad actually won. A few years later groups like the Beatles, the Rolling Stones, the Kinks, the Animals and the Yardbirds, who'd all started out as Trad Jazz Skiffle bands evolved right through Folk Music, Rhythm and Blues, Traditional Blues, Soul Music and Rock and Roll without the strict categorizations and ugly put downs that pervaded in the USA. So in 1949, as Traditional Jazz went into the Dark Ages in America Rudi and Hansi contemplated their next move.

What happened of course is that they criss-crossed the country interviewing surviving old time piano players, and shortly thereafter released the book that became known as the bible of the Ragtime Revival: They All Played Ragtime, in 1950.

Jazz always was a scuffle...

note: here is what Brian Bird wrote in <u>Skiffle</u> 1958 (forward by Lonnie Donegan):

"But at long last, about the year 1948, some record of this type of music was begun in America. A Harlem newspaper editor named Dan Burley made some piano recordings of numbers he used to hear as a youngster at parties in Chicago, which were called Boogies or Skiffles. He was accompanied by two guitarists, Brownie and Globetrotter McGhee, and a bassist, Pops Foster, and decided to call the group 'Dan Burley's Skiffle Boys'. A year later, in England, a Skiffle Group was formed within the 'Crane River Jazz Band', and in 1952 the well-known 'Ken Colyer's Jazzmen', one of the foremost traditional Jazz bands in the country, formed a Skiffle Group within its ranks, and another group was used in 1954, when a smaller outfit was required to play the sort of music that Burley had played in America, which was still called by the name he had used--Skiffle."

note: The only inaccuracies in Bird's narrative are the date of South Side Shake (1946) and the name of the group, which should be Dan Burley and his Skiffle Boys.

Once Bop dropped it was not be stopped, but perhaps Rudi didn't know that. The Train. The problem was even though in many ways my grandfather was totally right, this was a fight he was destined to lose. Although vindicated years later long after it mattered, Rudi Blesh took it on the chin for being a Fig. Because, of course, Jazz has to grow. Like Ragtime passing before Jazz now it was Trad's turn to stand aside. Still this cultural process, totally corrupted by personal ambition, greed, racism and rampant commercialism, was vicious and insulting. In this new post-war bizarro "Modern" Jazz world, scene creator Louis Armstrong was a square and an Uncle Tom. Jazz fans no longer danced. Bearded brooding Jewish and Italian American hipster intellectuals sat at tables, played chess, contemplated the deep art of it all then argued for hours about who was the hippest based on the which of their avant garde Black horn player idols exuded the most hostility towards Whites. Jazz was flagellating itself. Maybe Trad Jazz had been about the Blues and this really was the blues. But they were having none of it. No Blues, no Swing, no dancing. It wouldn't have mattered anyway if they wanted to dance there weren't many women making the Modern Jazz scene. Not many Black people either, except for the trend setting originators.

Rudi and young Barry Ulanov were involved with concerts for high school students sponsored by the Herald Tribune, Bands for Bonds. At these shows a Trad band (Sidney Bechet) would square off against a Bop unit (Charlie Parker) and at the end of the show the kids got to vote for Trad, Bop or both (hint hint). Rudi spiked the show however by having both bands play old numbers like Tiger Rag. To hear the Bopsters play the tune you wouldn't even have recognized it. It was said that at one concert the dressing room had to be aired out (from Parker's pot puffing) before it could be occupied by Sidney Bechet. Did they really jam?

A period photo shows Rudi another night after a Bop show at Birdland, sitting at a table with Charlie Parker and Dizzy Gillespie. Signed by Parker: "at last we meet, pleasant pleasant pleasant..." Also at the table, Ahmet Ertegan, who probably arranged the peace conference. All to no avail, after months of skirmishing and some vicious polemics (Rudi knew how to keep his end up), the forces of artistic and commercial progress, and a new generation of Jazz Critics, won out and the classicist/purist Traddies were banished from the American House of Jazz. The

44

Blues was denied. Needless to say, in the big purge Rudi lost the Jazz Critic position at the New York Herald Tribune.

It was a tip from Tony Parenti from New Orleans, who still called his performing unit his "Ragtimers", that set the ball rolling. What was this Ragtime Music that predated Jazz? No one had ever written much of anything on the subject, in fact, who was Scott Joplin anyway? Rudi and Hansi both remembered Ragtime from their childhoods but only vaguely, as a mostly forgotten sound that got just about totally superseded and swallowed up by another fresher batch of forbidden fruit: Jazz. Somewhat baffled, Rudi and Hansi first went to the Smithsonian Institute where they found a kindred spirit in Genevieve Norvell. Ms. Norvell did what she had to do to get them access to a huge body of information taken from turn of the century periodicals pertaining to Ragtime music. Clues by the thousands, let the hunt begin.

From there the researchers turned in Harlem, Dan Burley and also friend Kenneth Lloyd Bright *3, owner of the Lafayette Theatre where Jazz was often presented at that time. Bright hooked them up with a truly wonderful character, Shepard Edmonds in Columbus, Ohio. Shep had been a Ragtime pianist at the 1893 Chicago Worlds Fair, but was then best known for being "America's first Negro Private Detective". Shep's recall of the early Ragtime era was amazing, filling Rudi's and Hansi's notes with the memories of the early greats, people like Plonk Henry who never got to publish or record. Mr. Edmonds also gave Rudi two tips that made their searches much easier. First, never go anywhere without Hansi. Black people don't like talking to solitary White men. Second, always check with the local Black undertakers first. They know where every elderly person of color is in town and what their state of health is.

Either (both?) Burley or Kenneth Bright also put Rudi and Hansi in contact with Lottie Joplin, Scott Joplin's widow, still living in Harlem running a hotel, mainly for Black show business entertainers. She showed them what Scott had been working on when he died in 1917, some thirty years earlier, folios and other scraps of paper scattered on the floor in the basement. Rudi and Hansi took all the sheet music they could carry back to Circle and subsequently had some of it played by friend James P. Johnson. They also took with them the only known photos of Scott Joplin and copies of his opera, titled Treemonisha, saving all of it, a precious cultural legacy, from certain destruction, the fate of the the rest of the remaining material in Harlem unfortunately. *4

And so the quest for Ragtime began. In the space of six months or so Rudi and Hansi criss-crossed the country in Rudi's brand new streamlined Studebaker tracking down the surviving Ragtimers, many of them now unknown figures well advanced in age. From the Bowery, starting point for both Ben Harney / Williams and Walker to Scott Joplin's former hometown of Sedalia, Missouri, St. Louis, Kansas City, Chicago, New Orleans. Photos in the collection tell the story. Old Tom Turpin from St. Louis, owner of the bar near where Frankie could have gone to find Johnny, if you know what I mean. Pictures from Sedalia of a flowering turn of the century Black middle class, The George Smith College - a Black music institute, and also a negro gentleman's sporting club, The Maple Leaf Club, by 1949 a Black bar. In the period picture they retreived that's doomed Joplin associate Louis Chauvin with the guns and hunting dogs. Another time, another place, but (thanks to Rudi and Hansi) - the same music we play still.

At the end of their travels Rudi and Hansi had found evidence of all but one of the exalted trio they now called the Ragtime "Big Three". There was Scott Joplin starting from Sedalia Missouri and his young protege James Scott, but also a mysterious (White?) man known only as Joseph Lamb who wrote exquisite Rags in a most original manner. None of the other Ragtime originators had any solid leads on Lamb so Rudi and Hansi had just about given up finding out anything about the guy. Suddenly Rudi remembered there was one thing they hadn't tried, the Brooklyn telephone book. Sure enough Joe Lamb lived in Brooklyn, and he was willing to talk to Rudi and Hansi about Scott Joplin and Ragtime. After that he even wanted to write some new material and do his first recordings. Ragtime Lives!

The book that resulted in 1950 from all this research, They All Played Ragtime was never a best seller. But it did inspire thousands of people to reconsider the type of music formerly played too fast and without much feeling on tack pianos. The revelation that Ragtime writers like Scott Joplin, James Scott and others had considered themselves to be Black classicists was like a dream come true. Here was the source of the Black musical Art at the other end of the tunnel that narrowed down to one lane with snobby Modern Bop. As Hansi predicted, it would take another 25-30 years for the public to come to appreciate the Art Ragtime style as they had rediscovered it. This would have to wait until after poor old Scott's Melrose Music copyrights ran out and the Hollywood exploitation machine swung into action. That's why in 1973 so many people could identify Joplin's The Entertainer for example as the 1930s theme from The Sting by Marvin Hamlish. As Rudi knew all too well, commercial music knows no shame, especially when it comes to Black Art. Many books have come out on the subject subsequently but the story of Ragtime, the real Ragtime era story, was and is still best told in <u>They All Played Ragtime</u>, as any serious student of the music knows. Hurredly written *5, but with Hansi's indispensible help, Rudi's best work.

from <u>They All Played Ragtime</u>, Rudi Blesh and Harriet Janis:

"Industry thrived and money flowed up over the levee bank down into St. Louis, to gather like a golden pool in the Chestnut Valley sporting district around the bawdy houses and saloons of two notorious streets. It was on Chestnut and Market Streets that the professional gamblers waxed prosperous; that the madams piled up the gold their girls earned from rich cattlemen, traveling businessmen, and the idle, moneyed local sports. The money got around: the dapper, foppish 'macks' or 'sweet-back men' in their Stetsons, box-back coats, and St. Louis "flat" shoes got their gambling stakes from the girls.

These glittering thoroughfares were the heaven of the wandering musician. The joints rang with the archaic, jangling jig-piano syncopations that in only a few years would be a developed music to be dubbed ragtime. By 1899 it would be pleasantly tinkling in these two bawdy highways while on near-by Targee Street, as the legend goes, Allen (Johnny) Britt said to Frankie baker: 'Bye Bye Babe, I was your man but I'm just gone,' and Frankie pulled the trigger and then turned away, the smoking pearl-handled forty-four in her hand. Within a week the ragtime pianists would make a song of it and the pretty octoroons and the pimps would think up a hundred verses--many unprintable--for the district to sing..."

"In the center of all this, behind his bar at the Rosebud Cafe or seated at his upright piano, would be the one stable, un-moveable figure in thie whole licentious melee, Thomas Million Turpin, the tall, heavy imperturbable Negro of the rough manner and the gentle heart. He was the man who in 1899 would would count in the District, whether that meant music, liquor, or gambling. In his way he would be both patron and practitioner of the arts. His piano would seldom be silent. When not shaking under the force of his huge hands rolling out the rhythms of his rags, its strings would be yielding up the honky-tonk chordings and rippling runs of every ragtime pianist worth his salt who was to be found in St. Louis. It would be then, too, that Scott Joplin would find his way to the Rosebud and Tom Turpin, and between them the two men would make a long friendship based on the quiet, rich generosity and inward dignity that each possessed."

"The earliest ragtime--both East and Midwest--was a rocking music of medium tempo, though in the East this folk ragtime was called "slow drag." The ragtime of both sections consisted of syncopated pieces derived from the folk melodies and from the quadrilles and the schottisches. These rags were the four-themed compositions, including trios, with which we are familiar. While Scott Joplin developed this form through rising stages of complexity, he never deserted the essential dance quality or omitted his unfailing designations: 'Slow March Tempo,' ... or his familar 'Notice! Don't play this piece fast. It is never right to play 'Ragtime' fast.' Joplin took the country dance form and developed it classically without losing the original character of the music"

from The Author's Preface to the Fourth Edition (1971):

"it has been seventy years -- two full human generations as historians (and the electric computer) figure these things -- since a young Kentuckian named Ben Harney playing and singing a ragtime song in a Gotham vaudeville theatre, inaugurated a remarkable era. Seventy years -- long enough for an American music to arise and bloom, to enthrall a nation (and Europe too), to fade and be forgotten. And then to be remembered again." ... "Ragtime is an American word, humorous and deprecatory or not. Its second syllable seems to have been its key syllable -- for one thing, how its metrical time started music to swinging."

*3 - Kenneth Lloyd Bright managed (and his family owned) the Lafayette Theatre in Harlem, where Bessie Smith had performed in NYC. Loyal friend to Rudi and Hansi, Bright traveled out to LA to represent Circle in the licensing of the Jelly Roll Morton material, going up against prominent West Coast Negro attorney Hugh Macbeth.

*4 - Remaining Joplin material disappeared in the care of Wilbur Sweatman, self-appointed executor of the Scott Joplin estate.

*5 - Rudi told John Hasse TAPR was written in "three or four weeks".

In 1948 my mother graduated from Elizabeth Irwin High School. Hoping to become an artist herself she enrolled in the San Francisco Art Institute, then directed by old Rudi friend Doug MacAgy. Romance sometimes has other ideas and it wasn't long before she was back in NYC with her soon to be husband up and coming artist John Hultberg. A quick marriage in Harlem and a visit to Luckey Roberts restaurant club for a reception and the newly married artists spent their honeymoon night sleeping on the floor of his brother's kitchen in Brooklyn. Or maybe it was John's brother and his bride Ethel who slept on John and Hilary's kitchen floor when they (also) got married in 1949.

The Hultberg brothers, John and Paul had come to New York in 1949 from California in an old broken down car with my mother to make the scene in the newly emerging Abstract Expressionist School of Modern Art centered on the East Coast. The handsome Swedish descended pair both got married at that time, Paul to the former Ethel Lutsky and John to the daughter of Jazz critic Rudi Blesh. For a while John and Hilary lived with Rudi at 38 East 4th. Years later my father would sometimes recount stories of going to get 1$ buckets of beer at McSorleys ("rushing the growler") and hanging around with Jazz Musicians, the kind of people he had little respect for as a classical music highbrow snob.

Still, John Hultberg's paintings were expansive, bold, exciting. A Navy veteran, he seemed to have what the old 1940s Surrealist rehashers (like Rudi) had lacked, a compelling modern post-war vision. Hultberg's post nuclear war landscapes mascaraded as Abstract Expressionism with a dash of Freudian symbolism and action painting thrown in for good measure. His dream images were huge, deep, hypnotic, hard to ignore. The Descent into the Maelstom writ large. Breaking the new rules (by continuing to break the picture plane) Hultberg was one of the few who managed to preserve the idea of landscape painting in Modern Art.

I remember a succession of apartments in the Village as a baby, including my first clear memories of 47 Perry Street, a sublet from Folk historian Alan Lomax. The artist in residence John Hultberg had his studio adjoining our living area. As soon as I could walk I slipped out of my crib and tried my hand at this Abstract Expressionist School technique. Discovering my handiwork (brushes?) My parents set me up with my own canvas, archived today somewhere with the possibly thousands of other untold/

unsold Hultbergs. Things wouldn't be this idylic for long. John was working hard to make it in the gallery scene and with the death of his father he received a small inheritance. With that he jumped at the chance to go to Paris in 1953, leaving my mother, now pregnant again, totally in the lurch. After that event it was always his relationship with art dealer Martha Jackson which took precedence. I remember visits out in the Hamptons (before they became the Hamptons) as a five year old, the drinking ,word play, Karl Appel trying to teach me how to color in my coloring book "not like that... against the lines!" What an idiot. I remember going up in a small airplane and flying over the beach with Martha Jackson's brother and Bill DeKooning, I believe. In the airplane I was amazed my hand could cast a shadow that covered dozens of people on the beach. I was huge. They also let me fly the plane for a few seconds or so. Modern Art daycare 1955.

Between my father the artist, his friends and Rudi in his world, in my early years I was raised in a world of puns. It was only later that I found out other families didn't operate this way. I fondly remember grandfather talking about his own "calm pewter" age and ancient forms of "new clear" power. Hey, this is fun.

Back home now in Brooklyn things were miserable for my mother. Deserted by her now somewhat famous husband she struggled to support her now two children in the slums on a secretary's salary. She split her paycheck with a wonderful Black woman named Serena who took care of my sister Steffi and me, often out at her project apartment in the Bedford Stuyvesant section of Brooklyn. She lived there with her mother from Alabama (who'd never seen a telephone or an elevator) and her teenage boys who I idolized. Just like the famous musicians I'd seen at my grandfather's place these Black people were all Royalty to me. My greatest moment as a five year old was watching King Kong on TV with these really cool older Black kids, Serena's sons. Looking far down below from her high rise apartment window I could see Black guys in sharp clothes and hats getting out of fancy cars in front of the corner store. I remember playing in the fountain with all the other kids and looking down at my arm. What is wrong with me, why am I so pale and white?

Visits to Grampa Rudi's place on East 4th Street pretty much ceased at this point. I do remember earlier times though, some of my first memories, of Jazz men and their families, and the magic record player that Rudi hovered over. You're Feet's Too Big, The

Spider and the Fly, The Animule Ball - all played for the toddler. The 4th Street apartment was huge to me and full of (Surrealist) scariness that Rudi seemed to think was fun. Goodbye.

My mother's relationship with her father, always fragile, took a pretty much permanent turn for the worse at this point when Rudi decided it was Hilary's role to support her artist husband, no matter what. Somehow the sanctity of Art (with a capital A) trumped everything for Rudi, including human decency in this case it would seem. Rudi also took Hilary's small inheritance/ tuition money and later also tried to borrow funds from my impoverished mom for his recording projects. Frozen out from her only remaining family connection and now, a traitor to the art world as well, it looked like my mother was really going to have to go through this alone. A turning point for sure.

Despite having flunked out of secretarial school my mom became the personal secretary to famed Bauhaus architect/designer Marcel Breuer. Not really a bad job at all, though the pay was probably pretty meager. Christmas of 1956 she worked so hard after work to create a wonderful puppet theatre for me as a gift. The people in the model shop at the Breuer office helped and the thing was really a work of art, with working curtains and the faces of comedy and tragedy hand painted on it. I was thrilled when I opened it because it was so wonderful and large. Suddenly we heard a car honking outside the apartment building. It was my father and his art dealer lady friend Martha Jackson in her Cadillac bringing me another Christmas present. A big RCA television set. The puppet theatre got folded up behind the door and I never looked at it again.

Being young with a working mother I tried in my own way to help out. When Hilary slept late on Sunday mornings I would go to work. First I decided to practice being a barber. After giving my Steiff animal puppets each a trim I started in on my little sister Steffi's bangs. Darn it was hard to get them even, almost down to the scalp before they looked right. Sort of. I also liked to climb into the dumbwaiter and up on to the upper shelves in the kitchen. Like Isaac Newton I sought to investigate gravity except I used eggs instead of apples. I just wanted to see if they would all break. At one point my mother got a small check from Martha Jackson and invested it all in canned goods. What better way to help her out than to remove the labels from the cans? There were nights we had pineapples for dinner because my mother struck out trying to find a can of tomatoes. And mayonaise sandwiches when we were broke. At least we had each other.

Street level on St. John's Place in 1956 was really terrific, if you'd asked me. The tenements were teeming with kids, kid gangs and real gangs. If and when the tough kids from Butler Street (The Butlers) ever showed up we little kids were instructed to hide in the empty garbage cans and when we got the signal, jump out and fight using the lids as shields. We practiced this all the time but I don't remember the war ever actually taking place. I do remember watching grubby garbage men come to pick up and empty the cans, throwing them back across the sidewalk, bouncing around getting dented with a huge clatter and racket. That looked like fun. I'd watch the older kids (hoods) pitching baseball cards in the lobby and once asked one of them for a Duke Snider card, which I got for my collection. I remember these older kids talking about Elvis Presley, switchblade knives, using curse words I had not the slightest notion the meaning of. My mother was horrified when Anastasia, a Mob boss was assassinated in a barber's chair a few blocks away. I just thought it was all very interesting. Be bop a lula.

Probably the most memorable thing that ever happened to me in Brooklyn (other than walking all the way around the city block as a five year old, a feat worthy of Magellan) was the day I realized I could make myself any size I wanted to be, projecting myself above buildings or shrinking down among the ants. I practiced this form of psychic projection until I almost thought it was a muscle I could excercise. Already I was turning inward. I stared at the sun because people told me not to and when all else failed I would push in on my eyeballs until the greenish yellow moire patterns would begin. My childhood psychedelia. Also at this time or maybe a little later I began having a recurrent dream that over the years became known to me as The City of Enlightenment Dream. In this dream I am wandering around a strange city. It is unclear what the age is. I hear a group of people in a hall nearby. I listen through the window and am amazed that they are talking about the same things that have secretly concerned me. As I approach the door I am ushered in and immediately everyone in the room turns to welcome me. They bring me to the front of the room and ask me my opinions on the subjects discussed. I immediately find a way to speak my mind to everyone present and so the dream ends.

My Uncle Paul and Aunt Ethel Hultberg lived further up St. Johns Place (we were down by Grand Army Plaza). Paul and Ethel had kids roughly the same ages as Steffi and me, Cassie (my age) and Lorry (three years younger). Ethel's family had some money so Paul sometimes showed up driving an automobile, an amazing thing back then. Once he took us kids through the car wash, an embryonic journey for me. Another time Paul and Ethel took me to Ebbets Field to see the Dodgers practicing but it was raining so we looked through the fence at the empty playing grounds. Another time we bought kites but it rained again. There are pictures of me and Cassie playing Monopoly with Uncle Paul who had a big handlebar mustache at that time. I'm not sure we could read yet but I do remember keeping the Monopoly money in my pocket. Another picture from that period shows Cassie and me looking up in total amazement at the real Santa Claus. The fact that he looked identical to Grampa Rudi in a shiny red plastic suit was irrelevant. We saw Santa Claus.

Sometime thereafter my mother brought home a man she had been dating from work. A young architect from New England he impressed me no end when he gave me his ball point pen, a rare thing in 1956. Suddenly it was announced that they were going to get married, then we were going to move to Massachusetts, then to Holland. Great I said, finally we get to use the Holland Tunnel.

Right after they got married my new stepfather, Peter Morton announced that from that day forward I was to leave his TV (my RCA) alone. He also took his pen back. We moved to Marblehead where on the first day of school I did something, I think, and was told to stay after school. In Brooklyn I had been forbidden to step off the sidewalk (though I did). Suddenly as a seven year old I was faced with the prospect of walking about two miles across unknown suburban territory full of unmarked unsignalled intersections out to an island separated by a narrow windblown causeway wherever that was. A few months later I moved with the Peter Mortons to The Hague in the Netherlands where as an seven and a half year old I was to find my way to school daily across a totally foreign city. It's true sometimes I never got there but I always found a way to get by.

Den Haag

The first day of school in Holland, the maid brought me to school on the tram. See? It was easy, she explained in Dutch, just one transfer. The next morning with the strange foreign money in my hand I made it to the tram stop and onto the trolley. After that the strange alphabet soup Dutch street names reeled by the window with the streets all intersecting at odd angles. Which of these stops was the one she had told me to get off at? Older taller people would block my view. I'd miss the stop. So, on the long daily trolley route I got to study the city out the window in all kinds of weather. At the end of the line the conductor looked back at me curiously. Still on the tram as we went around the carousel to take the route back downtown. Heading from this direction I had no trouble finding the stop and making the switch to get to school. About an hour and a half late. Just about every day.

It didn't seem to matter that much. The International School in Den Haag was a chaotic place. Ah yes, the American boy who is always late. The classes were conducted in all kinds of languages. In addition to teaching us Dutch they also had us trying to learn French. In French class most of us seven year olds didn't have a clue so two twin girls from Brazil did all our work for us. I found myself increasingly puzzled. After living in Brooklyn it was English that was my second language. One day I asked the teacher how to spell the word "of". She said "sound it out" in her strange native accent. Obviously a set up because "uv" still won't pass for me. The recesses were pretty wild. The play yard was very small and the French kids, maybe about ten of them, would terrorize the place, joining hands and swinging around knocking everybody down. "Allez!" they would scream delirious in their bullying frenzy. A lifelong prejudice was being engrained in my tiny psyche. Small wonder I didn't want to learn French. If I could have caught one of them alone it might have been different, but they stuck together like glue. Merde!

We lived in an area of den Haag known as Scheveningen. When Peter had first pulled up to a policecar and asked where it was they gave him an escort. It wasn't easy to pronounce but I think we got it right by the time we left. Holland was the neatest most completely organized society I would ever see. Everyone drove a Volkswagen. In back of our block of row houses was an abandoned military base. "Stay out of there, it's still full of mines from World War 2" I was told. I took this advice to heart and thoroughly explored the place. I couldn't find any mines. At night the lighthouse would sweep through my room, every 90 seconds or so. There was no heat except a small coalgrate in the downstairs living room and one night the weather off the sea was so heavy it broke my window to pieces. Steffi and I had a nursemaid named Alyce who I adored. If I bugged her enough she would always take me to my favorite place, Maduradam, a miniature city complete with buildings and streets I could walk through as if I were a giant. When Peter and Hilary went off on a tour of Scandanavia Alyce decided to take me and Steffi to her family farm in the country. What a lot of fun that was. These hard working people let me play with their rabbits (I got bit), use an outhouse with real newspapers and watch the Walt Disney Show (in Dutch). The next day I got to go out and ride in the wagon as they brought in the hay. Getting back to Scheveningen I couldn't wait to tell my mother. When I did of course Hilary fired Alyce on the spot. Whoops.

It didn't hurt that I was from Brooklyn. Since I learned how not to get to school I also figured out how to walk home across Den Haag to save money. It was easy really. All you had to do was follow the canals that all went left to the ocean. As soon as you saw the first one you went to the bridge and onto the next. When you ran out of canals, there was the Kurhaus in the distance, a giant hotel by the sea. Our house was about ten to twelve blocks beyond that. On the way home each day I soon figured out that if I stood at the bus stop looking sad counting a few pfennings in my hand some older person would drop a guilder on me so I could ride the bus. I'd duck the bus, go around the corner and do the whole thing again. After a little while I had enough money to go into the store and buy Dinky and Corgi Toy die-cast model automobiles. My step father Peter Morton kept on my case wondering where I was getting these toys from.

The one thing Peter Morton trusted me with was the new record player he'd bought. He hated to get up and turn the records over, so when he found out I could do that okay, that was my job. So of course I used to play the records on my own as well. It didn't seem like such a big problem at the time but I do believe the Peter Morton family only owned three records in 1957. The ones I remember spinning were Oklahoma, My Fair Lady and South Pacific, the three records everybody bought back then. Those disks meant a lot to me. DJ Carl gets his start.

One day I talked another eight year old kid at the International School into walking home instead of taking the trolley. He told me his address and I was pretty sure I knew where that was. He was a dark haired kid with a reddish complexion. He looked kind of fierce but he was nice and he liked to speak English which obviously was not his original language. Getting to his house by walking instead of taking the tram was a big deal so he instructed me not to tell his parents. Going into their flat I immediately was struck by how tight the place was, stuffy, no oxygen. The parents seemed truly surprised that their son had brought a friend home. "From the United States of America!" Were they upset? No no. Here have some tea. Looking up at the hearth above the coal grate I could see an elaborate velvet sculpture, all tailored in different colors to look like a shrine or a monument of some sort. On this sat a massive steel plate with an image. An image of a hammer and a sickle. This must have something to do with the Iron Curtain I thought. I'd seen that in a book mislabelled as the Aurora Borealis.

One week Peter's mother Virginia came to visit from Marblehead Massachusetts and she gave me a music box that played On The Isle of Capri. That gave me an idea. I would go around the neighborhood ringing bells and hum along. You'd be surprised how many people put money in the little box. A Dutch friend had a big toy wagon which we rolled around the block asking for old magazines. All types of people lived in the neighborhood so we got copies of Der Speigel, Le Monde, Time, The Guardian, Punch, Mad, Playboy, you name it. My friend's blonde older sister worked as the weather girl at the Dutch TV station. She looked like Brigitte Bardot. She helped us organize the periodicals. Next step was to go back around the block with the wagon full, selling people their neighbors magazines. What a scam. Or was it recycling? It wasn't that I was particularly greedy, it was just that I loved those model cars and my new stepfather was incredibly stingy. The sad part of the whole story (from my point of view) was that when we were overweight flying back to the USA in one of the first Boeing 707 jets in 1958, guess whose little cars got left in the airport ashtrays for being too heavy.

But before we left the Netherlands, Peter had gotten the racing car bug himself. Weekly visits to the local Zandvoort race track, and then a stint taking his sporty Jaguar 3.4 saloon car (and my mother) on a road race rally across Europe.

56

Then, suddenly, who showed up in Holland but one of the subjects of this narrative, grampa Rudi Blesh to take me on a special boat tour down the Rhine River through Germany into Austria and Switzerland. In search of the Lorelei. On the way Rudi and I visited so many castles to be honest with you I don't care if I ever see another one again. We stayed in ancient hostels where the sound of the churchbells and Rudi's snoring was hard to ignore. In Austria we visited the zoo where (probably unbeknownst to Rudi) his old Vienna playmate Dr. Konrad Lorenz was studying geese. I got my first action photograph there with my little Brownie camera of a pelican trying to escape. We also visited parts of Vienna where Rudi had been as a child, a huge model train layout in Switzerland, and a series of art galleries where Rudi tried to expose me to the wonders of seeing originals by Gustav Klimpt, Oskar Kokoshka and others (a futile task). Also a few dozen more boring museums and a town records office where Rudi tried to find evidence of his Swiss ancestors before going back up to Luxemburg to hook up with Peter and Hilary, halfway through their road rally (they finished last).

The train trip to Luxemburg took Rudi and me through a section of Germany. I will never forget the sight and sound of those huge German border policemen with their big boots kicking open bathroom doors and terrorizing everyone on board. So these were the Nazis I thought to myself back in 1958. On this trip Rudi used to like to pose me for photographs. There are shots of me standing next to a big hurdy gurdy with the man playing it telling me to get lost, and back in Holland a shot of me with a Dutch girl my age in full local costume with wooden shoes. We look like we can't stand each other, two eight year olds of the opposite sex. Ick.

Modern Art USA

While I was living in Brooklyn and then, in the Netherlands, Rudi was back in Greenwich Village, the deposed Jazz critic, with Hansi quietly promoting the Ragtime book they'd written long before there would be any real general interest. Rudi also worked on a later edition of Shining Trumpets where he tried somewhat unsuccessfully to moderate the extreme positions he'd taken back in 1946 (he came out against Rock and Roll). He and Hansi also worked on a new edition of They All Played Ragtime with Sam and Ann Charters, the first in a series of revisions/corrections performed on that originally somewhat hurredly written story.

Circle had folded by 1952, the result of Bop, bad luck, bad shellac, bad business sense and probably too much good taste. Treasures that their record label now preserved are mostly there for the taking on CD from Jazzology. A labor of love that shows: Stride Ragtime/Jazz the greats: James P. Johnson, Luckey Roberts, Eubie Blake, and the newcomers: Dick Wellstood, Ralph Sutton, Bob Wilber, Dixieland Bands in their prime, This is Jazz, the Jelly Roll Morton Library of Congress recordings, Jamming at Rudi's, Wild Bill Davison, Mary Lou Williams, Bertha Hill, Pops Foster, Baby Dodds, the McGhee brothers and Dan Burley's Skiffle...

In 1956 Rudi began teaching, really what he'd been doing all along on the radio and on Circle. His classes were at Queens College and New York University. The circle of people who would be affected by my grandfather through his teaching activities would be ultimately enormous, both through direct and through secondary influences. The source. At NYU Rudi taught at night, adult education they called it. To a certain degree a waste of his resources but the (conservative) college in the Village just wasn't ready to jump in with both feet in the field of Jazz at that point. At Queens however Rudi was a full time teacher and so yes, you could say perhaps the ultimate "Jazz Professor" at the time. His students really loved him and the family collection contains momentoes of their appreciation, both for his knowledge of Blues, Ragtime, and Jazz, and also for his oddball humor. One photo shows Rudi with his famous phantom assailant trick, perhaps learned from Buster Keaton: Rudi is being strangled by a man with a bare arm in a doorway (actually his own arm, elbow hidden by the door jam). Another photograph is a gift from his students: a picture of Rudi doing a convincing vampire imitation framed in a chicken wire cage. Fang. Despite the come down, it must have been thrilling for my grandfather to be able to dispense such wonderful sacred knowledge (Blues/Jazz/Ragtime/Africa) to the most awestruck of fertile creative young minds, especially during the late 1950s - early 1960s cultural renaissance. Time to get out those wild shirts and ties from This is Jazz again.

It may be surprising today but Rudi taught African Music at Queens College throughout the 1950s-1960s. His association with Anthropologist Melvin Herscovitts while writing <u>Shining Trumpets</u> had given him a good background in West African music. Added to that was the good fortune, of even though being mostly unpaid for the sale of Circle Records to Riverside, the silver lining: some of the payment came in the form of a full set of African ethnographic LPs issued on Folkways, recordings made all over the continent from the Congo to Madagascar to the Sahara. Rudi studied these records closely covering the record jackets with his listening quotes, then used them to great effect in his classes at Queens College, sometimes with me as his assistant dropping the needle in the groove. It wasn't until the early 1970s that someone pointed out this great American injustice: Professor Blesh wasn't Black, how could he know anything about African music? Here we go again...

When he wasn't teaching at Queens (daytime) and at NYU (night classes), Rudi was still writing occasional articles for national magazines, liner notes for Traditional Jazz reissues and also the many revivalists and now of course, new articles, introductions to books and recordings in the growing fields he and Hansi had created: Ragtime History and Contemporary Ragtime. So there was life after Trad. He also continued on radio first at WNYC in the 1940s/1950s and then as an FM pioneer (before people were listening) on WFDR with his Dimensions of Jazz program, tied in with his Queens College degree program, the "University of the Air". Broadening his scope Rudi also did another radio show on Folk, Blues, Country, Bluegrass: Our Singing Land, and also Jazz Saga, yet another comprehensive Jazz program. The whole picture, once again only about twenty years too early.

In 1960 Rudi and Hansi sued one of the major television networks successfully for a prime time TV production, that featured Hoagie Carmichael, Eubie Blake and Bob Darch, but also used extensive portions of <u>They All Played Ragtime</u> without credit. Don't mess.

In the 1950s Rudi and Hansi also ventured often out to the (then) wilds of the Hamptons at the other end of Long Island to research, hobnob (and drink) with the emerging Art World stars from the Janis Gallery and others. Obviously Bill DeKooning, whose work now represents a big chunk of the Modern Art Gold Standard figures heavily in all this, though at the time he was still pretty much of the starving artist class. Hence the Hamptons, like NYC's Soho and Greenwich Village itself once a "low rent district". What a laugh. Rudi's book on the subject of so called modernist or abstract art: Modern Art USA came out in 1956, just in time to (almost) catch the big emerging cultural wave in formation. And despite Rudi's and Hansi's efforts to support women "Modern Artists" the book was still subtitled: "Men, Rebellion, Conquest", not too subtle. In this book Rudi also went out of his way to showcase the work of his errant son-in-law John Hultberg, my father, brilliant male genius. As in all of Rudi's life, in this case Art trumps all. I'm sure that made my mother, barely scraping by in Brooklyn at the time very happy.

In 1958 Rudi (and Hansi) published two monographs for the then notorious Grove Press. We say notorious because Grove had been responsible for bringing such lurid titles as Lady Chatterly's Lover and the works of Henry Miller, also occasionally racy Evergreen Magazine to American prep schools. (Of course today any child can see worse things on the Disney Channel, but back then...) Rudi's slim monographs for Grove were: a biography of Bill DeKooning written with Harriet Janis (DeKooning). - about the rising rebel Abstract Expressionist, then one of the Modern Art World "bad boys", and also a bio of Stuart Davis (Stuart Davis), one of Modern Art's original visionaries. Stuart Davis was particularly interesting because his 1920s work, though decorative, incorporated Jazz and Pop elements that would resurface heavily in the 1960s. DeKooning was heroic, a self mythologiser whose struggles on canvas (and with women) dated back to the late 1930s but whose life and family still preoccupy us today for some odd reason. Vaudeville perhaps.

Of course, as in all such similar situations, Rudi refused any work from these or any other artists he wrote about in compensation or gratitude or friendship, not even a sketch - as an obvious conflict of interest. We sure are glad he stood tough on that one.

from Modern Art USA (1956):

"They (the American Abstract Expressionists) will be long remembered as a remarkably rugged lot, with minds as well muscled as their bodies (Time calls Pollack "The Champ"). They are built like atheletes, and some of them, like Pollack and De Kooning, paint like atheletes."

"Something of the wild grandeur of these kids--space men of the brush and canvas--is conveyed in Time's quote of a remark by one of Hultberg's former San Francisco art schoolmates. Sam Francis, who is built like a wingback, is the "hottest painter in Paris," says Time...."

'I'd like'--Time quotes him--'to buy one of those flying platforms they just designed. Gosh, with one of those, you could hover any place you wanted, and you could make 40 ft. brush strokes'"

"Here then, is some of the newest new art. We look at young Hultberg's paintings and are reassured. No aping of success--or obeisance, even, to complete abstraction--in these extraordinary visions of ruined cities, broken houses, shattered ships. Nightmare lives in these pictures that are not quite like any pictures ever painted before. The private nightmare of surrealism and Chirico becomes the general nightmare of our time.

Then we look at Hultberg himself and are re-assured. He has the hulking build and the modesty coupled with quiet truculence which we have come to expect on our American modern painters."

(end quotes)

The Modern Art male beauty contest. You need big muscles to paint big pictures. General nightmare and broken homes indeed.

from Stuart Davis (1960):

"The most obvious thing about the painting of Stuart Davis is its American look: its gasoline pumps and highway markers, its bold-lettered signs, slogans and bits of "hep talk", its billboard and supermarket color. It seems to talk from the side of its mouth in "jive"--language caught in the act of growing, with fresh and undimmed meaning. But unlike slang, it refuses to date. As time passes it continually reveals new meanings, for its wit is like Mark Twain's and it's brashness like Walt Whitman's."

"In this interim [1927] a stage, empty and devoid of human beings, invaded the conciousness of Stuart Davis. He wanted no easy way out--even of subject matter that would guarantee a "modern" result. Though he felt compelled to reject the strong genre and illustra-tional elements that were part of the Ash Can idea, he still had to meet landscape on its own ground. The stage was his means of coming to terms once and for all with landscape and the literal idea."

from DeKooning, Harriet Janis and Rudi Blesh (1960):

"In 1953 another painter became identified with a woman--with a whole group of women. The artist was the American painter Willem de Kooning. The identity of the woman he had pictured was not known, but her appearance caused a deep shock. New York rang with cries of outrage perhaps not heard for forty years, since the 1913 Armonry Show had first introduced modern art to America."

"If De Kooning, with his seven gigantic, monstrous Women, had referred only to the Goddess and the Oedipus myths, he would have had a theme calculated to strike everyone in the deep defenseless dark of his [sic] personality. He brought even more to bear: a claustrophobic, strangling sense of space new to art. Never in our time had the magic of art seemed more like black magic.

The magic element seems to be increased rather than diminished when De Kooning tells how the paintings developed:

'I always started out with the idea of a young person, a beautiful woman. I noticed them change. Somebody would step out--a middle aged woman. I didn't mean to make them such monsters.'"

(end quotes)

Sad but true, to the mid-century American macho Art man, (rich?) middle aged women were monsters. It makes you wonder really how Hansi really felt about all this. The question is: has this honesty about sexism really made things any better, or do we now just have to live in its ensuing male echo chamber?

Back in the USA

For me, returning from Holland back to American life in Marblehead Massachusetts late in 1958 was still a small town experience. I made friends with the other kids on the Neck and we rode our English three speed bicycles all over town. Since we'd returned to the USA part way through the school year on my first day in class the earnest young third grade teacher asked her new student to lead the class in his favorite patriotic song. My what?

One of my neighbors on the Neck was named Josh. He had 25 pairs of shoes in his closet and his older sister drove a T-bird to High School. Their backyard was the old drilling grounds of the British Army before the Marblehead revolutionaries ran them out of town. We used to have great rag tag football games on that big flat field. Josh's father took us to the old Boston Garden, to a Boston Bruins game in 1959, back in the days when names like Gump Worsly and Johnny Bucyk still literally echoed in the hall. Another friend Peter Gamage's father owned the Lynn Item newspaper. We went on a class trip to their editorial and printing facility that had a big effect on the nine year old me. The Gamage family also took us lightweights up to Mt. Washington where we were very nearly blown off the side of the mountain by a windstorm. Gee it was great to have millionaire neighbors. This sure beats Brooklyn.

My very next door neighbor was my best friend Billy P. and next to where we both lived on Marblehead Neck was a giant bird sanctuary, the whole center of the island, just about the most perfect place for a kid to play. Trails that lead all over the place were mostly rideable on our bicycles. Looking up at the trees I could see owls and other wonderful forms of wildlife. In the winter we reversed our bedsheet capes from brown to white (as The Weasils), laying in the snow so the birders walking by couldn't see us. In the summer you'd find us hiding in the bushes waiting to set off firecrackers with time fuses to scare teenage lovers in the early evening. Ah the beauties of Nature.

My mother was obviously much happier than she had been in Brooklyn. She drove the family Jaguar now and even volunteered to be our Cub Scout Den Mother, taking us little monsters on field trips. At one point, perhaps later I was also enrolled in a sailing school out on Lake Winchester. After the whole summer of bashing about the lake in Turnabouts the head instructor Mary

Hogan realized she'd forgotten to give me my solo sailing test. Pushing me out into the lake alone, she watched from the dock as I was to round the various buoys within a few hundred yards of the dock. Suddenly, a freak wind storm boiled up out of nowhere. Not knowing to drop my sail I skated like a hockey puck all the way across Lake Winchester. Somehow I managed to skirt the wind along the edge of the lake and I got back to the dock about a half hour later, at least, exhausted. Ms. Hogan acted as if nothing had happened. Okay, you pass.

Each summer some of us in the family would go up to New Hampshire to the house in Gilmanton Rudi and Hansi had bought as Rudi's writer's retreat in 1951. The old inn house had once been an important stop on what was then the main road to Boston. It had been an illegal forge as well during the Revolutionary War, hence the name of the house: Hillforge. When I was little there was still an old giant bellows in a brick building across the road we used to play in and hay in the barn we would jump into. The summer place.

There was also an ancient Maxwell automobile out behind the barn. They said it had been bought by the farmer the dirt road was named after, Joe Jones in the early years of the century. Advertised as a 10 horsepower model, the crusty New Hampshire man had decided to put it to the test. Hitching up a wagon to the back he went down to Loon Pond and loaded it with sand, about the amount ten draft horses might be able to pull back up the hill. When the car failed (obviously) he drove it behind the barn and never touched it again. That's Yankee.

Together Rudi and Hansi restored the old farmhouse/inn in various period styles, decorating with antique fabric wallpapers, hand painted accents and filling it with beautiful old antique furniture. The two of them amassed what was probably the greatest collection of old marble dust pictures, Folk Art charcoal pencil sketches of castles and other novelistic themes done on sparkling marble dust paper (something like sandpaper). Over the years most of the sparkles fell off transforming these once sunny scenes into moody nocturnal Folk surrealism. Rudi had an eye for this sort of thing and with Hansi around their aesthetic sensibilities grew exponentially. I remember them driving around in Rudi's old Volkswagen, antiquing (and squabbling). There are pictures of me out on the Miss Winnepausakee boat with Botsie and Mary Jane Grossman and their daughter Mitty. They had a place in Wolfboro I believe. Ever since I first started going up to Gilmanton in 1951 New Hampshire has been this magical place for me, my once and future home.

Rudi did write up in Gilmanton, and when they summered there he had Hansi all to himself. Together they wrote another book, Collage about multi-media, found objects, even incorporating Happenings and other hip early 1960s ideas. Rudi said They All Played Ragtime was his book and Collage was Hansi's. But you only have to compare TAPR to Rudi's earlier Jazz book, Shining Trumpets to see how having Hansi as his collaborator had changed Rudi as a writer.

from Collage by Harriet Janis and Rudi Blesh (1962):

"... there is that quality in folk collage and in folk art in general which is called 'naive'. Specifically this means an ignorance of the artistic credos, tenets and theories; and practically it means that this ignorance frequently results in an esthetically productive freedom of expression. The folk artist, not hampered by preconceptions that a painting must be executed on a flat two-dimensional plane, blithely sticks on objects, builds up bas-relief, or even creates free-standing "pictures" in three dimensions. This "naive" freedom was purposely adopted by modernists from the beginning, and we will have ample and dramatic evidence of how, through its knowing deployment, they have altered art and expressed the challenging new concepts of our time."

"Almost immediately thereafter [1918] Schwitters found his medium, in fact his own personal idiom, in collage. He began collecting from sidewalk, dustbins, wastebaskets, and trash heaps, all their dusty tattered, castoff materials to paste into the extraordinary little pictures upon which his towering present reputation so securely rests. Granted that these mundane fragments can be transmitted through poetry and pure invention into important art works--and the smallest Schwitters collage, scarcely larger than a postage stamp, proves that they can--then a mere cataloguing of the castoffs he retrieved from the streets will show what an amazing variety of new materials he used, many of them for the first time in modern art..."

"It was in 1956 that Allan Kaprow transformed his own exhibit of collages at the Hansa Gallery into a carnival sideshow, a penny arcade, and the environment had been created. Kaprow is a quiet, bearded, family man and a college professor into the bargain (he has taught art at Rutgers University). As off-campus artist he is relentlessly unorthodox. Collage, by posing a challenge, became his springboard into the unknown.

'The environment came out of collage which is the prime mover in a kind of thinking which is 'impure'--that is, anti-classical and anti-traditional--and which hinges on accepting not only the accidental *but whatever is there.* Collage inflames the imagination: I began wanting to collage the impossible--to paste up action, to make collages of people and things in motion.'"

"Pop reports our whole subliminal, brain-washing environment: billboards and beer cans by the highway, neverending audio-visual chatter of the television commercials, traffic jam of food carts in the supermarket. Yet critics who presumably live comfortably with this environment are shocked by the art that reports it! Henry McBride, a great critic of an earlier generation, reviewing the Armory Show in 1913 put it straight. 'To be shocked,' he wrote, 'says well for the power of any painting.'"

(end quotes)

But then, a few months after <u>Collage</u> was published in 1962, while we (the Peter Morton family) were again living overseas, Harriet Janis, or Hansi as she was known to those who loved her, died suddenly of a malignant brain ailment.

Rudi was crushed. Standing alongside Sidney Janis over her grave at the Jewish cemetary, this would be a turning point for the man who'd come from Oklahoma to California, from New York City to New Hampshire. Stymied in the world of Jazz, having told the story of Ragtime twenty years too early, it must have been an especially difficult time for my grandfather.

But Rudi the author at least had already completed a compelling project in anticipation of finding some interest with the public. And it was in a field completely removed from the worlds of Afro-American music or Modern Art.

66

Buster

Buster Keaton had been a popular silent movie comedy star in the 1920s when Rudi was young. Whatever happened to the guy? Had anyone ever written a book? As it had been with the Ragtime story it was Hansi who had asked the original question. The instigator. Rudi investigated and found that nothing of real importance had been written regarding this compact extremely graceful doleful yet indomitable character. Determined to contact Keaton right away (1954) Rudi got in touch with the outfit whose job is to know the location of every star at any given time, Celebrities Incorporated. Where was Buster Keaton and what was he doing? The answer: Buster was on the steamship Normandy sailing to England on his way to France, where he still appeared as a headliner at that time. Not wanting to waste another minute Rudi immediately wired Buster by short wave radio, Ship to Shore. "Would he consent to allow Rudi to write biography" Rudi said that Buster was so impressed that someone would go to all the trouble to reach him on board ship that he agreed on the spot.

(Reference The Navigator)

Buster was from Kansas and Rudi was from Oklahoma. They both made their names in California. And they both had been pioneers in their fields and had been knocked off their perches. There seems to have been a chemistry between them which you can read in the book Rudi ultimately created, <u>KEATON</u>, Buster's only authorized biography. Rudi loved Buster. My grandfather once told me that Buster had confided in him: "I'm on the side of the animals". I'm not sure if there's any better description of Buster Keaton's life and philosophy.

(Reference Go West)

Buster was officially washed up in the 1930s. When he'd first come to California he'd married into one of Hollywood's leading acting families, the Talmadges. When Natalie divorced him Buster lost that ironclad connection. It would also have been his loyalty to his movie mentor Roscoe Arbuckle after Fatty's Hollywood show trial. Even though Arbuckle was acquitted, the powers that be in Tinseltown closed up ranks to collectively turn a cold shoulder on him and the other silent movie era stars. Charlie Chaplin, always a bit of a rogue was ultimately driven out of the country. Harold Lloyd made sound movies but who saw them?

Keaton made sound movies as well but he was drinking and he looks terribly unhealthy in them. They teamed him up with Jimmy Durante, motor mouth comedian from the Ragtime era. What a mismatch. Buster was so forlorn.

Buster Keaton had hung on to Hollywood for dear life. Fired by MGM he refused to leave the studio lot, parking his motor home (a 1930s Buster invention) inside the walls and never exiting. At night he would run big stakes poker games hoping to get one of the studio heads in dutch. No luck. It was always Keaton who came up short. Buster knew there was no life for him after he left that lot. What could he fall back on? He had been in Vaudeville since he had been an infant. Though obviously a genius he had never been to school.

But somehow Keaton found a life away from Hollywood. He made low budget movies for small distribution companies, instructional films, advertising promotions for wretched real estate developers, television commercials for Alka Seltzer, Phillips 66 gasoline and other products, most of which he directed himself so they're all pretty much all great. He was in pimply teenage surfing movies. He also appeared on television sporadically to recreate the Butcher Boy sketch he first did with Arbuckle. It is simply amazing to see Keaton the senior citizen standing by the bar counter, hoist first one foot up then the other falling about three feet straight down on his butt. But that's why his godfather Harry Houdini named him Buster. The original Buster. By the 1950s Buster Keaton had stopped drinking* and was finally ready to reclaim some of his artistic legacy.

*Rudi told me that when he lived with the Keatons in LA in the early 1950s, after Buster had gone on the wagon himself he would still mix his aged mother a highball every night. This he would send up to her room on the freightcar of a model train he'd designed to go through the walls of his house.

(Reference The General and the Electric House.)

When Rudi went to live with Buster and his young wife Eleanor in 1952 things were still pretty sketchy for the former silent film star. Eleanor had been a showgirl and she worked with Buster when he appeared at the Cirque in France where he was still considered a hero. But she was also eager to see him do better and make more money. A driving force on the elder comedian to be sure. As he was gathering material for the biography Rudi was approached by the Keatons and offered the position of managing Keaton perhaps as a non-profit venture. Rudi's answer was classic (for him): no, that would be a conflict of interest. Over the years Rudi also turned down other offers, paintings from artists he wrote about (Bill De Kooning, Stuart Davis, Mark Rothko), and I think perhaps other opportunities to manage estates. Perhaps his failure as a manager, his inability to find work for his New Orleans buddies during the Jazz Wars had soured him on the entire managing business.

No, said Rudi, he couldn't accept, but wasn't there a young man involved with silent movies locally, working with the Harold Lloyd estate perhaps? A fateful comment as it would turn out. Sure enough this person, associated with the art house Coronet Theatre in Los Angeles was eager to work with the Keatons. Enter Raymond Rohauer, a character deserving of a part in a silent movie if ever there was one.

One of the big problems for Rudi the biographer was actually getting to see Keaton's old films. He'd seen some of them thirty years earlier but what could he remember? What could Buster remember for that matter? But in this case, Buster had a plan. His old mansion in Hollywood had a secret room which contained copies of his old films. He and Rohauer would go to visit and recover the films. So they went. They rang the bell and the man who answered was new owner James Mason. "And what can I do for you... Buster?" was his supercilious greeting. Dubious at first Mason then let Buster and Rohauer in. Sure enough under the stair opened by pushing a secret switch a small room appeared filled with film cans. "Well thank you very much gentlemen" Mason replied ushering them out the door. Mason later made up a story about finding the films "after a renovation". A period of negotiations followed the upshot of which was that Rudi got the chance to sit through one long continuous viewing of the various films. This in the end, in the dark theatre, led to some confusion between movie plots which crept into Rudi's notes and narrative, making it easy for hotshot 1960s/1970s writers to take potshots at KEATON, the book, once the movies went back into some sort of limited distribution.

Because even though James Mason was obviously an SOB, Rohauer was an even bigger one. Once reacquired, all Keaton's classic movies came under Rohauer's control. That's why for about thirty years it was next to impossible to see the filmmaker's work. Rohauer simply priced the rentals so high that movie houses had to lose big money to have a Keaton festival. They could kiss his ass. The films didn't come out on VHS until well into the 1990s. Rohauer thought he knew how to milk a good thing. Poor Buster. Had he just exchanged one abusive family (Joe and Myra) for another? Starting in the early 1960s Rohauer and Eleanor drove the clearly ailing Keaton like an old farm horse. It is painful to see them on camera in a 1980s Buster Keaton documentary (Rohauer in a ridiculous baby blue polyester suit) wondering if maybe they might have pushed the old guy a bit too hard. This of course was after Buster Keaton the genius died suddenly in February of 1966 at the age of seventy.

If Buster lived long enough to see Rudi's biography, KEATON in print, it wasn't by much. The quote in the book says: "This is Buster as I knew him" Buster Keaton May 23, 1965. A photograph autographed by the star to Rudi at about the same time is written in Keaton's own shaky hand: "To Rudi Blesh, untill now my life was a closed book. Lord help me now!" The shot taken of the two of them together, pre-publication, shows Rudi and Buster looking at a dictionary. One last gag. Rudi had holed up down in Mexico City to finish the manuscript in the mid 1950s, but neither Rudi or his literary agents had any luck selling the book. Buster who? One publisher, Doubleday then did a doublecross and had a hack writer whip out My Wonderful World of Slapstick, a half hearted effort that killed interest throughout the 1950s. You remember the movie Sunset Boulevard? There are no comebacks for Hollywood silent movie stars. But by 1965 Buster's hard work in all those bikini movies had paid off and interest was gradually reviving in his earlier career. KEATON the book came out in print in 1966. Then of course Keaton died, so interest suddenly sparked in his movies and with the book newly in print Rudi dutifully did the rounds of the television and radio talk shows.

The Today show went well but when Rudi taped the Tonight Show with Johnny Carson sparks flew. No fan of TV ever, Rudi was perhaps prepared to make his mark. Upon seeing that the NBC television staff had cut and edited the precious films he'd brought to show, Rudi confronted Johnny on the air. "You cut the films!" "Yes, but what about..." Rudi clammed up, his arms folded tightly, glaring. He refused to answer and when they broke to a commercial he walked out of the studio. Yep, that would be Rudi.

from <u>KEATON</u> (author's Preface):

"There were two Buster Keatons. I met one of them at least forty-five years ago. This is Keaton the artist, and I met him then not in person but through his films. I recall his earliest two-reel comedies from 1920 on. No doubt I saw him even earlier (in 1917) in the Comique shorts featuring Fatty Arbuckle. I followed his work on throught he 1920's and well into the 1930's.

In the earlier decade there were three outstanding clowns or comic mimes in the silent films: Charlie Chaplin, Harold Lloyd, and Buster Keaton. Even then, I was impressed by the strong differences in their work. Lloyd could make one almost helpless with pure laughter, while Charlot brought tears with the laughter. Keaton made you laugh, then think. Lloyd, in other words, was pure comedy--laughter for laughter's sake; Chaplin was laughter plus sentiment and a kind of Victorian (or *fin de siecle*) poetry. Keaton was the serious one--from the never-smiling face on to extremely personal concepts of fate, which, for Buster Keaton, is man at the mercy of both chance and The Machine."

"If this story is not just the life of one man, with all its peripheral radiating connections, and is more a chronicle of a whole time-- seven decades--as seen from a particular vantage point, this is because there *were* two Buster Keatons. Beyond the man whom time inevitably corroded is the figure that time has burnished--the beautiful mime, the tragic clown, the artist, speaking through silence." (end of quoted section)

Everyone now knows Keaton was a genius. Here once again, an unaknowledged master of the arts, a film maker in this case, has been reassessed and through the forceful use of artistic literary persuasion, the articulation of enthusiasm, placed back on the pedestal where he belonged all along. Buster Keaton, once forgotten, is now at the top of most film students' lists largely because of of the earnest efforts of that dogged recurrent pesky persistent critic with the consumate taste. Rudi Blesh.

I got special permission to stay up late and watch my grandfather disappear on the Tonight show while at the the all-boys school I'd been sent to in Vermont. Before that, for almost four years the Peter Morton family lived in Rome, Italy.

Roma

After leaving the employ of former Bauhaus architect designer
Marcel Breuer, my stepfather Peter Morton had joined the new
venture started by Breuer's old mentor, Walter Gropius, the
original founder of the Bauhaus. The Bauhaus had been a design
school in Germany that pioneered modern design (and radical
socialism) in the 1920s. Among other things, the Bauhaus helped
develop the steel frame high rise building, as workers housing.
The fact that this design became primarily used to show off the
wealth of capitalist corporations is one of the great ironies of the
modern world. In 1959 Grop created a new type of architectural
company, a collective of sorts, to be known as The Architects
Collaborative. In Holland with Breuer Peter had helped design a
beer barrel factory and the new US embassy. After a short stay
back in the States (1959-1960), it was back to Europe this time to
live in Rome. The project they were undertaking was none other
than the building of the University of Baghdad. Peter's
assignment for TAC: to make sure they got paid.

You know how this movie ends?

Peter was a tough guy in a tough job. My mother says Gropius
used to call him his "Little Bulldog". Once while on assignment in
Iraq in 1962 Peter Morton witnessed the brutal first coup d'etat
set up by the Baathist Party. Sadaam was just a colonel back then
and I believe Peter worked with him at some point. During the
1962 coup, just to be sure everyone got the message the Baathists
executed the former government on TV. Now that's reality
television for you. Holed up with various informers, reporters,
CIA men, etc. on the roof of the Hilton Hotel, Peter Morton and
the others watched Hawker Hunters dogfighting with Migs
overhead. In the streets below tanks patrolled. A day or two later
an offer came to drive to the only flight getting out. It was risky
but Peter took the chance. Along the way the taxi driver was
stopped at an armed checkpoint. With machine guns pointed at
their heads the driver was asked which side they supported.
"Long live the Communist Revolution!" the driver exclaimed. All
the men at the checkpoint raised their guns to cheer along. "That
was close" the driver muttered as they drove away, "I just guessed
which side they were on". After getting back to Rome Peter was
one of the first Americans out of Iraq. He was besieged by the
news agencies asking if he had any film. Oh for sure he said, great
shots. They took the film, but true to his Yankee skinflint origins

Peter Morton used a tiny Minox spy camera (to save money on film). His pictures were great but you couldn't tell a fighter plane from a grain of film emulsion.

Years later when TAC had all moved back to Cambridge the firm fell into hard times. Peter's job had been to see that the company got paid by the Iraqis. Guess what?

I was also flirting with danger and Communism while becoming increasingly alienated and expatriated in Italy. Going to the wonderful Overseas School of Rome was a big plus. Classmates included kids from all over the world. My best friends were kids from China, Colombia and Italy. A few classmates were embassy kids from Communist block nations. The ruling clique in our class was the temporary Hollywood set, kids of parents like Jack Palance in town filming Cleopatra. Big deal. I never could figure out why the teachers made such a fuss over one tossle haired kid from England, Colin Thomas. Could it be that his father was that guy whose books my mother Hilary had on her bookshelf, the guy who went by the name of Dylan? Anyway I figured myself at least as creative as Prince Colin and other class star Holly Palance. OSR gave me a chance to try to prove that, right or wrong. I gained a great deal of intellectual self confidence in this children's community far from the dumber than you American public school experience. In the Fourth Grade we studied Greek History. In the Fifth Grade we studied Roman History. In the Sixth Grade we studied English History and in the Seventh grade we tackled American History. While still in Elementary School we put on a burlesque of Macbeth where the girls played the men's parts and the boys played the women. I was one of the witches, along with Piotr Parevich, the son of the Polish Ambassabor and a kid from South Africa. In music class with Mrs. Sparti we sang Woody Guthrie songs and did expressive dancing to Mussorsky's Pictures at an Exhibition. I was even picked to sing of duet on stage in front of the whole school with a girl, a song we sang in Chinese. In art class our teacher was the sculptor Bruno Luchese. For him I did an elaborate mural on paper depicting Hadrians Wall in Northern Britain. He put it up all around the ceiling in the studio and even my parents had to come to admire it. My short career in Art. For another class I crafted a little book of poems, puns and pictures on The Birds of Prey. School sure is fun when everyone is competing to be creative smart and cool.

Hanging out with the even cooler kids at the Overseas School of Rome, stories of getting to go to Holly Palance's apartment in the garden district with my buddies Fernando M. and Willy Wong. Hiding in her mother's vast closet Holly told us that her movie monster father was out to get us. What a laugh she and her dad must have had scaring the bejesus out of us. A little later Holly had us crank call Elizabeth Taylor. "God, it's Eddie!" she screamed and hung up the phone on him. "If he ever finds out about Richard Burton that'll be it!" she confided in us. What in the world was she talking about?

We lived in a district called Parioli. Rome was a massive puzzle for me. I had a map on the wall where I marked the neighbor-hoods I had explored. Tram fare varied, starting at about 15 lire (2 1/2 cents) for the ED/ES line that brought you part way to Via Veneto, below the Borghese Gardens. I found if you hung around in the back of the tram or hung on outside you rarely had to pay. Via Veneto was the place. They sold American comic books there, you might see movie stars at the cafes and the American Embassy had weekly English language movies at the MAAG theatre for armed forces personnel and their families. So you had to have American money. The US armed forces people were so strange to me. I visited a few of them since their kids were the same age as I was. This was probably my first experience with the rural minded American family. These folks lived in Rome but they ate Franco American canned spaghetti from the PX. They never learned a word of Italian except the swear words. Even when I was ten years old I could see these people didn't have a clue.

Above where Via Veneto snakes down to Piazza Barbarini there was an English language movie theatre known as the Fiametta. One evening I saw Some Like it Hot there but at least as interesting as Marilyn on screen was Anita Eckberg, hot off her performance in La Dolce Vita making out with her Italian boyfriend in the seats a row behind me. Via Veneto with it's hundreds of cafe tables scattered over the sidewalk epitomized all those things gracious and Italian, la Bella Figura, juxtaposed against it's most massive building, the palatial American Embassy. During the Cuban Missile Crisis there was a tank parked in front of that building. Whoever those people were, in there afraid of whatever, they didn't have anything to do with me.

The marines who guarded the embassy had a barracks near us in Parioli. We would go there and sell these young Southern White guys ladyfinger fireworks at a profit. They would use them to play tricks on their Black cook. Firecrackers. When I was eleven I'd taken a cast off USA Boy Scouts Handbook as my bible. Then I read that the US Marine guard contingent from the embassy had organized a Boy Scout troop at the Overseas School. I joined but was disappointed to find these clowns drunk, the only thing they knew to teach us was how to march around and drill with dummy guns while they lay around laughing and swearing like goons. America on display. Right on our own block below where we lived on Via Pezzana was an apartment with a balcony above often frequented by American looking bodybuilders. Sure enough after we yelled up they said they were Americans and invited us up. This was the pad shared by none other than Steve Reeves and his buddies, American gladiator actor stars. They offered us their autographs but for some reason we didn't want them. The place was full of jocks, smelled of sweat and these half dressed men admiring their muscles made me nervous. I found I was becoming more and more embarrassed to be around Americans.

No I was determined to be like the Italians, the nice folks who lived by the cancello downstairs in the small apartment block on Via Adelaide Ristori. These were honest sincere emotional people who took me into their modest home unquestioningly to give me a bowl of soup and some panini bread. People like the servants my mother now hired to help her keep the apartment and prepare meals. Inez, the civilian/child World War Two survivor as ugly as a witch in any movie and Rina whose husband was a Marxist so she came to work so timid working for the Americans. When Inez was a little girl the Americans and the Germans set up on either side of her father's farmhouse in Latina. Shooting at each other the soldiers managed to machine gun her and most of her family. Because she had been wounded in the war Inez rode the buses and got into all the local movies for free. She lived in a tiny room behind our kitchen and got paid 16,000 lire ($30) a month. She smoked the cheapest Italian cigarettes which she bought individually for a few pennies each. She told me that during the war they had just about starved to death. To waste anything was una vergogna (a disgrace). I took this message to heart.

I felt like her and the other servants because of course things never seemed to go well with me and my stepfather Peter Morton. Actually when we were alone together we got on fine. Peter liked to do all those things boys my age do: collect stamps, build and fly model airplanes, go skiing in the Alps, go skin diving, watch automobile racing. He loved to do all these things so much he really didn't want to waste any of his money letting me give them a try. Back in Marblehead we'd gone sailing together, even frostbiting in the winter once or twice. In Italy Peter took me skiing a few times and I managed to collect stamps as well though my collections in the end all seemed to belong to him. I also got the chance to follow his automobile racing hobby a bit, even getting into the pits at the Grand Prix of Italy at Monza collecting autographs of famous drivers of the day (1963): Jimmy Clark, Graham Hill, Phil Hill, Dan Gurney, Lorenzo Bandini.

The story of how Peter got to be in the GT (Gran Turismo) sportscar race that preceeded the Italian International Gran Prix was interesting. Having traded in his Jaguar for a Porsche for a Sprite for a Morgan, he met up with a down and out American hotshot race car driver and mechanic named Carroll Smith, at that point living with his Swedish girlfriend in a filthy apartment in Rome. I thought (wrongly) at the time maybe they might be druggies, whatever that was. Anyway, along comes Peter with his brand new Morgan Plus 4 and the racing bug. Smith took the car to a race car development garage in Rome called Giannini. There you could see Ferrari or Maserati V12's glowing red hot in sound-proof rooms on dynometers running flat out for days until they explode. When the Morgan was finished (a few legal modifica-tions) they were off to Monza for the big race. At Monza the car performed well and Peter had his first taste of big time race car driving. But the engine blew a headgasket about halfway through the race and it looked like it was all over. In the pits the young mechanic they'd brought along, Arthur Steinberg was all positive energy. Let's change the head gasket right here! So they did. Taking the head off the Morgan's Triumph four cylinder engine and replacing the gasket took 45 minutes, a new record. They finished dead last but they finished. Carroll Smith went on to work for another race car driver named Carroll, Carroll Shelby as the team manager for the Ford Motor Company assault on LeMans and was largely responsible for the FoMoCo winning efforts there in 1966-1969. Arthur Steinberg, the son of the world famous conductor of the Chicago Symphony was studying at the Academy of Rome. Arthur fell hard for Frederica (Freddy), the governess from Vermont of the family of Peter Morton's boss Louis McMillen, so they got married.

Louis McMillen was probably the impetus behind Peter's getting the racing bug to begin with. As a wealthy young man Louis had competed in the European racing circuit back in the day. One time, when we had first arrived in Rome Peter took me out to visit where Louis McMillen was living at a large estate in a farming district outside of the city. Peter left me there, and Mr. McMillen, after watching me play with some toy cars, asked if I'd like to ride in a real one. Sure. Outside he had parked a stable of fine sportcars. He chose an open top Jaguar XK-120 and we were off onto the long straight raised agricultural roads nearby, all but deserted except for an occasional tractor or farm animal. Sitting in the big leather seat with no seat belt in the low slung roadster, a few inches away the ground was rushing by at a furious pace. I gazed over at the speedometer which Mr. McMillen was also studying. 70 mph 80 mph 90 mph 100 mph 110 mph I felt my ten year old butt rising out of the seat. I grabbed onto the sides of the seatpad to avoid getting sucked out. Louis McMillen looked over at me. Afraid? No way. He slowed down. I'd passed some kind of test. Later after we'd lived in Italy for a few years his son Stocky (Louis McMillen Jr.) became one of my closest friends. Stocky was a totally unique human being who resembled no one more than a very young Aubrey Beardsley. Quite a decadent character even at the age of twelve. My Demian for sure.

My other friends included Filipe E from Colombia, and the M Brothers, Italian kids who'd grown up in Rome down on the Via Regina Margharita. We (Peter Morton family) had by then (1962) moved downtown, to Nomentana on a little quiet street called Via delle Isole situated behind a little park known as Villa Paganini. Fernando and Amadeo M's father was always away on business in America. Their mother cried all the time and Fernando confided in me that she thought his father had another wife and family in the States. We got back at his dad by selling the rare books in his glass bookcase at the local used bookstore. Just like the 400 Blows. Fernando had a record his father had brought back from the USA by Dion and the Belmonts. I borrowed it and I'm afraid to say, I believe I still have it, one of my oldest personal LPs. Fernando had another friend known as Wimpy, named after the Popeye cartoon character, a rotund American teenager who'd lived in Rome most of his life. Wimpy had lots of connections. He got us jobs working at Cinecita as movie extras in gladiator films, also jobs dubbing American movies into Italian, translating on the spot into a microphone. Early in the morning before going to school we also got jobs putting up posters for one of the political parties. The PCI, the Italian Communist Party, to be precise. The goal of the "afficheur" (even in Italy they used the

French word) was to get the posters up fast, and last. That's why they hired kids like us to run down the Via Cassia after all the other political parties had put up their advertising. With this team sports approach and more than a few thugs with broom handles the daily miracle was accomplished: hundreds of yards, a veritable sea of hammers and sickles as far as the eye could see running down the main road to Rome for the morning rush hour. What posters I managed to pilpher I sold at school later, mainly to American kids for US specie to go to the MAAG movies. So you see, even years before Russia and China got with it I was already trying to balance the forces of communism and capitalism.

In addition to the young idealistic people in the PCI, the other thing that probably saved me from becoming a total delinquent monster in Rome was music. The Peter Morton family had a scarcity of records that I played to death back in 1962. Mahalia Jackson's pounding In The Upper Room on ep (the source of Little Richard's Ooooos) and Frank Sinatra's swinging Chicago ("that toddling town"), my "borrowed" Dion LP, a few Italian Pop singles, Chubby Checker, Joey Dee Twist singles, some Circle Dixieland LPs, a Bales and Lingle record, the three Show tune records from Holland and that was about it. Help!

My friend Filipe from Colombia had an older teenage sister. We borrowed her collection of Elvis and Ricky Nelson records for some intense listening sessions / evaluations. Hmmm... Later, in 1962 when Filipe went to school in the USA he brought back early Beach Boy records that were really stoker man. She's real fine my 409... In My Room. Now it's starting to make sense.

Some of the young people I hung out with from the Overseas School of Rome were into American music. But where was it? Finding groovy teenage music in Italy was difficult, maybe even impossible. Short on money my favorite gambit was to go to a fancy Italian record store with listening booths to pre-sample songs. I would arrive with a list copied from someone else's list but more often than not the Italian music stores had never heard of anything I wanted to find: Please Mr. Postman, Mashed Potatoes, What I Say, Runaway, Shout! by the Isley Brothers. About the best I could do was Duke of Earl by Gene Chandler and Stand By Me, a worldwide hit for Ben E. King on Atco. I played that last song and the flipside On the Horizon, a moody piece over and over. Gene Pitney's Town Without Pity, Roy Orbison's Only the Lonely, Dion's Teenager in Love, Lonely Teenager... have some self pity for the price of one week's allowance. Another potential source of Soul/Rock and Roll was the quasi mythical Radio Luxemburg. A Pop force to be reckoned with in Northern Europe you couldn't really pick it up in Rome at all. My sister and I once caught a few minutes of a real Rock and Roll song (even possibly performed by genuine Black American teenagers) while washing the dishes on the maid's night out, but the signal soon faded. Another source of music was classmate Holly Palance giving me Four Seasons and Neil Sedaka records on my birthday, basically our only mainlines to what was a pretty much stale plastic USA Pop scene except for R&B in 1962. As far as we knew.

What I was seeking more than anything was: American Soul Music, Girl Group songs, Motown, Del Shannon, Roy Orbison, Ray Charles, Gary US Bonds. What I found instead was Italian spin offs: Pepino di Capri, Adriano Celentano and Rita Pavone. Pepino had a crack (American) Twist band and Adriano was ahead of his time, like an Italian John Lennon, although he looked more like Ringo. Celentano had transformed Ben E King's Stand By Me into a moving love song to a blind girl, Preghero (I Will Pray). Rita Pavone was almost like Cyndy Lauper, before the fact. Looking for American Soul one time I discovered what appeared to be the Holy Grail. At the Porta Portese thieves market a single LP filled with terrific Motown/Soul music. This is for me though it cost almost two dollars, about a month's wages. Getting it home I found that the songs were all lame instrumental cover versions performed by someone named Akky Aliong and his Licorice Twisters from the Phillipines. Ripoff. But another time my stepfather Peter brought home a record he'd gotten on a trip back to the USA. Don't Knock the Twist by Chubby Checker and other various artists turned out to have on it one absolutely killer song, the original Bo Diddley by Bo Diddley. Well alright!

The Twist was all the rage in 1961-1963, kind of like a natural evolution from the previous teenage sensation: the hula hoop. We had twisting birthday parties and the Chubby Checker and Joey Dee and the Starlighter records were everywhere. One night Peter and my mother took my sister and me aside and instructed us to be on our best behavior. The guest for dinner that night was to be none other than Walter Gropius himself, the father of modern architecture. That means no smart comments out of you Peter said, speaking directly to me. He must have been pretty peeved when Grop spent most of the evening talking to my sister and me, telling us cowboy stories and yes, we did demonstrate the Twist for him. From Bauhaus to the doghouse.

My other secret source for USA records was my grandfather Rudi Blesh (remember him?). Rudi sent me two records that certainly changed my life: Leadbelly's Songs for Children and another inspirational Leadbelly collection containing the amazing "Follow Me Down". I was hardly unique in this respect, but that was when I truly realized and understood I'd witnessed "where the soul of man never dies". Life changing. Amazing that a single song, sometimes only heard but once, could transform a young person's life back then. Perhaps it still can.

Rudi also sent a record he had just produced himself by the seminal but reclusive Stride Piano genius Donald Lambert that was fantastic. Just ridiculously good. Rudi had rediscovered the humble piano man playing in a Irish Bar in New Jersey and coaxed him out into a recording studio to do just about his only recordings. Of all the great Stride men: James P. Johnson, Willie the Lion Smith, Luckeyeth Roberts, Fats Waller, the virtual unknown Donald Lambert was probably the best. Not as a composer but simply as a performer. The Lamb.

Huddie Ledbetter, aka Leadbelly was one of the most influential human beings of the twentieth century. It was Leadbelly who had proclaimed that the Blues was universal, something that effects all men and women. That's all most of us White boys needed to hear, whether it was Eric Von Schmidt growing up in Connecticut in the 40s, Dave Snaker Ray in Minnesota in the 50s, or me in Italy in 1962 - the same. The connection. A little while later I began to hear stories my grandfather told me about him and Leadbelly. Grampa Rudi had promoted Leadbelly and his music back in the 1940s and had even made sure Huddie got home alright to his wife a few times when the artist had been drinking.

Another time Rudi told me he'd arranged to have the artist sing at a fancy reception put on by the wife of the mayor of NYC, Fiorello LaGuardia in the Empire State Building in 1945. Rudi knew it wasn't going to go well when the organizers insisted Mr. Ledbetter play while strolling around entertaining the high class diners eating and drinking, smoking and having their conversations. Rudi watched helpless as these rich people laughed at Huddie, asking each other: "who is this darkey?", blowing cigarette smoke in his face in disrespect. As they all left the event to take the elevator downstairs the White lift operator plainly told Huddie he could use the freight. Rudi said he saw Leadbelly's eyes go from blue to red and he knew that in a few seconds the great Folksinger was going to have another murder on his hands. Fortunately for all Mrs. LaGuardia stepped in and told the elevator boy Mr. Ledbetter was part of their group. Follow me down.

So, as far away as I might be in Italy Rudi still knew the source - and he made sure I got the Blues message. And Stride as well. I might have been in a mostly crummy situation with my stepfather but in 1963 at least I had my bicycle, Leadbelly, Bo Diddley and the shared idealism of the oncoming world socialist revolution.

I also was at the point where I spoke the language pretty well and could usually pass for an Italian. Looking at my blond hair people would ask: "You're from the north, right?"

Suddenly it was time to go back to America, just as my northern Italian vitelone bluesman commie twister surfer identity was starting to happen. America, the home of Blues Soul music and the evil capitalist imperialism. Was I ready for this? On board the Cristofero Colombo ocean liner I spent my time up in the First Class bar sipping shirley temples and reading American magazines. It seems there was this blind kid from Detroit who was my age and had already made hit records with his harmonica on Motown Records. Stevie Wonder, add him to the list.

Back in the USA Again

Settling back in at Marblehead Junior High School in the autumn of 1963 my mission was as plain as anything. Obviously the time was right to organize a Communist revolution in the USA. Working out of my locker at school I distributed pamplets (in Italian) and big posters with the hammer and sickle superimposed on the Italian flag. Actually I sold them. A few days later three girls screamed when they saw me in the school hall. "Look a beetle!" They cried out. Is that what they call socialists in New England? Or was it the long "surfer" haircut I had to avoid having to pay for barbershop visits? A few weeks later the principal of the American school, a Mr. Place, called me into his office. His hands were shaking and his face was white, like someone in the Middle Ages actually confronting an actual satanist. "You're in America, now Carl." "Yes, but don't you realize that the capitalist system is doomed Mr.Place? Have you read Trotsky? Have you?" He didn't have an answer did he?

A few days later someone killed the President of the United States. I suddenly realized there were two known Communists in America at that point in our country's history and I was one of them. Maybe it would be better to delay the revolution for a while, at least until things calmed down a bit. I was amazed at the reaction of the mindless kids on the American school bus after the assassination. "Did you kill him?" They laughed and joked. Had they ever had a serious moment in their lives?

Turning to the American AM radio dial I searched again for American Soul Music. Ben E. King had come and gone and in his place were Nino Tempo and April Stevens harmonizing (with harmonica) on the haunting Folk/Skiffle Deep Purple. Also Hey Baby by Bruce Channel a similar Skiffley harmonica driven tune, and the HiFi TradJazz of Englishman Kenny Ball's Midnight in Moscow. The Shirelles were there with Soldier Boy and Sam Cooke was still Twisting the Night Away but mostly American Rock and Roll was out to lunch, crowded off the airwaves by middle of the road shlock. The DJ on the Boston station, WMEX, Arnie Woo Woo Ginsberg was interesting and in his quirky offbeat personality lay the potential it would seem. Were Americans too clean cut these days to go for anything wilder than the Beach Boys, say, in their matching striped shirts singing about cars? Time would tell.

Back in the USA it turned out all the kids my age now had fancy imported ten speed racing bicycles. Gee I thought I would have been the only one, with my Harthener that I'd paid for myself in Italy. Teaming up with my old friend and neighbor Billy P. we took a long day ride north of Marblehead, through Salem and Beverly almost to Gloucester. We were hoping to soon organize a trip across the USA but for now twenty miles up to Cape Ann and back was pretty good for thirteen year olds. It was getting dark as we crossed the Beverly Bridge into Salem so we decided to stop at the Howard Johnson's and call our folks. Billy locked his bike but being full of the moment I said what the heck, this is America, not Italy. I was wrong because when we got back outside Billy's ten speed was there and mine was gonzo. It was Italy. You've seen the motion picture The Bicycle Thieves where the poor hero is walking down the center of the street ignoring all the vehicles in the search for his lost means of transportation? Well that was me in the fall of 1963 walking the four miles or so back to Marblehead Neck looking in everyone's garage and driveway. I felt like something had been torn out of my body. It was doubtful there would ever be anything to fill that space again.

Suddenly there was something. Something real, maybe to even replace the bike, the young president, the European grace now disappearing from my life. For my fourteenth birthday my mother had promised me a special present. Checking out her hiding place I soon uncovered the Beatle's first (US released) record. Carefully slitting the shrink wrap I had the LP played and mostly memorized before I put it back in the bag in the hiding place. She must have been suprised when I opened the present. So you know the songs already? My main problem was figuring out which Beatle sang which song and which Beatle was the coolest, the leader perhaps. My feeling it was John. Three days after my birthday the Beatles played on the Ed Sullivan Show. There they were. They were real. From then on it was pretty obvious John Lennon, as always a step ahead of us all, was going to change America, make it safe for Soul Music. Sitting with my junior high school buddies making model cars (fumes anyone?) and listening to the Beatles do those amazing songs on the AM radio who could deny the onrushing world transformation? Rock and Roll was now definitely here to stay.

Attending Marblehead Junior High School was a world apart from the Overseas School of Rome. Shaped in a square with a useless patch of grass in the center the school was run like a prison.

Talking above a whisper in the hall could get you "anowah" (an hour), as could walking too fast. Passing anyone else in the hall could get you two hours (detention). Of course they didn't have surveillance cameras yet so they deputized student rat "Hall Monitors" to stand every 40 feet to observe all behavior. George Orwell was here. Some of us would sneak into the girls room through the exit door just so we could run the length of the washroom and pop back out the entrance. We actually passed other kids and got away with it. Probably my greatest accomplishment while I was there. One day two local dogs got into the center grass patch. Every classroom facing inward got to see them at play. I'm not sure what they were up to but somehow the two dogs got stuck together back to back. I'm sure this had nothing to do with anyone's education plan back then. There were at least two tenured teachers, sisters actually whose skills in the field of education had long since expired. One of them, Sarah (or was it Mary?) I had for Science Class. After I'd told her I thought the Volkswagen was a great car she flunked my class project, a working periscope. You don't have to be taught to be stupid, but it sure helps.

The Principal of course was no fan of mine and when my stepfather announced I was going to go away to a boarding school, Mr. Place made a special effort to give me a negative recommendation. "...has shown absolutely no academic promise whatever". How would he have known? So suddenly I was leaving the family, this time for the entire school year excepting holidays. Vermont Academy was to be my new home and it was there that we left off the story of me watching Rudi briefly on the Johnny Carson show with my schoolmates.

VA was an interesting school back then, if you liked football. Their main claim to fame was that they were a small school of 210 (all male) students that took on 600+ student schools like Mount Hermon. Vermont Academy always lost but at least we tried. My job at the school was to try to get the huge semi-illiterate 20 year old+ Vermont farmboys the school brought in as Post Graduate "ringers" (linemen) to pass their French language requirement. To do this I was encouraged to tutor them, do their homework and help them cheat on the tests, although the "low shoulder" didn't help senior varsity quarterback Jim M. Try as we might he still flunked out without that French credit in my Freshman year. What does learning French have to do with football anyway?

Also in my Freshman year we youngest students played touch football regularly against two other area schools. Our secret weapon was the local townie Hotaling twins to whom we occasionally assigned the same number shirt. You'd be suprised how often no one caught on to that simple trick. It isn't easy to be at two different places at the same time (throwing and catching a touchdown pass, for example) but they managed it. Our two adversaries in the Vermont touch football league couldn't have been more different. The first bunch of kids we squared off against was the motley crew from Kurn Hattin, a local orphanage full of tough cast off Vermont kid thugs. These were ten to twelve year olds but we regularly got our butt kicked. Even if you're a fourteen year old it's extremely hard to catch or even touch a squirrelly little farm brat with a football. I also volunteered as a Big Brother at Kurn Hattin and learned a little bit more about what it was like growing up poor in that tough rural environment.

The other school we played touch football against as Freshmen was Putney School, a place with a history all it's own. We never lost a game to the pampered kids at Putney, even though some of them were seniors. You see at Putney they had no rules. You didn't have to play sports. You didn't have to go to classes. At VA we could be thrown into detention for simply failing to say Sir at the end a question. At Putney the kids routinely cursed out their poor exasperated coach and teachers, which of course was quite amusing to us young convicts. Putney was an experimental private school along the lines of Summerhill in England.

Also at Vermont Academy in 1964, as a freshman I heard another classmate, who I think had attended Putney previously, a red headed kid, sing and play a note perfect version of Dave Van Ronk's Cocaine on a six string acoustic guitar. Wow you can do that? He said he'd been a runaway and a few weeks later he'd run away from our school as well. Runaway with a guitar. The image stuck in my fourteen year old mind. Some of those kids from Putney really had their stuff together with this Folk music.

It was only much later, after I'd read Eric Von Schmidt and Jim Rooney's Baby Let Me Follow You Down that I learned about the real Folk/Blues kid originators from Putney School.

The legendary class of 1958.

First there was Debbie Green. Debbie played fingerstyle guitar, pretty unusual at the time. On a summer break in 1957 she'd ran off to Greenwich Village and got over involved with a much older Ragtime Bluesman Dave Van Ronk. Sweet Substitute. Along with a broken heart Dave passed on the secret guitar mojo and a repetoire of old English Folk Ballads to Debbie as well. Fleeing back to Putney the girl had had a Folk Music education.

Her classmate at Putney School was young wildman Geno Foreman who played Black style Blues Ragtime guitar and sang like he came from Memphis in 1927. Except he was a 17 year old White kid and it was 1958 in Vermont. Either way too late or a bit too early depending on how you look at it.

After graduation both Debbie and Geno gravitated towards the Boston area. Debbie enrolled at Boston University. It was there that she encountered the beanie. One of the things you definitely had to do in 1958 if you didn't want to be sent to a mental hospital was to wear a little cap when you were a freshman at college. If you didn't, the upper classpeople had every right to beat you ("hazing"). One of those quaint inheritances from the English Public school system. It must be hard to understand now, but conformist social pressure used to be so oppressive back in the 1950s that people could easily be institutionalized indefinitely for the simplest of transgressions, failing to cut one's hair, or refusing to wear proper clothing, for instance. That is why the Beatles unleashed a firestorm when they combed their hair down in 1962. No one had ever tried that, or at least that is how it seemed at the time. So back in 1958 at BU, the beanies were still a big deal. Debbie Green, original Folk guitar heroine, looked at the beanie and wondered what a girl from Putney School was supposed to do in this situation. She looked around and every other freshman had their stupid little skullcap in place. Every one, but one. A darker Madonna like girl also stood there looking at the ridiculous hat in her hand. Debbie introduced herself. The Spanish eyed girl said her name was Joan Baez (pronounced Bahz).

Joan also came from an unconventional background: her father Albert Baez was a former defense scientist who'd quit to become a Quaker and work for UNESCO. Joan's mother was a commited Lesbian activist in 1958. No Joan wasn't going to wear the beanie either. She and Debbie bonded immediately, and in the ensuing weeks/months, Miss Baez acquired some of the guitar mojo and most of the repetoire of old English ballads from Miss Green.

Joan also got her first real boyfriend, the wildboy Geno Foreman himself. Geno used to arrive at the Baez residence in Belmont at dawn after partying all night, tearing up the lawn with his motorcycle screaming out obscenities related to Miss Baez's anatomy for all the neighbors to hear. Poor old Al Baez, good Quaker that he was would come out and invite Geno in for breakfast. Geno went on to Europe, heavy drug use, Dylan bodyguard status and an early death in London. He never even slowed down enough to record anything it would seem. Joan went on to be the biggest superstar Folk had ever seen, due in no small part to the repetoire she had gotten from Debbie. Miss Green became the reigning beauty of the Cambridge scene after Joan went stellar international. Debbie was first Mrs. Rolf Cahn, another guitar master connection, then Mrs. Eric Anderson. I saw Debbie Green Anderson accompanying her husband at Club 47 in 1966 and I can tell you, she was radiant even in the background. But just for the record, it did all start at Putney School, where we played touch football as Freshmen in 1964, a few years after it mattered, back then when a few years mattered a lot.

Most of my time at Vermont Academy was spent in the woods, running/skiing cross country, smoking cigarettes, fishing, looking at old books and magazines in the library, trying to learn to play guitar, hiding out writing poetry. Sometimes a few of us would slip out at night to run in the forest. After a while we'd hear our running coach Mr. Rousseau trailing behind us, tracking us by the glow of our far off cigarettes, the sound of our panting, of course with the intention of catching us. That would have meant getting expelled for being out of the dorm at night, smoking, etc. We would play cat and mouse with the coach for hours at night sometimes, almost letting him catch us then running even further. The next morning we'd see him eyeballing us all at breakast, trying to figure out which of us he'd been chasing the night before. There's definitely some deep freudian symbolism in all this but I'm not sure I knew what to make of it at the time.

One of the older kids at the dorm during my Sophomore year was a Junior named Dawson Farber, one of the school's ruling student elite. He used to store Colt 45 Malt Liquor on ice in the wall. It was okay. His father owned the company. Dawson even had his own beer named for him. Who was going to tell him he couldn't pop a brew? Dawson's roommate was the Junior Varsity quarterback, Peter Larson. Together they had the greatest collection of early Rolling Stones records I used to listen to whenever I was assigned to cleaning their room as a "plebe". Now I could see that the Rolling Stones was where the spirit of Chuck Berry and even my man Bo Diddley still ran free. In this group it seemed like it was the rhythm guitarist Brian Jones who kept them on track, a Folk Blues purist probably. Another kid at VA, Michael D. was from Mexico. Guess what he brought back a pound of after Christmas vacation. Enough for the whole school in 1966. Time stood still and working in the cafeteria waiting on professors and their families was exactly like being underwater in an aquarium. Blub blub blub. One day running to get to morning chapel late I went out in only my Harris Tweed jacket over my dress shirt and tie. When I got to the cafeteria a little later they told me the temperature was thirty below. Thank goodness the Hebrides Harris Tweed wool jackets Peter Morton brought back from London were still thick back then. Other times I would bring a fish I'd caught the day before in a Vermont stream and the cafeteria people would serve it up to me like a king while everyone else including the headmaster got the same old eggs, cold cereal and gruel. Henry David Thoreau Jr.

As it was in Italy my ultimate salvation at prep school was music. A couple of the football player types were into Blues so when it got out I had Leadbelly records I was in with them. The other records my grandfather gave me, Staples Singers, Woody Guthrie, Chicago the Blues Today (produced by Sam Charters) were all cutting edge at the time. One classmate in particular, Robby Seaver was a truly poetic character as well as being a jock. Robby taught me that you could rebel in small ways, like not wearing socks or underwear and not brushing your teeth. His father had sent him to school with a collection of 500 mens magazines. Even in this compressed setting it was obvious to me that here was someone who was larger than life. Robbie played occasional guitar. Buck Mulligan to my Stephen Daedalus. We listened to his records, Dave Van Ronk, Fred Neil, Tim Hardin, Jesse Colin Young, Jim Kweskin Jug Band, Bob Dylan, Paul Butterfield and later, Judy Collins, Donovan, Yardbirds. Robby even took me to Club 47 in Cambridge a few times, to see Jackie Washington, Eric Anderson (w/ Debbie Green) and once in 1967, the Butterfield Blues Band. An offer to stay in a Harvard dorm room that night evaporated and I barely caught the last bus back to Lynn. From there it was a nine mile hike back to Marblehead Neck in the middle of the night in the dead of winter with the police following me. Maybe I had the Walking Blues now too, what do you think? At some point later that year Vermont Academy got around to

88

kicking Robby Seaver out of school. I wanted so much to write a poem to put on his former dorm room door, but I felt it would only be misunderstood. When I went up to see his old room I was shocked to see the door covered with poems by fellow classmen and even a couple by teachers. I guess that taught me something.

When I wasn't at school my stepfather arranged that I would be working at a job in Boston. As soon as I was old enough (16) I started in as a stockboy at Filenes in Boston on holidays and for two summers. Forty hours a week for a take home salary of $31.40. I would have had some money to spend but Peter also required me to buy my own clothes and books for school. The first year I worked in the beauty salon, sweeping up the cuttings and cleaning out the hair from the hairbrushes. Fellow workers included a Black lady whose husband was in prison. When the summer got hot I earned quarter tips running down to Friendly's to get lime rickies for the ladies under the hair drying machines.

My second summer at Filenes they stuck me down in the basement. You've heard of Filenes Basement? And the lower Basement? And the Basement below that? Well I worked in the basement two levels below that in the stockrooms filled with rats and leaking sewer water. My job was to assist the buyers who got merchandise from liquidation sales. Much of what they had was dirty, damaged, defective or in the case of foods and cosmetics spoiled. I was assigned to refill the shelves, the racks of clothes with stuff people actually might want to buy. It didn't take long for two of the buyers to figure out I could do the paperwork as well and after that I rarely saw them at all. Another one of my jobs was to open the doors to let the ladies in when Filenes had a sale. This was dangerous work, once you took the chains off the doorhandles the human wave pushed in like it was a Who concert. You had to be able to whip the chain out quick and run before you got crushed. The women who shopped in the lower basements were amazing. Big gals, they would fight over a 50 cent item and rip it apart right between them. They would try on clothes, even bathing suits right in the aisles. It was an education. I found that you could never get a rack of clothes down a crowded aisle pushing it forward or even pulling it facing forward, but if you pulled it facing backward like you were leading a horse everyone got out of the way. Go figure.

My co-workers in the basement were a strange subterranean lot. Did they ever go out in the light or even come up for air? One of the ladies printing out price stickers was a prim older gal who never missed a chance to tell me that she'd been married to a Mr. Heinz "and he knew 57 ways!" I'm not sure I knew what she was talking about. Another was a short stocky muscular fellow with a blond crewcut and an Elvis obsession. He favored the King's more recent movie work the most, putting him in the minority among the critics. I was amazed to find out he was pretty much totally illiterate. He had a wife he'd acquired in Vietnam and he never missed a chance to tell me what they had done in bed the night before. Again, I'm not sure I understood everything he was talking about. At one point in the summer of 1966 this person took me to a pool hall on the deep end of State Street where I attempted (unsuccessfully) to purchase a small amount of marijuana from a Black man wearing wraparound sunglasses.

On my lunch breaks I would wander around Boston Common, and also search out occult/hipster titles to read while browsing the local bookstores. Books I couldn't afford I would come in and read a successive chapter each day. Where the homeless alcoholic men (called "bums") slept on the grass of the Common I'd watch burley Boston City cops waking them up by aiming the exhaust pipes of their Harley Davidsons right at the poor guys' faces and gunning the engines. Nice wake up call. On the far side of the Commons there were music dealers, fancy salons where snooty salesmen sold Hammond organs and other fine instruments. It was sometimes fun to go in there with my hair combed down pretending to be in a hot Rock and Roll band. They'd let you play for a while if they thought you might actually buy one.

Further down towards the seedy side of State Street was Skippy White's House of Oldies record shop. Full of great titles and the weird greaser proprietor (with his own radio show) but a bit pricey. Skippy would really put you down if he found out you didn't know about some obscure Doo Wop title, which I of course didn't. I preferred the Salvation Army in Lynn, on the North Shore (bike ride from Marblehead on the weekends) with its bins full of pre-owned Negro 45s. One day there I got a single by a group on Atco (always a good bet) called the Hawks. She Don't Love You had that real Black sound. Of course later I figured out this was actually Levon Helm singing with The Band.

One of the records I bought with my summer earnings money in 1966 was Bob Dylan's Blonde on Blonde, a strange double record that totally dumbfounded me with it's romantic decadence. What could Dylan do to top this? Rudi had heard me playing The Times They Are a Changing LP at home at Christmas in 1965 and told me to take it off. Soon thereafter he gave me a Woody Guthrie reissue album on Mike Lipskin's RCA Vintage Series label.

On the radio I would wait for Sunday nights when WBZ would have a Hootenanny Show, playing safe (non-Pete Seeger) Folk Music. By 1967 I even had a crummy little reel to reel tape recorder (toy) from a Boston import store with a built in radio. I thought I'd really aced the system when I managed to tape Country Joe and the Fish off Dick Summer's show, now known as The Subway. No more money for the record companies from me! Soon thereafter the tape recorder chewed my precious tape and the whole thing stopped working.

Part way through my Junior year at Vermont Academy I ran away or maybe I just took a trip to New York City to stay with Grampa Rudi for a few days. This was in 1966. While there I took the opportunity to do a bit of club hopping. Going to the Village Gate Jazz Club with Rudi as a kid was oppressive. As soon as the managment (Art D'Lugoff) caught sight of the elder Jazz critic coming into the club a spotlight lit up our path. The pianist on stage (Errol Garner?) quickly segued into Memories of You or some other Rudi favorite. I sat squirming in my seat until I said I was going to hit the john.

Out on the street the West Village in 1966 was one wide open youth festival. Ducking in one door, a corner storefront I was suprised to see I was in the formerly world famous Night Owl Cafe, now a grubby poster shop with small raised stage. But instead of the Lovin' Spoonful the band was some bunch of kids my age I didn't recognise. With limited funds I slipped out of there before they cornered me for any money. I realize now that that band was probably The Flying Machine with James Taylor and Danny Kortchmar. But by now I was across Macdougal street where the Cafe au Go Go promised a show with Howlin' Wolf. No shit. Half of my total net worth, three dollars got me a seat in the back at a table and a glass of ginger ale. First up was the local Blues outfit Siegal Schwall. They were okay but not the Paul Butterfield Blues Band with Elvin Bishop so I wasn't that impressed. Next up was none other than Tim Hardin still in his prime. He did most of the songs now so well known right to the heart though I don't think he opened his eyes once. Now the moment of truth and sure enough right before my eyes appeared the man who Memphis record producer Sam Phillips once referred to as his greatest discovery, Howlin' Wolf. (Sam Phillips also discovered Elvis Presley). Where the heart of man never dies. Wolf sat in a chair at audience level rocking back and forward playing the harmonica while his crack band in gold seersucker suits (Buddy Guy?) pranced back and forth in perfect synchronization without ever looking at the audience. Absolutely amazing especially since Wolf sang most of the songs directly to the people in the table right in front of me when I moved up. As far as I could see the one he was singing to there especially was Davy Jones of the Monkees. Wild. Returning to Rudi's apartment I had to make amends for having ditched him at the Village Gate. Telling him I'd seen Howlin' Wolf didn't hurt.

The next night down to my last three dollars I was corralled into what looked like an abandoned church, The Players Theatre on Macdougal Street without paying a dime. Appearing on stage the strangest Rock and Roll act possibly ever, the Fugs. Despite the group's obvious amateur qualities, lead singer/poet Tuli Kupferberg was absolutely mesmerizing when he chanted and sang. Jack Off Blues of course the preppie lament. The Fugs bass player was Charles Larkey, soon to marry Carol King. The young Fugs guitar player (sixteen just like me) was Jonathan Kalb, little brother to Village guitar legend Danny Kalb (Blues Project). At the Players Theatre that night young Kalb played a huge load of Blues Psych lead driving songs like Tuli's Morning Morning into strange dervish territory. Light My Fire before Light My Fire. Still, experiencing the Fugs was a stange unsettling experience, like hanging out with the homeless. With the three dollars I'd saved I bought a copy of their second record which I gave to Robby Seaver when I got back to VA, right before he was expelled.

All through my Junior year at Vermont Academy I was the Proctor of a Freshman Dorm. Stressed out from being a homework mill for the football and hockey teams, driven to distraction by having to deal with adolescent brats in the first years of the psychedelic revolution, I snapped, getting thrown out of Vermont Academy for being drunk on the job in the middle of the night. One of the only times I ever drank hard liquor and definitely the only time I ever drank coffee (force fed) in my life.

Just as things were looking grim a hidden guardian angel appeared. It seems not crying when the speedo hit 110 had earned me a benefactor back in Italy. My stepfather's boss Louis McMillen was advising Peter to get him to try sending me to a different kind of school. His son Stocky, my old friend from bicycle and trampoline days in Rome was doing pretty well at the Cambridge School of Weston, a small somewhat non-traditonal coeducational institution west of Boston.

So it was that in the fall of 1967 I went to be a boarding student at The Cambridge School, an alternative academy with a long history in the Boston area. Coming in as Senior transfer student out of the Vermont woods I had a lot to try to make up. My classmates were the children of the rich, intellectuals, geniuses, the Overseas School all over again. Even though my interest was deeply into Theatre at the time I let my stepfather talk me into taking advanced Physics and Calculus courses which proved to be a nightmare for me, barely scraping by. But in the Theatre classes I did well, especially after my Drama Lit teacher realized I was Rudi Blesh's grandson. Whitney Haley had been a film and stage actor in Britain, now functioning as a sort of Arthur Treacher style expatriate Englishman at this posh prep school. Whitney always seemed to have a bon mot for me and I started to be able to come up with them for him as well. My favorite quote: "The secret of life is a sight gag". Whitney did love Buster Keaton... and banana peels. I appeared in productions of Aria da Capo, Idiot's Delight, The Mad Woman of Chaillot and some Edward Albee plays.

One of my friends at CSW was fellow misfit Jim W. With his firey eyes and wild kinky wiry hair Jim had the school uptight. The administration was after me for a while as well, for alleged hard drug use that turned out to be the brush on shoe polish I used to shine my shoes. The rap on JW was radical politics, he was like I was back in Italy full of the Trotsyite fever, the YSA (Young Socialist Alliance) were his mentors and their magazine was his rag. One day I put on an informal Minstrel Show in the quad where Jim and I managed to offend just about everyone. About this time I also was in a disasterous stage production of The Death of Bessie Smith where I put on blackface and forgot most of my lines. Terrible play, anyway. To make amends at the end of the year I took the only Black girl in school to the Senior prom, but she ran off with the soul band from North Carolina. Jim W. was a rebel, kind of like Robbie Seaver at VA but no one at Cambridge School seemed to like him but me. I took Jim with me when I had to register for the draft in Cambridge Mass which was probably a mistake. We ducked out of there right after I got my card, but just as the police were being called. Radical, man.

When Cambridge School kicked Jim W. out for no good reason I resolved to go and visit him at home. This was no easy matter. But somehow as a just eighteen year old I drove my tiny Austin Mini micro car all the way to Delaware and back (from Weston Mass) in a single weekend. You have so much energy when you are that young. I don't think I slept a minute. On the way down to Delaware I took the wrong turn into Camden, New Jersey at one AM. Despite the fact that I had just recently played in a Vermont Academy production of A Happy Day's Journey to Camden and Trenton, at this point in time (1968) you did not want to be in Camden NJ at any time of the day or night. It was like something right out of my mysterious father's paintings of deep post industrial human hell. I'm not sure how I got out of there, an illegal U turn in front of a toll booth I believe. Getting down to the suburbs of Wilmington Delaware at six AM Jim's mother was sure suprised to see me at their door.

Jim was a gracious host. He took me to a YSA discussion group and to a staging of The Dutchman, a play where a Black man gets raped by a White woman on a subway. My buddy Jim would have had no way of knowing that the author of that play, LeRoi Jones (now known as Amiri Baraka) had singled out my grandfather Rudi Blesh in his bestselling book Blues People as a despicable White Jazz critic who had no business criticizing Black Art. I'm not sure I even knew that back then. At the YSA discussion I put forth the idea that marijuana might be having a bigger effect on young people than world socialism. Pretty clever on my part I thought. Of course I was roundly ridiculed by all the faithful present. You obviously haven't read Marcuse! Already I hated these kind of doctrinaire Marxists. They weren't anything like the idealistic earnest young PCI people I'd known in Italy. Returning northward to Massachusetts I picked up fellow Cambridge Schoolie GW at the entrance of the New England Expressway and somehow we got back to Cambridge School on time despite losing the muffler connection and blowing a radiator hose which I fixed with a bicycle tire patch. Blasting the little Mini flat out on the New Jersey Turnpike I'd clocked in on radar at 72 mph. My stepfather Peter couldn't believe I got an 850cc to go that fast. I couldn't believe it how the State of New Jersey suspended my driving privileges when I didn't pay the fine.

At Cambridge School I volunteered as a Big Brother as I had at Vermont Academy. Going into gritty Central Square Cambridge I worked one afternoon a week hanging out with a couple of troubled elementary school kids. Misery loves company. In my second English Class I struggled to get through some Faulkner novels. The professor, Howe Derbyshire let me slide, writing poems instead of review papers. My recurrent out. One of the other kids in the class was Kate Taylor, a really nervous chick who spent all her time chewing her fingernails to the bone. Her fingers were covered with bandages and mercurichrome. Mostly she never made it to class at all, transferring herself into Macleans the famous sanitarium in Belmont. Hey, can I do that?

One night I went to a performance of The Importance of Being Earnest at Brandeis with Amanda Powers, a fellow acting student.

After the play was over and the audience was starting to file out there was a strange rumbling, strangely reminiscent of Cream doing Sunshine of Your Love. As it got louder it seemed to be getting closer and suddenly, rising up out of the elevator orchestra pit was Kate Taylor and the Macleans mental hospital band with Danny Kortchmar on lead guitar. In addition to the Cream number they also did a smoking Rock version of Leonard Cohen's Suzanne. We got up and danced onstage. When she got going Kate could sing just like Etta James. Wow, that was talent. As 1967 became 1968 the buzz was all about her older brother James, a seriously original fingerpicker and songwriter. Tom Rush had covered a couple of his songs on the album Circle Game where he also premiered the work of other singer songwriters Joni Mitchell and Jackson Browne. On The Circle Game LP the James Taylor song Sunshine was actually about Kate. The Taylor family rumours were all somehow intertwined with the new Beatles venture, the record company they were forming after the Magical Mystery Tour and their world-wide talent search.

Stocky McMillen was also in my class at Cambridge School but I think we saw even less of him than we did of Kate Taylor. Off on another cloud he spent his days perfecting his effete walk or creating simple semi-abstract line drawings of female genitalia. Privileged characters it seems Stocky and his brother Leander arrived when they felt like it in Stocky's 3.4 Jaguar (just like Peter's old rally car) and Stocky never attended any classes except Art. When I tried to talk to him about the old days in Italy he just looked right through me. One of the people I met at Cambridge School was a beautiful sophomore named Ann O. who lived in nearby Lincoln. By some strange quirk of fate she was also good friends with Robby Seaver. It was Ann who had given Robby the hash we'd smoked in a cigarette in Dublin NH in 1966. That would have been the first time I really got it, the first time I ever played records and listened to a really good McIntosh stereo, you get the idea. The day the die was set. At Cambridge School Ann appeared with me in my production of Edna St. Vincent Millay's Aria da Capo. I spent the night at her family's house in Lincoln shortly after her mother died, listening to Leonard Cohen's first record, accompanying her and her father on an art gallery tour on Newbury Street in Boston the next morning. To make the symmetry complete Ann became Stocky's girlfriend shortly after that. The connective tissue of life and love. Right after leaving Cambridge School Stocky went to London to join the Beatles, just like James Taylor. But while JT made his first (and in many ways his best) LP while at Apple Records, Stocky was notorious for hanging around and you guessed it, drawing pictures of girls' you know whats. In the movie Let It Be, If you look at the scene where the various Beatles are arriving at Apple to do business, that's Stocky hanging out of the doorway right before Ringo shows up. The kid really knew how to position himself. In at least one of the Beatles history books Stocky is mentioned as one of Apple's more ridiculous indulgances. Returning to America Stocky McMillen worked for a while at TAC before joining the Guru Maharaji cult and giving away the family mansion in Concord. His father Louis got written up in the Boston Globe once in the 1970s for cracking up his AC Aceca on Storrow Drive (he was unhurt).

Upon graduating from Cambridge School (actually getting kicked out the night before graduation for attending a party) I didn't go to England to join the Beatles. Instead I decided to go back to New York City, a place that had begun to figure heavily in my poetic images. Applying to New York University I checked the box that said Uptown Campus on the application. That must mean 14th Street right? Wrong. The Uptown campus of NYU was actually in the Bronx at that time, up on the University Heights overlooking the Major Deegan Expressway. Another world. Fortunately another Cambridge Schoolie, GW had made the same mistake so we went into the unknown territory in an uncertain condition together. The guinea pigs of the psychedelic age.

It was 1968 and many of the world's bonds of familiarity seemed to have already evaporated or expired. Living in the miniaturized NYU dorm rooms or in squalid tenements also known as the Puerto Rican slums preppy dandies like us might as well have come from outer space. It was 1968 at NYU and all the Freshmen were still required to wear the beanies. Being from WASPy New England I thought the Jewish kids had really fancy ones, held on with hair pins and extra side curls. No we didn't wear the beanies.

Local Burnside Avenue empties out down at Jerome Avenue where the 6 train took us all the way downtown to Astor Place. To the Fillmore East or to visit Grampa Rudi a few blocks away on East 4th Street for a dinner at Sing Wu. Further up on Jerome Avenue in the Bronx was a wonderful record store called Disco Pop and Son run by a Black vet and his Vietnamese wife. We duly pre-ordered copies of James Taylor's first Apple album. A few months later after working as whackos at the local WNYU college radio station we got promo tickets to hear James sing every night for a week at the Bitter End coffee house where he was opening for corporate Rock act McKendree Spring. The Spring were about as plastic as you could get at the time (1968). They had a sensitive singer songwriter who looked and sounded like Tim Buckley, the bass player looked like Jimi and the guitar player was the spitting image of Johnny Winter. The "crowd" at the club each night was almost all Mob record company people checking up on their investment. The group was nervous and they didn't really have any good songs. James Taylor as the warm up act was at the top of his game. His unbelievable unique finger picking just made anything sound wonderful. After a few nights he picked up on us being his only fans in the club so he did different numbers each night, reaching back to interpret Folk numbers like Woody Guthrie's Pretty Boy Floyd and also Beatle George Harrison's If I Needed Someone, among others. One night I was so tripped out I inadvertently followed the performer into his dressing room area. So sorry big guy help me find the door.

The Fillmore East on Second Avenue was a massive magnet for us. Three acts for $3.50 in the balcony of this big old Jewish Theatre was hard to beat. The balcony seats were actually the best because you looked down on the groups and didn't get withered by their amps. I saw Pacific Gas and Electric, Steve Miller Band (trio), Cat Mother and the All Night Newsboys, Spirit, Crosby Stills Nash and Young, The Jeff Beck Group, Procul Harum, Jack Bruce with Mitch Mitchell and Larry Coryell, Mountain, Grand Funk Railroad, Aynsley Dunbar, Family, The Who, John Mayall (with John Marks) and some others I don't even seem to remember. The best was the first act I saw there: Traffic/Albert King/Staples Singers. A dream set, also my first acid trip. Other highlights: Steve Miller, Spirit, and Neil Young with CSNY. The worst show I saw at the Fillmore was the Who, at an undersold matinee they treated as a sloppy soundcheck. Unprofessional. One peak night at the Fillmore, with future Disney songwriter Alan Menken - we experienced Spirit and so resolved not to stay for the headliners, some Top 40 hit band. Creedence Clearwater Revival. Oh well. The big challenge at the Fillmore for the dopehounds (GW and me) was getting out between the acts. There'd be about ten to fifteen minutes and we needed a plan to realize our objective. The kids who worked the door at the Fillmore were nice, but tough. You go out you're not coming back in. The Fillmore men's room was a cold dark filthy unventilated hole, a zoo of some sort. So G came up with the idea of running to get an egg cream for the guy at the door. An egg cream is just a NYC soda, kind of a milkshake with syrup, no egg or ice cream at all and it ran about 35 cents. The answer from the door was usually okay but make it quick. Out on the street we quickly headed for East 7th Street where we knew there would be hippie pot dealers sitting on the steps of certain buildings. Sure enough there he was. We were teen preppies from New England looking to score a pound or more. What did he have? Try this. Anything better? Try this. Wow, okay, like we got to go now and get the money. Off we run back first to the Gem Spa (to get the egg cream) and then back to the Fillmore just in time for the massive rush and the next act. This routine went like clockwork until we tried the same trick with the same guy twice on Seventh Street and got chased back up the avenue. We also forgot the egg cream that night and didn't get back into the Fillmore at all.

Our other extra-curricular activity, after radio, live music and various forms of "experimentation" in college was protest. It was great to be attending a university with an active war going on in Vietnam killing hundreds of American soldiers every week and the draft board breathing down your neck about your deferment. Whenever we could in 1968 we listened to Bob Fass on WBAI to get our (anti) marching orders. A year earlier the Yippies had been brutally beaten for tearing the hands off the clock on the wall at Grand Central Station, so hundreds of us gathered to lay a wreath at the spot. Of course none of us got anywhere near the station but we had lots of fun faking out the cops going down one way streets so they couldn't follow us. At one point one of the signs broke off and I picked up the stick to walk with. Weapon cried a cop lifting his nightstick over my head. Stop yelled someone else, an undercover detective I guess, grabbing the policeman before he could bear down on me. I ditched the stick and left the two cops wrestling on the ground. In the end we Yippies decided to go to Sheeps Meadow in Central Park, but upon arriving, through the darkness and the fog, we witnessed an ominous sight. The rim around the sunken part of the meadow was lined all the way around with mounted policemen just waiting for the chance to beat our heads in. At this point we dispersed. All you had to be was against the war or have long hair and you were pretty much guaranteed a threat or even a beating in those days. The wonderful 1960s, Peace and Love, man.

In 1969 I went down to Washington for the biggest anti-war rally ever. There were thousands of people and hundreds of police. For some reason some of us decided to drop acid before the event, perhaps for the magical effect. At the start of the rally we were hemmed in by crowds and police, ending up in a small store which sold (no lie) hot dogs and pornography both prominently on display under a glass counter. Outside folks were surging back and forth against the police. People filled the national museums, sitting under the displays resting and nursing wounds. Outside the tear gas was everywhere. The manager of the local 5 and 10 cent store gave away all the store's handkerchiefs so people could breathe. As we faced the police in the large open space in front of the federal buildings I watched riot cops start to charge at us shooting teargas grenades while the wind carried the gas back at them. Watching them rushing at us as if in slow motion, I suddenly recognized the photographer working next to me. Jim Church from Vermont Academy. "Have you heard anything from Robbie Seaver?" Jim asked me as a tear gas canister rolled by our feet. "No what's up?" "I heard he fell in love with a married woman and when she wouldn't leave her husband he volunteered for Vietnam..." Just then the police were upon us and we were being beaten and dispersed as a crowd.

Back in NYC I fell in with the usual bunch of Bronx hippies. Part of our scene revolved around Charlie and Glen. Charlie was a larger than life kid from a prominent Jewish family. His sidekick Glen had a sister who was Bob Dylan's housesitter up in Woodstock. At one point these guys decided they wanted to go upstate to look for land. So we all piled into my car, the tiny little 850cc Austin Mini (clown car) Countryman station wagon. Somehow the four of us including the rather large Charlie all fit in and somehow the tiny car made it up all the hills. Another time Charlie and Glen organized a bogus campaign for the NYU student senate running the old gag line character from a WC Fields movie, Carl LaFong. Please don't ask how that is spelled. Predictably the guy from the movie won, creating all sorts of problems for the administration.

A little later NYU decided to fire their only Black professor at the uptown campus. That was it, we SDS students at NYU decided to swing into action. Breaking into the Pantheon like History building before dawn about a dozen of us pledged to hold the building until NYU reinstated the professor. As we waited for the police to come in and beat us all to a pulp, images of the brutality at Columbia a year earlier were still vivid in our minds. Suddenly the door opened and a young history professor came in to negotiate. "Can I have my building back?" he asked and offered

100

the NYU Student Union as an alternative (university approved) demo site. After lengthy consultations between the various radical leader types (including one dude who went around in an army jacket with a large armor piercing shell on a chain around his neck), the answer: yes the consensus was we were ready to move our demonstration to the student union lounge. The marble steps in the history building were cold and the police were the next people we were going to have to deal with there.

(The history professor/negotiator who made a name for himself at that standoff: Bronx native Jay Oliva, future President of NYU.)

I wish I could say there was a lot of great feeling of solidarity between the White student radicals (SDS) and the Black militants in the Katara group we were supporting but there wasn't. After risking our academic careers (and our academic draft deferments) as well as our personal safety for the common cause these Black kids were still not about to welcome us to their demo. Their bitterness and racial mistrust trumped everything else we were trying to raise up as an alternative. This was certainly an education for me. I attended rallies and wrote "agit prop" anti-war street sheets with a weird anarchist guy named Peter Scucciamari. Radical man. In the fall of 1969 some fellow NYU uptown radicals organized the hippies, mostly big hulking Bronx Jewish giants ("shtarkers") into an amateur "touch" football league team. The intention of course was to challenge the NYU ROTC geeks to a friendly game they were not likely to survive. Assault training techniques and concealed weapons were all part of the hippie game plan. Peace and Love. When the ROTC trainees arrived it was pathetic. They were just tiny little Chinese and Puerto Rican kids trying to put themselves through college on the Army. One look at the Freaks and they scattered. A year or so later I heard the NYU ROTC hq a block off campus was destroyed in an arson attack. The Bronx responds.

One day in 1968 Grampa Rudi stepped in a puddle on the sidewalk on East 4th Street that turned out to be an eight inch deep sunken square of concrete. The owners of the local parking garage, the Hitners found Rudi a good lawyer and he successfully sued the city for his broken ankle. There was one problem however. With his leg in a cast grampa couldn't drive his car. So for a few months, in addition to my so called studies, theatrical appearances, anti-war activities, weekly trips to the Fillmore and consciousness related experiments I also became Rudi's assistant at Queens College and NYU (downtown). This was when I finally started to take my grandfather's full measure. I knew something of his reputation but up until this point I had never really seen him in action. Driving him, and cuing up the records he was about to discuss I fell into the routines which have carried me through the rest of my life so far.

Rudi was a very entertaining and enlightening teacher and his students often took to the message with a messianic devotion. One of his students, Alan Raeburn had an interest in learning the Blues guitar so Rudi set him up with lessons from the Reverend Gary Davis. Of course there were others. Rudi told me that in the early 1960s Paul Simon had been in his class at Queens College. Later, on his first solo record after Simon and Garfunkel Paul worked with Ragtime Blues guitarist Stephan Grossman and used a Dixieland Band. The multi-platinum multi-culturalist gets his start. Carol Klein, soon to be known to everyone as Carol King had also been a student at Queens College in the late 1950s but she quit early to write hit pop music songs with her husband Gerry Goffin. I don't think she ever studied with Rudi but I have always imagined Paul Simon could have gotten at least part of what he has to offer the world from studying with Rudi Blesh.

Ragtime to Hendrix

When my grandfather Rudi Blesh taught Jazz, Blues and African Music at Queens College in the 1960s one of the other professors was the young William Bolcom. One day, in 1966, Bill poked his head into Rudi's office area and asked: "What's this I hear about a Scott Joplin opera?" Many date the modern Ragtime revival from that meeting. Certainly the world's rediscovery of Treemonisha (from the folios entrusted to Rudi and Harriet Janis by Lottie Joplin) *6 started a lifelong friendship between Bolcom and Blesh, two true lovers of music. And new life for the Graceful Ghost.

Rudi's other classes, at NYU held their own surprises. Often Rudi would end one of his evening study groups with a trip to a local club or even a performer like Eubie Blake right there in person. One time during my assistantship in 1968 Stride pianist (and RCA producer) Mike Lipskin demonstrated different piano styles for the class. Mike loved the old music and paid for RCA Vintage reissues by producing the Jefferson Airplane and Hot Tuna. In the 1980s Mike confided in me that they were both "shit groups".

Mike Lipskin was the one who introduced the Tuna to Ragtime/ Blues violinist Papa John Creach. Big improvement.

(note: in the 1980s Mike told me he was upset with Rudi for having typed him (and fellow Stride pianist Ralph Sutton) as Ragtime piano players years before the era of The Sting - Ragtime revival. I really didn't have much sympathy for Mike on this one to be honest. Rudi didn't have anything to do with The Sting)

Another night in 1968, not on class time, Rudi took me to a small club in the East Village known simply as Slugs. A plain room off the street with a few tables and a blanket on a wire for a curtain, the place was filled with menacing Black power types and blank faced White hipsters with sunglasses. Suddenly from behind the blanket there was a huge commotion of steam and presence and a huge Black man with wrap around sunglasses charged out playing three horns at once. *6 This was Rahsaan Roland Kirk the blind saxophone genius whose music defied categorization. All that power blowing at you from a few feet away can be a life changing experience. This was certainly that for me. Whether he was bringing the Blues, or Swing, or Bop, or Pop back to life it really didn't matter. Rahsaan's music had a sweetness to it that others could never even imagine. Nectar was the only word to describe what I received that evening. And Rudi knew it too.

Because, after his initial shock at Bop back in 1946 Rudi Blesh had warmed to the mellower (less angular/mechanistic) Modern Jazz where elements of the Blues were reintroduced into the Bop mix to create a moody soundtrack to urban existential life. Discordant elements persisted however. Once Rudi told me that he'd been out walking with his buddy and fellow Jazz author Marshall Stearns around Washington Square when they ran into Miles Davis and his beautiful blond wife. Bending down to admire their baby Rudi was pushed aside by Miles Davis. "Keep your white hands away from that child." Shortly thereafter Rudi gave me a copy of Miles' Bitches Brew with it's twin album cover sides, the pictures of the beautiful Black woman and the horrible White hag. "Here's some of the most important music being made right now" Rudi told me. Had he outgrown the grudge? Or had Modern Jazz simply outgrown it's punk roots and re-assimilated the older (eternal) elements? Rudi wrote an elegy for John Coltrane for Life (or Look?) Magazine after attending Coltrane's funeral in 1967. A Love Supreme was one of Rudi Blesh's favorite records.

They all played Ragtime, right?

They All Played Ragtime the book was a slow but steady seller. You could find it in many public libraries. For many folks, piano players in particular TAPR with the Ragtime scores in the back was the intro into a life of Ragtime music. This was admittedly sometimes little more than a classical exercise, and as in it's day, the ragged music still sparked controversy. Scott Joplin himself had written "Don't Play Ragtime Fast!". But that's all people had done for decades, making of it a joke element for period movies. The Black "professor" entertaining the clientele at the house of ill repute. There was an element of truth in this, but Scott Joplin himself spent his whole life trying to disprove that notion, dragging the charming lilting music into the world of popular sheet music sales. With his training at the George Smith College of Music in Sedalia he found a way to clearly annotate the clever syncopations he had learned from the banjo pickers, traveling piano players and such. Next stop for Scott should have been the established music schools and the finer concert halls but that had to wait until the 1970s and the expiration of his copyrights. Along the way They All Played Ragtime remained the major initial impetus for most people, the Ragtime Revivalists' bible carrying them through the lean years with it's messianic message.

"If a book can start a ragtime revival, this one will do it." Alan Lomax, 1950 New York Times review of They All Played Ragtime.

Some people got it right all along. Max Morath, who became a lifelong friend of Rudi's learned to play this style from his mother who played in movie houses in Colorado. (His dad set off the fireworks every year on Pikes Peak). Max's touring show, his television series on Public Television and records for Vanguard were always instructional and inspirational. But of course I didn't really know about any of that when I hit NYC in 1968 as an ungrateful NYU undergrad. One of the first things Rudi did was to take me to Max's one man multi-media show. Max Morath at the Turn of the Century, at the Jan Hus Theatre. Using slides and movie clips Morath created a television program on stage. Dressed in period costume he ran down the social history of the Ragtime Era like a stand up comedian instructing from laugh to laugh. His visuals were amazing, much better I thought even than the light show at the Fillmore East. Every time Max would refer to a song that was popular, of course he would sit down and sing and play it with all the feeling it had in it's day. You could learn a lot and be much entertained by Max Morath. Kind of like They All Played Ragtime as a one man musical show. After the Max Morath show Rudi took me backstage and afterwards, I went with both of them to a local bar. Max offered me a beer and I had to be honest with him. I was eighteen and I'd never tried beer, only pot and LSD. That got a laugh. So I drank the brew. Didn't you have to support the Vietnam War to drink beer? (That's the way it was in Marblehead - the potheads vs the beeries). "No way" said Max, "I drink beer and I HATE the Vietnam War". I was still learning stuff. A few minutes later Max decided he should also try to teach me how to pick up women at the bar. I didn't actually realize it at the time but I had just gained an honorary uncle. *7

Another Ragtime connection of course was Bill Bolcom. Now recognized as America's premier composer, in the 1960s Bill was an up and coming musician who had studied with Darius Milhaud. (Rudi's favorite story he'd heard from Bolcom about Milhaud involved the composer's family after dinner, when they would all pull out matching silver toothpick cases.) At the time when Bolcom was starting to hook up with Rudi to bring Scott Joplin's Opera Treemonisha back to life Bill also recorded a series of records (for Nonesuch) that seemed to play Joplin's and some of the other early Ragtimers' piano music at just the right tempo, not too fast and not too legato. Stately but still, lively.

At the other end of the spectrum from the tack piano/speed demon school of Ragtime piano playing was young Joshua Rifkin. A former member of the Even Dozen Jug Band (with Maria Muldaur, Steve Katz, Stefan Grossman, Peter Siegel, John Sebastian, Dave Grisman) Rifkin recorded Joplin for Nonesuch (Elektra) Records at a pace that was close to sonumulant. Slow. With no actual association with Rudi the Rifkin approach defined the boundaries of the studied delicate classicist school. You couldn't imagine anyone actually dancing to a Josh Rifkin Rag interpretation but they did make for charming easy listening background music in stores. With aggressive marketing Rifkin's Joplin recordings on Nonesuch were the big sellers of the 1970s Ragtime Revival era.

So, now you had the Rifkinites doing artistic / commercial battle against the Rudiites represented by Bolcom and Morath. And that meant the Jazz Wars all over again. The axe again, I'm afraid. Rudi was big on principle. Rifkin played it wrong (too slow). Bill Bolcom played it just right for the classical approach and Max Morath played it right for the period - historical approach. The speed merchants like Knocky Parker, Jo Anne Castle and to a certain degree, Ragtime Bob Darch, and many others playing way too fast with little or no feeling on their tack pianos represented the evil stereotype. It was simple.

One day in the mid 1960s Rudi got a call from a young man in the West Village. He said his name was Donald Ashwander. It was obvious from his accent he was from the South. Mobile, Alabama to be exact. He gave Rudi the usual They All Played Ragtime changed my life story and of course Rudi loved to talk to people like that because they usually had something interesting to tell him. What Mr. Ashwander had to offer was the fact that he wrote Ragtime music right then, in 1966. This wasn't actually all that unusual. Max Morath also wrote his own Rags, one of them dedicated to Harriet Janis. Bill Bolcom was experimenting with the form, later that was to be one of his claims to fame. Rudi asked the young man on the other end of the telephone line if he could play him one of his Rags and so Donald pulled the telephone receiver over to the piano and played Rudi his Business in Town Rag right on the spot. It was really a great Rag, full of melody and that wonderful lilting quality that of course would be epitomized by the gracious city of Mobile. They made a date to meet so Rudi could hear more. About a half hour later Donald Ashwander called Rudi back again. "You're not going to believe this Mr. Blesh but my apartment building just burned and I have absolutely nowhere to go." So Donald came over and stayed on the old day bed at Rudi's East 4th Street apartment until he could get himself a new place to live. After staying with Rudi Donald Ashwander kept writing Rags. One of them, Astor Place Rag, was dedicated to Rudi's favorite liquor store.

During this period there were many suspicious fires in Greenwich Village as landlords did what they thought they had to do to get out of what was perceived to be a doomed market. Hundreds of tenements in the Lower East Side were abandoned by landlords falling into the hands of drug dealers, squatters, derelicts, arsonists. Or were burned intentionally for the insurance money. The saying went that if you had a nice landlord he would let you know before they torched the place. It would appear that Donald's landlord wasn't one of the nice ones. The sad thing was that if the property owners could wait it out, the NYC White flight real estate panic of the late 1960s / 1970s finally played out when White people figured out that Fair Housing laws didn't destroy the neighborhoods and Black and Puerto Rican people were mostly great people to have as neighbors. The folks who waited out the 1960s-1970s stupidity panic stood to gain richly as values first dropped and then rebounded mightily in the 1980s.

One day in 1967 after Donald had found another apartment he and Rudi were having lunch together at Ratners, a Jewish dairy restaurant on Second Avenue that was actually right next to the Fillmore East at that time. Eating their blinzes they were a bit surprised when a young Black man came over and said he would like to shake Rudi's hand. He said that he had recognized Rudi and wanted to pay his respects. Rudi thanked him very much and the young guy went back and sat down at his table. "Nice young man" Rudi commented. "You don't know who that is?" Donald asked him. "Not really". "That's Jimi Hendrix sitting over there at that table, Rudi..." "Jimmy who?" So Rudi went out and bought Jimi's first record. Most of it was just too fast and furious. "The Blues should always breathe" Rudi had told me when I'd eagerly awaited his reaction to Cream doing Robert Johnson's Crossroads.* But one cut on the first Jimi Hendrix Experience album just knocked Rudi out. The Wind Cries Mary. It's hard to believe but that one slow Blues was one of his absolute favorite songs. The two sacred touchstones of the Blues for Rudi Blesh from then on in were always: Robert Johnson's Hellhound on my Trail and Jimi Hendrix's The Wind Cries Mary. Though each somewhat unique, the two songs resemble nothing in the world more than each other. Just like bookends.

*In addition to the Blues "breathing", the other sacred Rudi rule for the Blues was that your song had to be about yourself, a true personal lament. This got complex when you had someone like Billie Holiday who sang both Pop music and her own sad songs.

One of the things Rudi recorded in the 1940s of course was Skiffle, rhythm music from the rent parties where people made noise to dance to mostly without horns or violins, the usual lead instruments. Also known as Jug Band Music, this, along with Jump Jazz, the stomping piano from the Southern turpentine camps, the Blues, Black/White Spirituals and Cowboy Songs became the original basis for the tough pulsating music later known as Rock and Roll. Rudi put out South Side Shake as Skiffle, but he wouldn't have called it Rock and Roll. In the same way, he'd disparaged Elvis Presley in a later edition of <u>Shining Trumpets</u>, but for an interesting reason. Why would anyone want to hear primitive Black Folk Music sung by a White imitator?

Cut to the history of the Minstrel Shows from the early plantation days, to Ben Harney in the Ragtime era, to Bill Haley and Elvis to Mick Jagger. They may have lost the blackface but the combination of derision and adulation in the traditional Black imitator show is pretty much a constant through popular musical history. Rock and Roll is here to stay. Rudi would put down Eric Clapton for his lack of finesse or Ray Charles imitator Stevie Winwood for his "fluffs" but he had genuine respect for some of the young recording artists of the 1960s playing R&B. Whenever I played a classic Rolling Stones cut (with Brian Jones) for example, Rudi was always impressed. "Those guys can really lay down a shuffle." " Sounds just like Jimmy Reed." Obviously the Stones with Jones knew how to make the Blues "breathe" back then. Likewise Doctor John who started as a strange Voodoo character, The Night Tripper. In those days I thought this would be too far out for Rudi but of course, as Donald Ashwander then pointed out to me, that type of psychedelia was an old New Orleans tradition. Traditional Psychedelia. Okay...

So how would Jimi Hendrix have known about Rudi Blesh? There are two possibilities I can imagine. One of course is that he might have read Shining Trumpets. What going to the library in 1946 - 1966 and looking up Robert Johnson in the card catalog would have brought up most likely. I would wager Jimi, Eric Clapton, Brian Jones and Keith Richards all read Rudi's elegy in Shining Trumpets dedicated to Robert Johnson. Until Sam Charters's Country Blues came out in 1959, it was really the only thing in print on the subject. Bill Wyman refers to Shining Trumpets explicitly in his Bill Wyman's Blues Odyssey book.

Stripped of all biographical information or even a picture of Robert Johnson the artist, writing in the mid 1940s, my grandfather had simply reverted to poetry:

"The voice sings and then--on fateful descending note--echoes its own phrases or imitates the wind, mournfully and far away, in huh-uh-uh-ummm, subsiding like a moan on the same ominous, downward cadence. The high, sighing guitar notes vanish suddenly into silence as if swept away by cold autumn wind. Plangent, iron chords intermittently walk like heavy footsteps, on the same descending minor series. The images--the wanderers voice and its echoes, the mocking wind running through the guitar strings, and the implacable, slow, pursuing footsteps--are full of evil, surcharged with the terror of one alone among the moving, unseen shapes of the night. Wildly and terribly, the notes paint a dark wasteland, starless, ululant with bitter wind, swept by the chill rain. Over a hilltop trudges a lonely, ragged, bedeviled figure, bent into the wind, with his easy rider held by one arm as it swings from its cord around his neck." -Shining Trumpets 1946

One of my favorite writers is Peter Guralnick. His first book was a short monograph on Robert Johnson. In it he takes Rudi somewhat to task, for his florid language I suppose. Here's what Guralnick wrote about Rudi Blesh:

"Sometimes I can evoke the breathless rush of feeling that I experienced the first time that I ever really heard Robert Johnson's Music. Sometimes a note will suggest just a hint of the realms of emotion that opened to me in that moment, the sense of utter wonder, the shattering revelation. I don't know if it's possible to recreate this kind of feeling today--not because music of similar excitement doesn't exist, but because the discovery can no longer take place in such a void. Or perhaps there is someone right now who will come to Robert Johnson, or a contemporary pop star, or a new voice in jazz, or some music as wild and unimagined, with the same sense of innocent expectation that caused my friends and me to hold our breath, all unknowing, when we first played Robert Johnson's songs on the record player. Let me just quote a passage from Rudi Blesh on which an older generation of blues enthusiasts--Mack McCormick, Paul Oliver, probably Sam Charters--was nurtured and which expresses, I think that same sense of pure romantic surrender. It describes Johnson's masterful "Hell Hound on my Trail" in words that come close to mocking their meaning and yet evoke that same sense of awe I am trying to suggest."

The only part Peter got wrong was the self mocking part. Rudi loved those old nineteenth century words. Remember he was a spelling bee champ back in Guthrie. There were certain phrases he would pull out for special sacred occasions. I'm sure there were tears in my grandfather's eyes when we wrote those lines about Robert Johnson.

So perhaps Jimi understood as well what it was Rudi was trying to express about Robert Johnson in <u>Shining Trumpets</u>. Lord knows both artists had hellhounds on their trails. The other possibility is that Jimi Hendrix knew Rudi Blesh from sitting in on a class at NYU or perhaps a public Jazz film showing or talk Rudi had given locally. Jimi Hendrix was virtually homeless when he lived in the Village, before being discovered by Chas Chandler and being whisked off to England in 1966. A free lecture on Jazz on a cold day with a girl friend would have been just the thing. But whatever the reason for the introduction, the bond was then created on both sides Rudi to Jimi and Jimi to Rudi. That's really the Blues that breathes.

*6 - Wilbur Sweatman could also play three clarinets at once but lost all of Scott Joplin's musical legacy, everything except the materials salvaged by Rudi and Hansi. There was also music R&H promised they'd return to Lottie Joplin. It broke their heart to have to give these unpublished Scott Joplin compositions back ("Pretty Pansy Rag", "Recitative Rag" and others). On Lottie's passing they fell into the hands of Mr. Sweatman and were never seen or heard from again.

*7 - In addition to Max Morath, Terry Waldo has also put together Ragtime period retro-orchestras over the years that have always captured the enthusiasm, the youthful spirit of the original era. A true believer, Terry's also still at it today.

Rudi, Race and Sex

Growing up with my grandfather and his legacy, in my teens I often felt uneasy about it all. Part of it was Rudi's contentiousness that I couldn't really understand. Why is it so important to know the exact person who created various styles? Wasn't the purpose of music to just have fun? And this was a big part of our break out in the 1960s, but as soon as it got started it was obvious that without some sort of musical historical honesty, our anti-commercial youth rebellion wasn't going to get too far. And that was certainly the position of the British Invasion post-Skifflers, unbeknownst to me at that time, also set off by Rudi. So even though Lonnie Donegan himself was an impersonator and also a copyright creep, the Skiffle he created was part of Trad Jazz, where you paid dues. The Beatles, for example never bullshit anybody. They acknowledged Black originators, like the Rolling Stones did. It was easy to see that when Eric Clapton fell out of the Cream super group in 1969 how Rock split in two, one half still respectful to the Blues (Americana) and the other (Punk/Metal/Disco/Pop/Rap) mindlessly claiming self origination. Obviously Rudi had been on to something with his insistant purist approach to Black race music.

So what drove my grandfather to champion the cause of Black music in America? What caused him to support and more important, seriously befriend performers and composers who were considered "low class", outside the boundaries of middle class respectability in the 1940s? Rudi was a "Negrophile" back in the days when this was not really acceptable at all. And of course to a degree it was his example, his influence (in the press and on the radio) that now informs the near ubiquitous "hipster" mentality of racial equality and social/artistic acceptance. I believe Rudi was driven to be color blind by a confluence of forces. One of these of course would have been his family. The spirit of non-conformism and rebellion was alive and well in this boy. Rudi was obstinate, a willful child, what better way to get back at his snobby European cultured family than to drag Negroes into the museum, so to speak? Then to ignore all convention and have a Black drummer, Baby Dodds as his roommate. And of course, in full sincerity to develop those deep lasting friendships with Black performers: James P. Johnson, Dan Burley, Eubie Blake and others.

To bring them into the family as it were. But more importantly, as a cultured artistic person to join their family, the bi-racial world of Jazz. Another reason Rudi would have gone for this music is that, to a certain degree it was in the air, an insider/underground element just waiting to break into the mainstream. There were others who had been pushing Black culture all along, archivist/documentarians like Alan Lomax, record label power brokers like John Hammond and the Ertegans, other Jazz critics, but I think few did it with as much consument taste, such truly exquisite enthusiasm and at least for the time, so much historical research. I now see my grandfather to be one of a handful of influential people who swung the pendulum of popular opinion towards acceptance of Black Art back in the 1940s.

But also with that important qualification: acknowledgement of the real roots originators, however Black, indigent, wicked, sinful, alcoholic or druggy as they might be. And here of course lies the rub. For in the deal that gave acceptability to Black Art, the side baggage, what the White morality crew had feared all along, came along for the ride. Whatever the code word is for human despair, what some call Blues or maybe nowadays: "clinical depression".

In her book In Search of the Blues, Marybeth Hamilton addresses this very issue, as an unacknowledged subtext to Jazz:

"Even as early as the late 1940s, that sense that black city life as somehow pathological was trickling into the work of jazz critics, beginning to qualify their celebration of the vitality of the African American urban experience. Even Rudi Blesh expressed something of it in his 1946 book Shining Trumpets, denouncing the pernicious influence of race recordings of unscrupulous black entertainers who had been 'corrupted by city ways'. Such musicians, he suggested, were effectively perverting black musical traditions, hearing in the blues simply a 'lascivious song,' echoing with 'drunken snores in the barrelhouse, the snarl of the hop-head, prostitutes' shrill laughter.' Although the music did 'have all these things in it,' such listeners missed the underlying tone of lament: the fact that, 'in all of this, a lost race is seaching for home.' The core of the blues, Blesh suggested, was a spirit of alienation. In the years that followed, as more white writers latched onto the music, that claim would become an article of faith."

What Ms. Hamilton is pointing to is the basic quandary of the White Jazz critic, perhaps as appreciated first by my grandfather. How do you exalt the music of the house of ill repute? This was as true of Ragtime as it would be of Jazz, and later, Rock and Roll.

To seek to emulate the vitality of the expatriate, sexually attractive (but often ornamental) African American matriarchal family man is to risk falling into the traps of his hedonism and excess. The causes of these pitfalls are irrelevant. It's the traps themselves we were supposed to look out for. Whoops.

But the music was always so seductive. In the 1900s it was Ragtime, in the 1920s it was Jazz and Blues and by the time I was growing up it was the Blues again and the thing Skiffle turned into: British Invasion Rock and Roll. And if this isn't Art then as now... what is? What do you do when the greatest composer in Jazz is also a card shark, pool hustler and a pimp? Well, you spend a fortune licensing the man's spoken word recordings from the Library of Congress so the artist can tell his story himself. An interesting parallel would be Modern Jazzman Charles Mingus who compared himself as a Black composer to Jelly Roll Morton in his autobiography <u>Beneath the Underdog</u>. Nothing so elemental as Music or Art is ever as simple as it seems at first.

And don't forget, some of the European genius school, the so called "Classical" composers were no angels as well, and they weren't the children of slaves. Uh oh. Here of course is the biggest trap of all. Because after you get finished championing Black Art as some kind of immortal symbol of human suffering and forebearance, guess what? Many Black people, Strivers especially, won't want to have much to do with your concepts of High Art, universal saintliness and most especially: Black suffering or alienation. Can you blame them?

So now, in some way thanks to Rudi, we have a world where White people have the Blues, and Black people claim they don't. In mostly Right Wing Country music human emotions boil over, while White Bluesmen (and their disrespectful Heavy Metal clones) scream out personal pain and anguish, evoking the spirit of once virtually unknown Black man Robert Johnson in every note. Be careful what you wish for. The Blues is irony if nothing else. I'm not sure Rudi saw any of this coming but I'm sure the paradoxes were never lost on him. As the Old Indian once said...

Then of course most of these same ironies and contradictions spill over into the zone where another great dividing line is set across humanity: gender, or sex if you will. Rudi's attitudes towards women were intense and also varied. On one level his instincts were exemplary, especially after he paired up with Harriet Janis, very much his equal or more so in their concurrent fields of artistic endeavor. And yet, those old attitudes die hard. I remember what Rudi told me they used to say back in the Ragtime Era: "She's as pure as the driven snow... but she's drifting." and later, in the 1920s what they called the "easy" girls: "roundheels". That obsession with feet persisted into the 1970s when Rudi would gripe to me about the humorless hardcore militant feminists: "the sound of women in boots marching". At least he was being honest, and that, along with being confused is perhaps the best any man can do until the next renaissance.

In the meantime Rudi and I both got to experience the paradox of the modern subsitute for renaissance, militant feminism when we would go to the formerly all male McSorleys Ale House on East Seventh Street to have a quiet beer. As Ragtime Bob Darch, or Max Morath would say: "Saloon...." McSorleys had been picketed by the gals in boots in the mid 60s and by the time I got to go there, back when the drinking age was still eighteen in 1968, the place was sexually integrated, including the one and only restroom. So it was and for now will have to be that until we humans can find a way to recreate our sacred temples (for men and for women), this "unisex" thing would have to do.

The other part of the ideology (of women) that I might have inherited from Rudi could best be described as "sexual realism", something I think he would agree could best be understood through the ambiguities of an old Folk song like Careless Love, one of his absolute favorites, or perhaps one line from the Black Folk Blues vernacular in particular: "You cheat and you lie and you're no good... I'd be the same way if I only could." Equality between the sexes? Right!

Still for Rudi the example was everything and artistically, following his own inclinations or influenced by Hansi, he had done pretty much all he could to include women in his pantheon of Jazz Art. From Bessie Smith to Bertha Chippie Hill, Mary Lou Williams, Hociel Thomas, if there was a chance to showcase women performers he jumped at it. Lovie Austin and Lil Hardin Armstrong, both interviewed for Shining Trumpets, were women whose artistic sensibilities and creative output Rudi took very seriously. Outside the framework of Traditional Jazz but still high up in my grandfather's post Shining Trumpets aesthetic universe, Billie Holiday. As Rudi would often remind me, her singing style, based on Louis, was ultimately as influential has his. And also in

114

the world of supposedly Fine Art, where Rudi and Hansi supported artists like Jacqueline Lamba, Janet Sobel and Joan Mitchell against the grain of the prevalent male genius norm.

Around the turn of the century a few ladies had written Rags at home and so had mostly bypassed the usual historical channels. Rudi had heard of May Aufderheide and her Thriller Rag through Bunk Johnson, who knew her published material well. But the complete story of the female Ragtimers still remained to be documented by Ragtime musician and historian Max Morath on his The Ragtime Women LP (1977), a solid Rudi favorite. When my grandfather played that record I could almost imagine him thinking: Gee I wish we'd known about all these gals, it would have made another great section in They All Played Ragtime.

Rudi would have said it was the romantic in him, the same feelings that had attracted him to Ragtime to begin with, the lost lady of American Music. For my grandfather the Art Nouveau era was all a great celebration of Woman, from the sensual sinuous curvatures of the decorative arts to the breathtaking lilt and sigh of both Ragtime and Debussy in music. Woman as idolized of course is still pretty judgemental, and here as in the subject of race the pitfalls are everywhere if you stick your neck out.

One real life male/female relationship my grandfather attempted to pass judgement on was that between my father John Hultberg, and his daughter, my mother Hilary. In coming down heavily in favor of the Artist, Rudi's purism came up short. Way short, and for that he paid dearly. And so, after Hansi's passing, Rudi's bitterness about life fed both his cynicism about women and his own self-pitying depression. The maelstrom.

But of course whenever I had a girlfriend over Rudi always charmed them totally in his effortless way. So many of life's contradictions so little lifetime really to figure even half of them out. It could be said that on one level Rudi Blesh was definitely a product of his times, a typical male if you will. And yet whenever he had the chance, Rudi moved to redress the imbalances, the injustices in culture and society that he perceived. So I would say all in all, my grandfather was a great supporter and benefactor to both causes, racial and sexual equality.

It just wasn't easy.

The Dixieland Curse / Bop Menace

Coming up as I did in the shadow of the slide trombone it's easy to see now how easy it was then to get everything backwards. Of course forty to fifty years later how much easier could it be now to get it all wrong when there's so much more to try to understand.

In a nutshell, it was that Traditional Jazz thing called Dixieland. In Rudi's day it was vital and punk, the source from which all Blues, dance and modern music flowed. But to me it was these truly corny conservative White people who tried but really mostly couldn't swing and obviously had never really had the Blues. Wrong end of the telescople of course but at the time all the evidence pointed that way. Stereo Hi Fi sure didn't help. Most of the big Traddies who went for the big sound with all the instruments recorded separately and then mixed back together shouldn't have bothered. All they were trying to "recreate" was the live ensemble sound to begin with, but the genius producers had to prove they could do it. But they couldn't. Because by the time the music got pressed into crisp glorious Hi Fidelity, the musicians had long since died of solitary repetitive boredom.

Because of the generation gap, Dixieland became like Frontier-land, or Tomorrowland, another bizarre Right Wing fantasy. Red striped shirts and straw hats. Happy Negroes strumming banjoes on the Old Plantation. But of course that was wrong. Dixieland began with Black people, was unbelievably cool, the source of all Cool perhaps. Just listen to these scratchy almost unlistenable vintage reissues, making mental corrections for the acoustic recording methods of the time. All this took time to sink in. In the meantime there was commercial Trad Jazz in all it's stereophonic glory. Midnight in Moscow by Englishman Kenny Ball for example, on the radio in the USA in 1964, just weeks before the Beatles' full scale British R&B invasion. Zzzzzzz. No, the problem with stereo Trad was that this music wasn't born to be cleaned up, recorded in little modules and reconstituted like frozen orange juice. Real Trad had to be fresh squeezed.

But of course we kids never realized that until we'd made a similar journey through the Blues. I remember the first time Rudi played Robert Johnson for me when I was young. I thought the style was archaic. It stopped and started in vampy ways that modern R&B, Rock and Roll had stripped away. Still, when RJ got honking on his open E, open A string Dust My Broom, the origins of R&B

were quite apparent. Soon I found myself able to disregard the recording deficiencies, and immersed myself in Johnson's different styles, each a unique self portrait of the artist as a unique self defined human being. Journeying back into 78 territory, scratchy Son House and Skip James recordings now spoke to me as Leadbelly once had done, outside of the framework of the rest of the world problem some struggle so hard to overcome. I was there at least for a moment as some semblance of a natural man.

So it also became with Dixieland. Playing the frantic 20s originals on 78s, Circle 1940s revival era recordings, reissues, and modern New Orleans revival material with Rudi I could appreciate the excitement, the rawness, the genius of its youth again. It's like Dixieland was happy and the Blues was sad. But both truly real.

The biggest problem Dixieland had was it's own success. The kids who weren't cool enough to be into Hot Jazz in the 1920s made up for it by recreating a cleaned up modernized Dixieland that just oozed with their own personal success stories. Dixieland music, originally created by poor Blacks, got appropriated by rich White people. Just like the Blues is now Heavy Metal or conservative Country Music. Or like certain rugged sounding Native American tribal names that now belong to rich college football teams.

But underneath all the success, the overfed White faces, the car dealership sponsors and the often spiritless, flabby Dixieland music being played, behind the behind, there was and is another Dixieland. Another Trad Jazz story. Starting with Bunk, King Oliver, The Original Dixieland Jazz Band, Louis Armstrong, Sidney Bechet, Jack Teagarden... on to Fats Waller, Bessie Smith, Bix, Basie, Lester, Billie, Cab Calloway, Joe Venuti, Eddie Lang, Lonnie Johnson, the Boswell Sisters, Django Rhinehardt, Muggsy Spannier, Wild Bill Davison, Mary Lou Williams, Chick Webb... then back to the Preservation Hall Band revivals in New Orleans.

And just like with the Blues, this journey is another life changer.

I remember a night in 1967 when a friend of my stepfather, a fellow race car driver (and car dealership owner) took Peter, me and Rudi in a V12 Jaguar on a high speed tour through Western Massachusetts crashing late night Jazz parties. You can't believe how people reacted when Rudi Blesh walked through the door. A real eye opener for me and I got to play drums. Hey, this is Cool.

On the other end of the music universe (supposedly) sat Bop. An original Black Art music in every sense, definitely the precursor to Black Power in American culture for better or for worse. The sit down strike in the Swing horn section gets ugly. Protest Music - its not a dance, its a demonstration. Until the rediscovery of Ragtime, Bop was the Black Art Music. By dredging up the history side of it Rudi somehow managed to even the score, or perhaps just broaden the field. So, ambitious young Black minds found out they didn't have to actually be ashamed of their musical origins - their history, it hadn't all been houses of ill-repute. And Rudi could stand aside this time.

But still, all this was even more confusing, especially to young minds in the 1960s, mine for instance. Lets get this straight. According to Grampa Rudi Swing was out. Don't even bring it up. Bop is bad. More like evil perhaps. Trad is great but not so great in it's modern form and the Blues is awesome but not if it's played by kids like me. Oh and Ragtime is also great but not like you've always heard it. Got it?

The real trouble was that for me, no one in my world but Rudi saw things this way. It was important for him that I get indoctrinated correctly, but what of my peers? I got nowhere arguing with Rudi about Skiffle's connection to Rock and Roll. He just didn't see it that way. Modern versions of Robert Johnson or Woody Guthrie were abominations. Instead I was to try to learn to appreciate Modern Dixieland. This wasn't going to get me too far in the real world, as we all knew it then. So I stuck with the Blues artists and Gospel people Rudi gave me.

At Cambridge School in 1967 I bought two records at a student sale: a Wes Montgomery LP and Blue Spirits by Freddie Hubbard. When I got around to playing them for Rudi I found he also (secretly?) revered this kind of music, and he spent some time showing me how it had evolved back into the Blues after being Arty brittle early Bop. I also found he loved all kinds of people who really were Swing: Django, Bennie Goodman, Fats Waller, Count Basie, Billie, Lester Young, the Boswells, even (shudder) select recordings of Duke Ellington. And, in his weaker moments, even some of my favorite Rock and Roll, Folk and Soul Music.

So there was hope after all.

118

In 1970, when I was twenty, I spent the entire summer with Rudi in Gilmanton while he wrote a book on Jazz for teenagers. It was an ill advised project to be honest, the only really work Rudi Blesh wrote not totally based on his own original research. I was to provide the teenache context. I got a job working on the Laconia Business Directory, driving around in my tiny Mini Countryman verifying people's names and addresses. The woman I worked for was such a racist she told me the Vietnamese "weren't really people" and that the American troops couldn't do enough to wipe them out. You should have seen her face when I told her she'd convinced me to enlist. Actually I had to help Rudi finish his book. After getting some interesting original interview material with people like Gene Krupa and John Hammond, Rudi was having a terrible time finishing by his deadline.*8 It just wasn't going to be that exciting a book. Ultimately titled <u>Combo USA</u>, it was simply a collection of mostly rehashed biographies, one each representative of each of the instruments in a Jazz group, plus the singer. It was a big fizzle and didn't represent a renewal of interest in my grandfather's writing but I guess I can proudly say I had a hand in making it.

From <u>Combo USA</u>: (The Sound of Jazz 1957 - "Fine and Mellow")

"It was the sound of jazz and it was the sound of the past: Billie's voice, sad as ever, and that other voice, Prez's sax. It was Billie, still beautiful but ravaged by drugs and loneliness and all the inner torments she had carried since childhood. And it was Lester, his face wooden with despair. The television cameraman had the feeling to come in close on Billie as Lester played, and caught her dark eyes as they softened and filled with tears..."

At NYU I majored in Drama at first. Sitting through directing and play production classes, attending Broadway and off Broadway shows, appearing in student plays I got a taste of the world of New York theatre. Some of the kids in my class were the Jewish genius types, they acted, they sang, they were photo models, they made TV commercials, they danced, they tap danced, they wrote musicals, had theatrical agents. You know, the usual thing. Our drama professor was Murray Vorenberg, a real Jewish Indian. A real creative force in his cowboy boots, a Castaneda like character, another Whitney Haley type theatrical presence. Too bad I was too spaced out to really connect. At that point traditional theatre, street theatre, radio improv, anti-war demonstrations... all of it mixed together in my mind. Who knew which was real?

One day the infamous Living Theatre showed up at the drama center to give us undergrads a demonstration of Yoga breathing. I already knew about that kind of thing from my mother so I fell in with them. The Living Theatre were known for their guerrilla approach, sometimes even taking the audience hostage when the police came to bust them for nudity or obsenity. The Doors Jim Morrison spent his later Rock career trying to outdo the Living Theatre but got busted before he even really tried. I got on pretty well with the Living Theatre people, Julian Beck and Judith Malina, they even let me tag along when the Living Threatre did the Yoga thing at Fordham and CCNY but it turned out I just wasn't scary enough looking to join the troup doing Frankenstein.

Probably a good thing.

The uptown campus of NYU had something the downtown facility lacked, a campus. It was great to have a big lawn to sit out on and those NYU Security rent a cops protecting us from the real police. There was even a hookah out in plain view on the grass for weeks on end. One day some kids from Bard College dropped by including a girl named Katie I admired from afar. I decided to transfer.

Bard was definitely different than NYU. In this tiny school with a alleged old radical tradition I suddenly found myself in an Anthopology Department that had exactly one professor. Going "Down the Road" meant going down to the tiny Annandale town center were there was a great local bar known as Adolphs. It wasn't unusual to see Johnny Winter or members of the Band just hanging out there, probably trolling for undergrads. Outside the bar was the old town pump, missing it's handle. They said Bob Dylan had been up at Bard chasing some chick in 1965. Can You Please Crawl Out Your Window was written about this girl who seems to have been having an affair with a professor as well. Katie lied? Other apparent Dylan/Bard references included The Mighty Quinn which seems to refer to local Sheriff Tom Quinlin who had drug raided Bard College in 1965 with his "must bust in early May". (This event was also referred to later by Bard grads Steely Dan in their Never Going Back to My Old School: ".. up in Annandale, it was still September when your daddy was quite suprised to find you with the working girls in the county jail").

The missing pump handle outside Adolphs, lost for decades through some college prank (remember them?) also figured in the lyrics of Bob Dylan's Subterranean Homesick Blues. "The pump don't work 'cause the vandals took the handle" (Some people also said the line "Badge out, laid off" was actually "Backed out of Adolphs" but I doubt that.) A few years later my friend Dan Lewis was getting ready to graduate from Bard (after I'd dropped out) He was helping to move some old cabinets in the Physics lab and he found it. What? The handle to the pump of course.

After sliding through as part of the crowd at NYU a spotlight was suddenly being shone on my academic career. My what? In between demonstrating against war and exploring the humanity in our minds by different means, learning about music and art and the opposite sex we were supposed to be preparing for some sort of career? Wassat? In my Junior year I was faced with something Bard calls Moderation. An oral exam by your professors covering all aspects of your field of study. Some people don't make it and get flunked out occasionally remaining nearby as local hippie types. I actually passed Moderation but the bad blood that lingered afterwards doomed my college career. Central to my particular interrogation was the question of what kind of anthropologist Carl Hultberg Morton intended to be. I got no laughs with the line that I had no intention of becoming an anthropologist. I told them I wanted to study native peoples so I could become a native person. Not amusing.

My ethnology professor, kind of a New York Hippie, was all hepped up on my paper about the Hopi Coyote Trickster traditions of the Southwest. This study I'd spent some time researching at the New York Public Library. It was his enthusiasm for my work that got me through my Moderation. Right after that ordeal he announced that some of the Hopi elders from New Mexico would be visiting Bard and he intended that I should be their official welcoming committee. After thinking about it I realized I had no business interacting with these people in such an artificial setting. This really burned my prof and it wasn't long before I was given another evaluation where I was a labeled as a "dilletante". Whatever that is I'm sure I would rather be that than ever be called an anthropologist. Years later I met this professor of ethnology at a party in New York City. He still seemed totally wounded and so bitterly disappointed in me. What could I say? Had he never seen a kid drop out of college before?

While at Bard I lived at a run down old Jewish summer camp, Camp Daro in Hudson with some other Bard students in a semi communal living arrangement. It was communal until it came time to do the dishes. I drove my little Austin Mini station wagon around and gave informal Yoga lessons I'd learned from my mother. One of the other residents was an arty guy named Richard F. Richard was a real Jewish Prince, but also a real humanist of sorts deep in his heart. He loved Bob Dylan more than anything in the world, and listening to the man on Richard's reel to reel I got much deeper into it all. Ah, bootlegs. Maybe it was his steady supply of hash as well. Richard was an art major. His father owned a bingo supply company out on Long Island where Richard had started as an artist painting the numbers on the little balls. I would visit Richard in Oceanside and we'd go out to Nathan's and order frogs legs in a little take out box.

Richard aspired to be part of the NYC art scene and indeed Robert Motherwell's daughter Jeannie was also attending Bard at the time. Once Richard and I went to the Marlboro Gallery in New York City to see the last Mark Rothko black and white post-suicide show. Richard was certainly impressed when I greeted the widow of artist Bill Baziotes, Ethel, there making some arrangements regarding her husband's work. She was Rudi's girlfriend. One day at the Bard Art Gallery I noticed a familiar name from the past on the bulletin board. John Hultberg was having an opening and a show at what was left of the Martha Jackson Gallery, now being run by her son David Anderson. Not really knowing the reason why I journeyed down to NYC and went to see the show. I signed the guestbook but to no effect. No contact with my father came about at that time (1970).

That fall Richard's brother Robert showed up at Camp Daro from Colorado. With him was his faithful dog Chica, half shepard, half coyote. Robert ended up doing about three month's worth of dishes and telling everyone off as phoney hippies. Good for him. Next time he came to Bard Robert had two of Chica's puppies... did I want one? No way, too much responsibility, man. One look at the little big footed brindle pup - my mind was instantly changed and Nikita became my dog for the next fifteen years.

Living in Marblehead in the summers between school years at NYU and Bard had become a totally different experience after my mother put her foot down and got Peter Morton to move the family into town from off the snobby Neck in 1967. Living downtown in the house where the American revolutionary and third Vice President Elbridge Gerry had been born was a gas. For one thing the place was full of ghosts. Gerrymanderers. You could hear them walking up and down the stairs, or perhaps on secret stairs in the walls that had hidden people during the Revolution. Steffi and I had the whole top floor to ourselves with India prints everywhere and rooms lit up with different colored lightbulbs. My sister had an art studio adjoining her room. I had a little library where I would sit and smoke and watch the street below while listening to the radio revolution being waged on WBCN in Boston. All obscure amazing album cuts all the time. Everyday was an incredible music lesson as crack DJ's like Peter Wolf (The Wolf) and Matt Siegel (The Seagull) revealed new dimensions for youth music appreciation. Rock Music, the big new Pop monster was being born. On the FM radio, up until then the format for snobby Classical Music and that was it.

On WBCN we got to hear unreleased Beatles stuff, real Blues, old Folk Music, Psych, Bert Jansch, Pentangle, Fairport Convention, early Fleetwood Mac, Ten Years After, Pink Floyd, Marvin Gaye, Otis Redding, Aretha Franklin, Taj Mahal, Linda Tillery and the Loading Zone, the Youngbloods, Joni Mitchell, Tom Rush, Richie Havens, classic Jazz, Modern Jazz, even Classical Music itself. And more. Totally eclectic. With little sponsorship, WBCN winged it beautifully during it's struggling glory years, 1968-1970. Oddly enough the station had been managed by a neighbor of my stepfather's mother Virginia on Lee Street in Marblehead, Mr. Deardorff. I knew his son Asa. Mr. Deardorff was losing money big time playing Classical Music on BCN (Boston Concert Network), so he threw open the doors to anyone wanting to sponsor a show. In the earliest days WBCN Rock Music listeners like me had to wait through various types of programming including a Bible study hour to get to the cutting edge shows by DJ's like Blues expert Peter Wolf (later lead singer for J. Geils Band). Finally, I'd found Soul Music (and much more) on the American radio. And as if that wasn't enough, in those pre-FM car radio days there was also the Mighty WILD, a Black AM station operating in Boston playing Soul Music... I mean the real thing all the time. It's counterpart in NYC: WWRL. Well Alright!

One day in 1969 a hippie girl in town approached me asking if I'd drive her and her girlfriend to the Newport Jazz Festival. Why not? Like Woodstock a few months later, at Newport that year fences were broken down and the festival was declared free.

123

Whose idea was it to let Rock groups in anyway? Most of these kids had zero respect for Jazz, that was for sure. Groups like Led Zeppelin, debuting for the first time in the States were nauseating, in my view. Why should I want to look up at some guy's crotch? This was worse than prep school. Zepp's obviously disrespectful debasement of the Blues was a sad prediction of things to come. Yecch! A cut above that in my estimation was the Jeff Beck Group, with then unknown Sam Cooke imitator Rod Stewart as lead singer. I'd seen them at the Fillmore East and they got the job done. Jeff Beck had basically been the Yardbirds; he should have inherited the whole scene. But at Newport in 1969 the Jeff Beck Group's set was preceded by a Jazz master I'd also already seen before in New York City, with Rudi, Rahsaan Roland Kirk.

Coming onstage and facing a hostile crowd chanting "We want Beck!" Rahsaan was unfazed. He immediately warmed the kids up by calling attention to the scent of weed burning in the air. Being blind he then did a great routine on men's magazines vs. the hands on approach when it comes to women. After that it was on with his own patented history of Black music in America. Rahsaan playing in the old styles, from Field Hollers through Spirituals, Blues, Jazz, Swing, Bop, R&B, Soul, Pop. Continuing and playing with two sometimes even three horns in his mouth at once Kirk channeled the living spirit of John Coltrane and Burt Bacharach's sweetest Pop. By the end of his set that young outdoor audience was his. The kids called the artist out for three encores and started filing out as soon as Beck and company began walking on the stage. Rod Stewart offered some lame excuse about their "shitty equipment" but the fact was they simply couldn't follow Rahsaan Roland Kirk. He was in a different league altogether. Jazz won that battle that day.

Back at home in Marblehead there were big changes in the Peter Morton household. My mother had simply burst out of her shell. The assassination of Dr. Martin Luther King in 1966 propelled her into action. She went to the local newspapers with a proposal to build a teen center in nearby Lynn, home to a large poor Black population. Raising money in Marblehead she partnered with a former director of the NAACP in Lynn, Clarence Jones. A benefit for the "Teen City" was arranged at Lenny's on the Pike, a Boston area Jazz club. Pianist Jackie Byard played and yes, Rudi Blesh was there. Byard was an excellent choice because he was like Rahsaan, a member the Modern Jazz fraternity who still loved the traditional styles. Byard would often break into that choppy

Stride rhythm in the middle of a more fluid Modern Jazz trance, a unique stylistic twist on piano that Rudi of course loved. After money was raised for the Teen City Project Peter Morton did the design for the retrofit of an existing building in Lynn and we all got to work, Black and White volunteer labor doing the gut renovation. Soon there was a gleaming new Teen City youth center in Lynn with pool tables, juke box, soda machine, ping pong tables, pinball machines. A few weeks later someone burned the place down to the ground. You could call it a failure but nothing that involved that much cooperation between different populations could ever really be judged that way. That energy just got put on hold if you ask me, just waiting for a chance to be retapped. I was never prouder of my mother than at this time. What a star.

A couple of years later Hilary initiated another new project, becoming the proprietor of the first health food store in town, Marblehead Natural Foods. My mother worked hard to help people in town eat a better diet, a vital job that remains undone for most of folks to this day. Way ahead of her time in 1972. My little sister Genny remembers working in the health food store as a kid and waiting on George Martin, the former Beatles producer then living in Marblehead while producing Seatrain. I did stock work, sold on the weekends and also drove the VW bus into Boston to purchase wholesale natural food products and produce from brand new distributors like Erewhon. Working behind the counter with a (non-veggie) burger in my hand one afternoon I took the time to read one of the books on the rotating display. The Secret of the Mucus Free Diet by Arnold Ehret. Not exactly a snappy title but definitely a life changing read for me. I immediately went on a week long lemonade fast and swore off all meat after that. Thanks Mom!

*8 - In 1949 Rudi's writing style with Hansi was to get up early and write until noon seven days a week. She had notes from the field in her cryptic shorthand, which she transcribed onto cards. From these Rudi wrote the prose in his immaculate longhand. This was then checked over by Hansi who made notes. Then Rudi typed the whole thing up right away, doing all the revisions. It seems hard to believe but Rudi told John Hasse he'd written They All Played Ragtime "a chapter a day", finishing the job in two weeks. This estimate he revised somewhat to three or four weeks on reflection. Added to the six months of traveling and research this must make They All Played Ragtime the quickest write in history. Written by hummingbirds. Obviously up in New Hampshire in 1970 with only me as his writing companion, there was no such stimulus.

By this time there had been another big change in my life. Not just a couple of cats and the dog but also an ex-girlfriend I seemed to have acquired from Richard F., friend from Bard College. Her name was Rachel and her father had been a socialist organizer in the early days, a conscientious objector in World War 2 and one of the founders of the original (1930s) Coop Supermarket chain in Harlem. Rachel's mother was a dyed in to wool Maoist radical, the secretary at the War Resisters League in the Village. Rachel herself was a lovely half English, half Jewish blonde beauty. What was not to like? Her family seemed to like me and she liked being with me and my funky dog. We lived in an old broken down half renovated house in Tivoli near Bard. We both dropped out of college and I got a crummy job managing the Sears gas station in Kingston. I had long hair, a Volkswagen bus with an eight track player with the sound track to Easy Rider constantly blasting. Rachel didn't seem to mind living in poverty in that freezing house as long as we were together. Soon we decided to get married hastily inviting people setting things up at the local church. In my hurry I somehow forgot to invite Rudi which did not go over well though he found out and came of course. While there I took Rudi up to visit another former Bard person and friend, Larry Abrams. Larry lived in the past. Literally wearing stiff shirt collars, spats, pince-nez glasses the other fashions from years before. He drove an antique car and ran a repair shop in Tivoli for player pianos. Probably with his nose still out of joint Rudi was unimpressed. "Marcel Proust!" he harumphed.

Rachel and I then moved to Salem Massachusetts the neighboring town to Marblehead and settled into new crummy jobs, me working as an optician and Rachel as a tag girl, filing in with the immigrant ladies at the local shoe factory. But rent for a nice little apartment in Salem was $33 a week in 1972 so not having money wasn't as tragic as it would be nowadays. We lived on love while I worked grinding lenses and selling health food on the weekends. Visits to my wife's mother and father, both living separately in Harlem were always interesting. Her dad lived in the same apartment complex (Morningside Heights) as Rudi's ladyfriend Ethel Baziotes. A few blocks down on 125th Street in Harlem proper there were little record stores where you could buy Slim Harpo and Miracles 45s. Soul Music Mecca.

126

After a year or so of grinding lenses for $2.60 an hour I was starting to figure there had to be a better way. I had sworn off marijuana for over a year and in that period had settled down to the bottom of the economic ladder. I just didn't seem to have any imagination anymore. One day a fellow worker at the opticianry, R. Dube (that's right) offered me a joint downstairs in the stock room. "No way I'm clean man." "No, you need this if you work here." "Maybe you're right." A few months later I enrolled as a student at the New England School of Photography and things took a turn for the better. Maybe there is a life after all.

At NESOP my natural artistic talents started to come out. All that anti-art programming from my childhood, unconcious or not had had an effect. Watching exciting poetic photographs forming first on the viewing screen and then under the enlarger light, a part of my spirit held captive and silent for so long was released. A journey to self expression. Although I trained in both large format photography and miniature camera technique my best shots were documentary images of demonstrations, the poor working class and destitute people in Boston. Living in a dream book (The Family of Man), thinking that I could somehow become another Walker Evans or Henri Cartier-Bresson, I made plans for a long American trip where I could somehow get to the heart of the visual aesthetic that now had a hold on me. Click!

There were other factors at play. Starting with the Teen City project, Marblehead Natural Foods, and on through Mind Dynamics and other programs my mother was seriously rattling the cage of her marriage. Sometime in 1973 my sister Steffi joined the Divine Light Mission, the Guru Maharaji people, introducing a totally new wild card element. During the next six months my mother Hilary joined the Divine Light Mission as well and Peter Morton ran off with his secretary at TAC. In a short time the entire Morton family crashed and burned. The Maharaji's were as hypocritical as they were sanctimonious. Human crimes were widespread in the movement but covered up since everyone had the "perfect knowledge". I felt fortunate that Rachel received an inheritance at this point. With that we could move to the South where I felt I could work as a subsistance farmer and avoid both the unpleasantness of the family meltdown and the impending collapse of the capitalist economic system (still waiting?).

So with the former family all looking down at us from their newfound lofty states of permanent enlightenment, Carl and

Rachel set off in the Volkswagen camper bus to find America with a camera a guitar and a dog. The first stop was New York City where the camera was stolen. The next stop was Hendersonville, North Carolina, home of the Mother Earth News, the magazine where I got all my ideas about how easy it was going to be a grow all your own food farmer. Somehow the Mother Earth News wasn't that impressive in person so we continued into the Polk County section of North Carolina looking for like minded back to the Earth types. But at that point we got cold feet and moved across the line into South Carolina where we rented a funny little half finished mill house in a hollow. The outhouse was across a long bridge. One cold morning out in there I felt a muscle against my foot and behind the door there was a copperhead snake getting ready to strike. Killing this creature was difficult and we hadn't even started farming yet. Our landlady expected me to tend her garden. What's that? It didn't look easy at all.

I should have known I couldn't really escape. In the tiny mill house in South Carolina we had no television, central heat or running water. Instead of TV I read books out loud: Edgar Allen Poe, the Adventures of Sherlock Holmes. Other than that our only outlet to the "real" world was the FM radio. Wouldn't you know it, as soon as I got the tuner hooked up the first voice I heard was Grampa Rudi plugging the Ragtime Revival on NPR back in NYC. Another time it was Rudi's associate George Buck on his Jazzology show pushing the old Circle releases out of Columbia S.C., the family Jazz connection. Yet another day it was a picture in a magazine of historian Rudi Blesh adding his respects at Scott Joplin's newly commemorated gravesite ...with a maple leaf from off the ground nearby. The Ragtime Man.

At this point I decided I should get a job so I took another step backward and starting working as a lens grinder again. We started a doomed hippie clothes store in Greenville. R's sister F moved down to be with us and by then I definitely started to lose control of the situation. Because something else was happening with my wife Rachel. Wrapped up as I was with my photo Art project (documenting the South) I gave her little notice. We were drifting apart without my realizing it at all. Typical stupid male.

And so, to keep a short story (Country Western song?) short, my sojourn in the not so sunny South ended suddenly in 1976 and I headed back up to live in Salem Massachusetts. I was on my own now, it was just me and the dog.

All this time Rudi had been plugging away as a college professor at NYU and Queens College. Sometime in 1974 after the sudden deaths of his two closest friends Marshall Stearns and Doug MacAgy - everything suddenly came to a halt and my grandfather was no longer able to keep things organized. Papers piled up in the apartment. He quit teaching and with no tenure from NYU, fell back on living off Social Security. He still went up to the farm in New Hampshire each year but the place got no upkeep so it was gradually falling apart. The giant barn eventually collapsed.

Grampa Rudi showed up in Marblehead at one point in the early 1970s, while we were living in the Gerry Mansion, but got no encouragement to stay. Nothing in the bank between Rudi and his daughter, nothing to draw on in his hour of need. My grandfather's girlfriend after Hansi passed away was the beautiful widow of modern artist Bill Baziotes. Ethel Baziotes was heavily into psychology and she got Rudi hooked up with the Paine Whitney clinic where he was treated for "clinical depression". None of these treatments seem to do him any good but they did keep him busy and they earned him points with Ethel who seemed to mean a lot to him. They would visit the gravesites of their deceased loved ones together or go out to dinner when Rudi could afford it. Not much more than that.

Rudi was sinking lower and lower without receiving much solace from those he might have expected to be close to. I remember writing to him from Massachusetts in 1978 and trying to explain how I felt - about the legitimacy of despair, and the selfishness of depression - but the only response I got from my grandfather was that the lines in my letter weren't straight. At one point in the 1970s millionaire record collector/record label owner Nick Perls showed up at Rudi's 38 East 4th Street apartment and pretty much cleaned out the cream of my impoverished grandfather's 78 record collection, mint Gennetts and the Robert Johnson records, for a cool $5000. The low point for Rudi perhaps. Various titles now available on Yazoo Records.

For me, living on my own in Salem Massachusetts in 1977 was liberating. I worked for a local printer doing all kinds of process photography, artwork, layout, printing, a great education -- but working for a habitual liar was nearly impossible. This guy would disemble even when it served him absolutely no good. I never knew when I was covering for him or just inventing new fictions to avoid the truth like him. His greatest talent was as a card counter. After losing thousands from mismanagement he'd drive to Las Vegas (this was pre-Atlantic City/Indian Casinos) and earn back all the money playing Blackjack that he'd lost in the printing business. After that I managed various photography departments at Jordan Marsh and then worked in Cambridge at a horrible clipjoint camera store chain. I was living with a new girlfriend M, from New Hampshire but there was obviously still something very big missing from the puzzle.

An important clue arrived when my sister Steffi, still very active in the Divine Light Mission announced her marriage to another cultist "Premmie" Chris B, also from Marblehead. Chris was a giant, about a foot taller than my little blond haired sister. He came from a family of brick merchants in town. The wedding was to take place at the Unitarian Church in Marblehead and suprise of suprises my long lost Aunt Ethel and Uncle Paul Hultberg came to attend. The wedding was a bit awkward at times, a Guru Maharaji ceremony in a Christian setting. Uncle Paul took these hilarious pictures of the various family members all looking in different directions. It was amazingly refreshing to see Paul and Ethel after over twenty years. Their wit and sense of humor was so oddly familiar. Suddenly I figured it out, that's the way I am. Ethel had been a force in my childhood up to the age of six when last we'd been together. Deeply intellectual on many levels and mostly hard core Left Wing she had always symbolized something engrained in my subconscious mind. Now seeing her again after all these years it was just like reclaiming a part of myself that had been lost. I wanted to suggest something but she said it first: "I want to get you back together with your father". It all sounded so simple but of course it wasn't. John Hultberg had managed in alienate just about everyone in his drinking phase. It took a lot for my aunt to volunteer her house as a place for me to remeet my father. After the meeting occurred by her pool at the house in Pomona New York at least I had that. John was open to me coming to visit him in New York City and there was even talk of a house on Monhegan Island in Maine I would be welcome at.

Seizing the opportunity I moved in with John Hultberg in his loft in NYC, above the Cupping Room at the corner of West Broadway and Broome Street. Since the death of his benefactress gallery owner Martha Jackson he'd been the ward of her somewhat reluctant son David Anderson. It couldn't have been easy for

David to have to continue to pay the bills for his deceased mother's former lover. But pay he did, in return for paintings. Before John and his wife Lynne moved to the big loft on Broome Street, David Anderson had paid for them to live for years as horrible drunks at the Chelsea Hotel. He'd also paid so they could live as "artists in residence" in Hawaii. Must be nice. The Broome Street loft was a huge former manufacturing facility with fifteen foot ceilings. One end looked out on Broome Street and the other opened on to West Broadway around the block. The place was gigantic but there was no room. Unlike John whose paintings (if he was painting) were whisked off to the David Anderson storage facility, John's wife (#3) Lynne Drexler had no such outlet. Coming out of art as therapy when she had been institutionalized, Lynne did paintings and embroideries obsessively, sometimes a dozen or more a day. Starting in one corner and working her way around until she filled up the canvas or board, she painted little circles, big circles, nothing but circles. Everywhere, from the floor to the ceiling, in racks above the rooms and all down the open aisles were stacks and piles and piles of her dirty dusty horrible boring circle paintings. *9

John and his mate lived at opposite ends of the space. They rarely met or talked and when they did it was usually a spat. John was in his first years in Alcoholics Anonymous and Lynne was trying to be supportive. It wasn't easy. Though he had quit pouring the sauce down, my father was still an extremely difficult person to be around. I moved onto the little settee by the Broome Street door. A filthy hard old couch of some sort had been John's landing place when he still drank. Outside the big factory window the cars and trucks shot down into the intake for the Holland Tunnel. Sometimes you would look out and see open top trucks full of dead animal parts. Other times empty car carriers would blast by ("rattlers") shaking the building like machinery being destroyed.

John and Lynne were welcoming and suspicious. That was their nature. I had never been around people who did nothing. Lay around until it was time to make dinner. The place was filthy. I clean and painted the window frames white to make things brighter. I opened up a tiny room next to my father's writing hovel (he didn't paint much anymore) for a darkroom/bedroom with a fold down door off the street for a bed/table. John and Lynne remained cautious. What was I after? "Idiot Savant" my father called me. Maybe he was right, I had to look it up.

In his tiny bed area my father had three or four color TV's left over from Nam Jun Paik art events, piled up on each other, left on tuned to different channels. The Visualist. I spent time trying to edit John's narcissistic roman a clef memoirs (collage?) all cut up and deeply encrusted with whiteout, a thankless task. In that book (Vagabondage, unpublished) my father is Carl Axlehammer rising art star and I am Kurty and it's 1954, the year he goes to Paris to become famous. Trying to make amends perhaps, or more likely just revelling in his former glories and conquests. *10

Then in June suddenly it was time to go up to Monhegan.

The house on Monhegan Island twelve miles off the coast of Maine had been a gift from Martha Jackson "so John would have some place to visit with his kids". What a joke, I'd never even heard of the place and as far as John's other child, my sister Steffi, John hadn't seen or talked with her since she was three. My father used to joke that he might pick her up in a bar by accident. I told him to try the Guru Maharaji Temple. I was really going to have to make some adjustments to be around these people. They had obviously put themselves through a lot and it had coarsened them considerably.

But Monhegan was a joyous place full of sunshine and natural magic in the Summer. Arriving on the island John and Lynne immediately went through total personality transformations, becoming old Maine codger types in a flash. John had his fisherman's hat and he held down conversation with all the Monhegan folk, the old time lobstermen and the artists who have been coming to the island for generations, the sons of the artists who were now lobstermen and the sons and the daughters of the lobstermen who were now artists. The local Winterworks home handicraft industry produced sweaters and hats made from local wool. Across from the boat landing was another much smaller island, Manana, a grim looking rock where lived a semi-famous hermit in a falling down shack on the side of the hill. Lynne fit right in on Monhegan as well, mixing up the gossip with the best of them. So this is where they were themselves, a few months a year in this salt water, oil paint and kerosene lamp world.

* 9 - My favorite Lynne Drexler quotes: "Art will out. You are only an artist if you can do nothing else".

* 10 - other unpublished John Hultberg literature included a children's opera Junior and the Space Dogs, leading characters: Rudi (and me).

Rudi and Me

Returning at the end of the season I moved back in with John and Lynne on Broome Street. Gone were the sunny dispositions from Down East. I felt the chill again and wasn't sure what to do. The more I helped these folks the more they laughed at me in their cruel, callous way. I'm sure they could have respected me if I had been harsh like that as well, but I couldn't be that way. I stayed and worked in the darkroom or got out when I could.

The other people in the old manufacturing building were all so interesting. One old hippie upstairs made a living selling copies of thousands of stock photo negatives he'd found in a dumpster. I did the printing for him at $1 a shot. Other ex-neighbors Trish and Myrna had a pet food store grocery on Broome Street (Little Arf n Annie - named by my father), where I worked. Directly upstairs at 495 Broome lived a solid character from Jamaica, Twilight. Twilight made shoes, any kind you want. He had a wall covered with wooden forms and ladies would come by with pictures torn out of magazines of the style they liked. He'd measure their foot (a thrill I am sure), take a form off the wall, whittle it a bit or add some padding and then select the leather. Working it sideways with his broad smooth hammers he would shape the perfect shoe for any lady's foot. For this service people paid plenty. Twilight lived in a loft the same size as John and Lynne's but instead of being filled with dirt and dusty paintings it was filled with light, and beautiful blonde and brunette ladies, his roommates. Not that he was possessive at all, he just like having lovely women around. Sometimes I would go up to smoke or play Reggae music on guitar with his other buddies. Years later I saw him in a Rolling Stones video, sitting in front of a brownstone. That's Twilight next to Keith on the steps "Just Waiting for a Friend". What's he doing hanging around with those bums?

Every week I would have dinner one night with Rudi at his favorite (only) restaurant, Sing Wu on Second Avenue. Rudi had been going there since the 1950s, before that the place had been a Roumanian Grill. There was a back room where they had had at least one birthday party for Eubie Blake. Rudi ate there every night he could afford it and his routine was always the same. While looking at the menu the waiter would approach: "Drink Mr Rudi?" "I'll have a Stinger". I would order the ten ingredient vegetable loaded up with mustard and dried noodles. This was usually my one good meal of the week. Rudi liked to compliment the Chinese owner on his beautiful wife. I could see the restauranteur wince when Rudi laid that on. You know Rudi, Chinese people don't appreciate you admiring their women, it's like you want them to give them to you. The owner used to get back by holding the main course up a bit. "Another drink, Mr Rudi?" Well, alright. The drink would arrive and then the food. Rudi would look at the food for a minute, poke at it while I gobbled my stuff down. "Take home Mr. Rudi?" The refrigerator at 38 East 4th street was filled with brown paper bags. On each one Rudi had written in his exquisite penmanship what it was: "Fried Chicken" "Spare Ribs" and the date. I used to make fun of this system but it seemed to work for him. We had a song in the family we used to sing, about that second drink: "Sing Wu, sweet chariot who's going to carry you home?"

This night at Sing Wu in 1981 Rudi had something he wanted to talk to me about. He had been giving a lot of thought to what Ethel had been telling him and he'd decided he was going to check himself into the mental hospital as a patient. But you know Rudi it's not always so easy to get out of those places... He was adamant and he gave me the keys to his pad to look after the place. I went up to Payne Whitney ("Pain Whip me" my father called it) to see Rudi and it was as I thought. They'd put him in the room with a huge Black teenager who had to listen to mindless disco music all night to sleep. The Third Circle of Hell, Mr. Blesh. I talked to the doctors, there was no way Rudi was getting out of there in under six weeks. Poor guy.

This was my opportunity. Almost without realizing it I went to the apartment with intentions of cleaning it up a bit. You have no idea what the place looked like. There hadn't been any cleaning or organizing done for about ten years. Before that it had already been cluttered. There was a front room (actually two) that hadn't been seen in decades. The big sliding doors that once separated the parlor from the anteroom in the old merchant house had been shut since the 1960s, maybe earlier. Every now and then Rudi would slide the doors open a bit and throw something in there. The pile of furniture, boxes, paintings etc. reached right up to the chandelier. On this side of the sliding doors was Rudi's sacred listening room, jammed with records from the floor to the ceiling. Except over the Zenith record player. There there was a large flat cityscape painting by Evsa Model. A narrow pathway from the record room through the former dining room, now a canyon of papers etc. led to the kitchen, another canyon where the papers covered all of the kitchen table except one corner where instant coffee and an occasional soft boiled egg was made. In Rudi's bedroom, another canyon, the bed was 2/3 covered with papers books and a few items of clothing. On everything was about 1/16 inch of pure black Detroit diesel dust from the Hitner rental trucks idling outside. The windows in the dining room were black. Scraping a hole through the dirt you could see the back of the buildings and the fire station on Great Jones Street (East 3rd). This place was going to take some work.

Lucky for Rudi his landlord never found out what a mess the apartment was. If he'd known he could have evicted my grandfather and this story would have already been over. Living off the Bowery had never been easy of course. That's why Rudi was there, because the area was full of illegally parked trucks and alcoholic men ("Bowery Bums"), a low rent district. Occasionally the apartment got broken into. One time in the 1960s, a man from one of the shelters broke in and stole the stereo and some of Rudi's clothing. How did Rudi know who did it? The guy left his wallet with his veteran's card in it when he changed clothes. Not exactly a master criminal. Of course Rudi never reported him to the authorities. The Bowery people were a colorful lot, some were really Celtic poets at heart. Like homeless people often are, many were sensitive souls, the victims and not the victimizers. The losers. During the summer seasons some of them would sober up, clean up and get jobs working as kitchen help and busboys at Jewish resorts in the Catskills. Their second job. It was not unusual for me to see a man leaning against metal fence at 38 East 4th Street drinking. My mother remembers stepping over prostrate men in the doorway when she came home from high school. The Bowery. I'll never go there any more.

Across Cooper Square, on Fifth Street, back in the 1950s/1960s we could sometimes see people filming TV shows right on the street in front of ABC Stage City. I have dim memories of being told not to worry about shootouts being staged there for Naked City. I think I also saw a scene being shot there for Car 54 Where Are You, another TV show, at one point. In the square, above my head the big advertising signs I could see as a kid were: a huge painted ad on the side of one building for Hartz Mountain Seeds (a favorite of Jazzmen?), and also one for a local business: Cooper Square Tire. As you can imagine, Rudi used to have fun with me with that one.

Of course the street Rudi lived off of had a long history going back to the beginnings of NYC. And the Bowery had figured heavily in the history of Ragtime music. Originators like Ben Harney, (Bert) Williams and Walker and later Ragtimers who even made it into the television age like Jimmy Durante had all started there. Irving Berlin was a tough singing waiter down on the lower Bowery before the turn of the century. The Bowery was the poorman's Broadway, with it's own racy theaters, brutal clipjoints and nearby, Chinatown with it's opium dens. What the Bowery became is now known as the freak show, the amusement park, porno. Some of that history is in They All Played Ragtime, and also Gangs of New York by Herbert Asbury. By the early 80s the Bowery was changing. The alcoholic White men who'd lived in the shelters and on the street were then being replaced by de-institutionalized mental hospital patients from other states and angry young Vietnam Vets. It wasn't unusual for a judge in Boston to give a person suffering from mental illness 15$, a bus ticket to NYC and an address on the Bowery. The human dump. As the 1980s progressed the bottles disappeared and the crack vials were everywhere. The Bowery had finally hit rock bottom.

Inside the apartment in 1981 what happened next was that I worked just about as hard as I ever have with a bucket and rags cleaning and sorting, cleaning and sorting. I would go into the bathroom after working for eight hours straight and be as black as a coal miner. There was nothing easy about this type of slap dash archeology. Most of what was on the top seemed to be whatever Rudi had been doing when he left off teaching. Student papers were everywhere, most of them terrible. Having to read this stuff would drive anyone crazy, I thought to myself. I searched in vain for Paul Simon's student masterpiece but no sign. So many mimeographed course schedules, tests, paper plate, letter from Marcel Duchamp... I couldn't take anything for granted, every sheet had to be scrutinized. The superintendent of the building warned me about putting too much stuff out on the curb for the trashmen (this was 1981 pre-recycling). He also told me not to put anything valuable out because "the bums" would rip the bags open. In my desperation I put some stuff around the corner on the Bowery where an uptight upstairs resident saw me, ripped open the bag, saw Rudi's name and address on a piece of paper and made a complaint. Welcome to the neighborhood. Every day I had bags and boxes and all kinds of items nobody in our family was ever going to need. Newspapers and magazines from the 1940s, Hansi's old cateye sunglasses, thousands of copies of Art

Hodes defunct Jazz magazine The Jazz Record, also Rudi's pamphlet This Is Jazz, and behind all that stuff - a hidden room full of the last shipment of Circle Records that never took place, hundreds of copies of MaryLou Williams doing Sposing, all center warped from having been stored horizontally for years.

This was where Baby Dodds had had his bedroom.

Baby had been Louis Armstrong's original drummer on the Mississippi River boats when Jazz started moving out of New Orleans in the teens. Baby Dodds was one of the first to nail his parade drums to the floor to create dance music. He also invented the first foot cymbal. His brother Johnny Dodds was the originating Blues clarinet player, the man Benny Goodman ultimately measured himself against. Rudi had brought Baby Dodds and the equally magnificent Pops Foster (original hand plucking bass man) up from New Orleans with promises of work in the City. The Trad Jazz revival was in full swing and things were going well in 1945. But folks didn't like renting to Black people. So Rudi took Baby in as a roommate.

There were evidences of Louis Armstrong himself in the apartment as well, in the form of letters written to Rudi in Louis' characteristic green ink. "To the man who has made us all happy" one autograph reads, another calls Rudi: "a very fine fellow indeed". Armstrong was the mahatma of Jazz, a perpetually benevolent character whose huge personality filled the world along with his music. No one could believe that Louis could play the way he did. Experts in England search his horn in vain during the 1930s to find the device which enabled him to play with such remarkable sustain. They should have checked his lips, the secret of his amazing embouchure. Louis had not a bad word for anyone. Even gangsters who had shaken him down, threatening to bust his precious lip were only written off with: "that cat hasn't figured out how to dig life yet." One of Louis' secrets of course was that he was a devout herbalist. Rudi said that once, after getting caught growing weed on his windowsill, Louis had convinced the judge he'd thought they were marigolds. Turns out the judge was a Jazz fan so it worked. The trick back then was to separate the cannabis seeds from the mix in Hartz Mountain birdseed. That was the brand guaranteed to make your canaries sing. And of course, you can't argue with success. If Jazz was the music then Louis was the man. The Pied Piper.

Back in the filthy apartment in 1981 the extreme clutter problem surely called for dire measures. I remembered how things got done in Italy, the street peddlers, the Porte Portese flea market. I found four broken folding shopping carts and made two good ones out of them. Loading them up with good stuff, including packs of copies of The Jazz Record and This Is Jazz I headed up to Astor Place. Italia here I come! Surprisingly enough there were already some other peddler pioneers right there across from the subway station. There was Ali a tall Black man who also sold on the sidewalk down on Canal Street and another hippie character who went by the name of Jerry the Peddler, a former anti-war protester who'd started out in the Army and before that Texas. Jerry was a politico squatter connected inadvertently to the dubious local would be Yippies being run by disreputable warlord Dana Beal. Jerry sold collectible comic books and he knew how to fight with the police. That's right in New York, peddling (aka reuse, recycling, etc.) was strictly illegal. My kind of scene.

With the 1940's-1950s street level time machine I was an instant hit where we peddlers set up in front of a large parking lot owned by Cooper Union. The school would sometimes called the cops but mostly I was lucky. Every week I would show up with two carts bulging and overflowing and return back to the apartment with about $300 a small fortune back then. Of course I sold good stuff. And at far less than someone else might. Antique stores were amongst my best customers. Having thousands of copies I sold The Jazz Record magazines at their 1947 face price 25 cents. it wasn't unusual for me to go into a fancy store and see my copies, now wrapped in plastic being offered for $35- $40 each. People would ask why was I doing this? Someone has to put the magic back in the system that everyone else is taking out. What? Did I make mistakes? For sure. One day I looked in horror as a collector walked off with Rudi's copy of the Mississippi Rag sheet music. The first published Rag. This probably belonged in a museum and that guy got it for $5. I hope he appreciated it. Mostly I got it right and every week a new area of the apartment was cleared out for human habitation.

Underneath all the junk and paintings and furniture in the sealed off front room there was a desk, all in pieces and when I assembled it, the size of a small car. This was the famous Duchamp-Ernst-Tanning piece, nicknamed "L'Elephante" Rudi told me later. For the first few weeks I used it as a bed. The windows in the front room were all cracked and full of holes, the source for

138

the black soot that came in from the Hittner trucks parked outside. I taped the cracks and sealed the windows the best I could. I fixed the radiator leaking on the floor. I scrubbed and scrubbed until there was a room.

Obviously it was going to be a room for me.

Six weeks sounds like a long time but when I finally managed to spring Rudi the job on his apartment was still a work in progress. Picking Rudi up he seemed in good spirits. Don't do that again, I pleaded. No way. Hey Grampa, you in a good mood? I asked as he opened the door. I don't think he really noticed for a few minutes since I hadn't really touched his room or the kitchen yet. Slowly it began to sink in. I was there to stay. Rudi was nothing if not independent. There was nothing good for him in what I'd done in his eyes. That trash was sacred and now it was gone. That monument to his mourning for Hansi, that protest against life itself could never be reclaimed. I hadn't expected any thanks but his wounded look hurt. It would take a long time for Rudi to accept my living with him.

After Rudi came back from the hospital I still continued to sell the old stuff up at Astor Place. I would get up early Sunday and set up for the day playing my guitar wearing an army helmet under a large American flag I used for a awning, some of those items found in the trash and reused. The street giveth and it taketh away. I met a guy named Danny A. who'd read Rudi's books at NYU studying with pianist John Lewis, was thrilled to meet the man and also turned out to be an early NYC bicyclist like me. The month was August I believe.

City Cyclist

Looking at New York City now bikers are everywhere but in 1981 the only cyclists you saw were the strictly local death defying delivery boys riding on the sidewalks and the guys who carried their bikes on their cars to race around Central Park. When you saw another cyclist on the street back then you usually waved. I made it a point to take my bike everywhere in the City, just like I had ridden in Rome. Taking pictures from the bike I captured lots of great NYC shots. Street parades, punks, celebrities, Bowery bums, prostitutes, police busting street vendors, the beauty, the grit. I was pretty lucky but I had some close calls.

Once riding around in Harlem I came across a classic scene. The summer street was filled with Black men, some hanging around, some sitting at tables in the middle of the street playing cards. The sun was streaming down like a spot light on the elderly gentlemen. I had to get this shot. Of course I was the only White guy on the whole block. Raising the camera up to my eye I was just about to snap when I felt a jolt. Putting the camera down I was facing a huge Black man who was holding my handlebars like a vise grip. His arms were covered with scars like he'd gone through a plate glass window. This was it. I thought fast and remembered an old Blues lyric Rudi loved: "I could be your best friend and you'd never know it!" I quipped sticking my finger in his face, stunning him momentarily so he let the handlebars go. In a flash I was out of there looking back to see him laughing, my buddy.

Another time I was getting some really great shots of a couple of Hells Angels sitting on their doorstep on East 3rd Street. Again the sunlight was streaming down. I knew this would make a great Kodachrome. Suddenly a little kid snitch starting yelling "He's taking your picture! He's taking your picture!" All I could do was get the camera back into handlebar bag before these two Angels were right on me. "You taking pictures?" the big one asked. He had no hand, just a stump. Not me... I pointed in back of me. "You better not" Not me.

The worst photo related incident occurred deep down in Coney Island. If you follow the avenues south in Brooklyn eventually you run out of alphabet. And sometimes out of luck. Avenue Q, R, S, T.... and then you start getting closer to the beach. Back in the early 1980s this was rough country, before the collapse of the

Soviet Union - after which it became known as Little Odessa. In 1981 it was really seedy. One day I had a clear shot of a group of prostitutes standing in front of a block of run down houses, shot with a telephoto lens from about a block away. Real grit. Some kid had the sharp eyes again and as quick as a racer he peeled out to get me in his car. Outrunning an accelerating motor vehicle on a bicycle is a short term proposition. This guy was clearly out to simply wipe me off the road. In the nick of time I ducked down a one way street and he was blocked by another vehicle. Time for a little relaxation down by the water.

Most common comment encountered while cycling in the early 1980s: "Hey, you don't belong on the road!"

Another time I rode far into Harlem, on up through the Bronx and all the way up to Connecticut where my little sister Genevieve Morton was a competitor in a national bicycle race in Meridian. You can bet Genny was suprised when I pulled up next to her at the start of her race with my bicycle all loaded down with books for training. The gun went off a second later and she was off. That was the one time when she was probably right that I psyched her out and it didn't help. Then in 1983 Genny competed in a woman's race in downtown New York City, the first of it's kind, around Union Square just north of where Rudi and I lived. It was a big thrill for Rudi to see his granddaughter (almost) win that race. The person who won that woman's race was Betsy Davis. She was built like a high school football halfback. Maybe if her shoulders hadn't been so broad Genny could have gotten around her on that tight course. It was like freaking roller derby. By the end of 1983 we got the good word: Genny Morton Hood was now the New England Womens Bicycle Racing Champion. She was also invited to join an elite racing team (Seven Eleven) and to go to the training camp for the 1984 Olympics. Way to go Gen.

In another one of those strange (non?) coincidences, my sister Genny's Olympic cycling coach was my NYC neighbor, former American Olympic medal winner Oliver Martin. He had a bicycle store around the corner on Great Jones Street. A fierce competitor and an Olympic Champion back in the days when no one knew much about the sport of bicycling in the USA (1959), it was sad to see Oliver Martin reduced to fixing kids bikes for a living. Of course now as her coach, being a neighbor I got an earful when Genny started screwing up. "You need to talk to your sister Hultberg". Seems that she was putting on weight, hanging around the real hard party types on the team and losing her training edge. From the peak of her regional championship the really hard work started and Genny slid back to Marblehead, the only real world she'd ever known. Square one, you might say, but always the champ in my mind and certainly in Rudi's.

On another bicycle run, to Central Park I observed one of the oddest cyclists I'd seen yet in the city. A wiry guy with long flowing white hair and beard dressed in purple tie dyed clothing, riding a purple bicycle with a purple trailer. He was stopping at every pile of horse manure and sweeping it into a bucket which he then emptied into containers he had on the trailer. All the while he was muttering and cursing to himself. I had him pegged in a minute. Some public cleanliness freak on his own one-man sanitation project. I pulled up alongside of him and said "hey, stop complaining, old guy, you could use all that stuff for a garden if you knew what you were doing". He looked at me as if I was insane and went back to what he was doing. A couple of years later I met this gent more formally. Adam Purple.

While I was off bicycle photoing, the person who really made my stay with Rudi work was Nikita my dog. Actually by now he was Rudi's dog. Rudi took to Niki like a true friend. Called him "His Nibs" and supervised his feeding and walks. You don't need a psychiatric ward if you have a pooch. Now in his eleventh year, Niki loved everything about NYC, especially the smells, the piss, the female dogs, pizza crusts, the few patches of bare earth where he might perform his sacred duties in peace. Rudi used a little string leash but as far as I was concerned Niki was free. My relations with the Sanitation cops writing summonses for dog offenses resembled my rapport with the police busting us as street vendors. I developed an invisible leash technique holding out my arm while attempting to stay a fixed distance away from my puzzled dog, as if there was a leash. Across the square, flatfoot usually figured there was. Off loose, Niki was great about waiting at the corner or catching up when I got there first. He didn't need no stinking leash. And he sure as hell didn't want or need anyone messing with his poop activities.

My bicycling buddy from the street Danny A proved to be a great companion at certain bars, especially Dan Lynch's on 2nd Avenue south of 14th Street. Next to a locksmith shop this quiet little Irish daytime watering hole at night became one of the things you could never find in NYC in 1983: a great Blues bar. National and local talent like Bill Dicey, the Holmes Brothers, Bobby Radcliffe, Jonathan Kalb (formerly of the Fugs), Kevin Trainor and his band Needle Dik. For the price of a beer you could sit there all night listening to some of the most heartfelt music you might ever experience. Bill Dicey was an older (White) guy who could do Sonny Boy Williamson. I mean it. He'd recorded for Victoria Spivey's label. He was a classic and he always had a hot young guitar band he was nurturing. The Holmes Brothers were a polished family act, Gospel derived Blues a little like the Chambers Brothers. Jonathan Kalb was the same kid I'd heard at sixteen screaming leads for the Fugs. His brother is Danny Kalb, like Dave Van Ronk and Sam Charters part of the Blues Ragtime Revival guitar originator club in the Village. Danny Kalb's band had been the Blues Project (with Al Kooper). Jonathan Kalb was simply terrific at Dan Lynch's, a Blues master, did he ever make records? Bobby Radcliffe still puts out CDs and was/is as slick as any White boy who ever came out of Chicago, one of the few White boys who can do Otis Rush, with the intensity intact. Kevin Trainor was just a really gifted goofy kid from Columbia University who could play just about any style with his band.

At one end of Dan Lynch's bar there were Barnard girls, at the other end the Hells Angels. The most innocent looking girl in the place was actually Bill Dicey's daughter, a total poolshark. Many the night she suckered somebody into a high stakes game while her dad was knocking everyone out with his harmonica playing. At Dan Lynch's Danny and I would sneak 40 oz bottles under our coats and nurse one beer mug all night. Whatever money we had we threw into the kitty, the only money the musicians ever made. One night Kevin Trainor used the giant metal (spitoon) kitty tub as a slide for his guitar, playing the theme from the Beverly Hillbillies. We had hundreds of hours of fun there for very little money without a single incident of human stupidity. How likely would that be today?

The Ragtime Society

Life with Rudi in the newly cleaned up apartment started to take on an aura of normalcy. There was a cleared out middle room where we could sit and play cards. Rudi's lady friend Ethel Baziotes even came over to visit for the first time in years, making allowances for "bachelor living" she would even sit down on the chairs if I put a towel down first. The chairs were Rudi's own special design. Ultra modern in the 1940s, he had copied the line drawn for him by a chiropractor friend to create the design in wood. The chiropractor must have been trying to get more business because as sleek as they look, Rudi's lowslung butt recepticles only made cripples of the people who sat in them regularly, myself included. The towels may have been a new item at 38 East 4th Street. Because as I hard as I tried, I could find very much evidence of Rudi bathing. That didn't mean he smelled bad. On the contrary, the smell I most associated with Rudi would have been a honey-like odor, as if honey even had an odor. Rudi used to say that women were attracted to the scent given off from behind men's ears. Human musk from behind the mask. I would say this is what he had, combined with a complete lack of the smell of fear. The ultimate distillation of Jazz purity perhaps.

In the front room I found paintings of Rudi. Portraits. Each one illustrated a facet of his life and career. The oldest was from the 1920s, painted by Valente DiAngelo in San Francisco, it shows the young beardless furniture designer with pen in hand. The next portrait was a thickly impastoed portrait done by Walter Gaudnek of the expatriate Rudi in Tahiti. Rudi never made it to Tahiti, but after seeing the film Tabu in 1931 it had been his dream. The only thing that held him back he told me was the $5000 deposit required of all Americans to pay for their repatriation should things not work out. The lost dream. The last portrait was a depressing one, the sad eyed Rudi on his way to the mental health clinic in the 1970s, painted by close friend and former NYU Jazz student Ronnie Elliott.

Ms. Elliott had been a well known model in the early days (1920s), posing for Frederick William MacMonnies and other famous sculptors. "The pocket Venus" was her nickname. Turning the tables on the genius male artist society she became an artist herself, turning out great work in a new style each decade she persisted. Socialist People's Art in the 1930s, Surrealism in the 1940s, Abstract Expressionism in the 1950s, Pop Art in the

144

1960s and Jazz Art (influenced by Rudi) in the 1970s. The woman was unstoppable. I went over to help her with her art cataloging project at the brownstone owned by her and her husband, a former reporter for the AP in China. After a while I also took over as the unofficial superintendent for the building, repairing things when they went haywire. Her downstairs tenant was the flambouyant former manager of the Strand Bookstore, a guy with some literary pretensions of his own. Ronnie Elliott the artist was waiting everyday for a letter from her art dealer in Paris. One day the letter with French stamps appeared on the top of the mailman's stack of letters as he put them in the boxes. Oh there's my letter she exclaimed reaching down for it. No you don't the burly (temporary) mailman said grabbing her so roughly he broke her arm. After that things were never the same. Her arm healed badly in the cast. She'd gotten the show in Paris but had lost the use of her right arm. We went to the opera and concerts together but she was unconsolable. About a year after that incident with the mailman she died, from a broken heart as much as anything else. Beautiful talented woman.

Rudi had other paintings as well, more than would fit on the many walls in the apartment. In addition to the large Evsa Modell, a dingy ugly Jaqueline Lamba, some canvases by Jimmy Ernst, a few Hultbergs and all the paintings from Rudi's own first and only show, there was also a mirror on which my father had painted a fractured self portrait. I was somewhat relieved when the paint peeled off revealing a usable mirror again. Also on display: a small Hudson River School landscape, an unsigned Stuart Davis street scene, a bright tightly painted dreamscape by Charles Howard, Victor Brauner's Cat into Woman (an early morph) and a rather dimly lit small canvas by Bill Baziotes. These last three fine paintings were liquidated to pay bills during my grandfather's later lifetime, usually through the Sidney Janis Gallery, Rudi's last link to that world he had once so inhabited with so much flair, poetic presence and heartfelt expression. By the 1980s these were his last cards to play in that big stakes game.

In addition the apartment was overrun by Folk Art, which as others have mentioned, could be just about anything from a Cornell box to a Marcel Duchamp replica, Village Jazz poster, Art Nouveau sculpture, Baby Dodds' drumsticks, Buster Keaton's hat, Scott Joplin's folios, antique toys, found objects, Hansi's art constructions, gallery announcements, ancient Mexican artifacts, seashells, neolithic goddess figurines, ancient Buddhas, Native

American objects, rattles, African masks, drums, band horns hung from the ceiling. Also hung from the ceiling, a huge hulking antique whirlygig (moving weathervane) from Pennsylvannia Dutch (Deutsch) country of a fierce 1770s Prussian (pro-British) mercenary soldier with rotating swords for arms. I always hated that thing. There were also "The Immortals", De Chirico like wooden heads on the mantle that were actually hat forms from the 1920s found by my mother in a nearby deserted store. And don't forget the Max Ernst Kachina dolls and a few Karen Karnes pots from up in Stony Point, among (many many) other things. And one stunning item, moved up in New Hampshire: an antique Rudi found under the El on the Bowery, an upright secretary covered in white enamel purchased for $20 because Rudi could feel the grain of the birds eye maple under the paint. Some people's aesthetic understandings know no bounds.

Rudi and Hansi had those two Burmese cats given to them by Wild Bill in the 1940s. These large creatures managed to claw their way through anything antique and upholstered, especially Rudi's endangered personal reproductions. From Little Italy in 1981 I brought in Giulio, a Maine Coon kitten I carried home in my hand and a little later, Tofu, an alley cat refugee from a Chinese tofu factory on Broome Street. Rudi and I would play with these cats, rolling aluminum foil balls down the long alleyway that ran through the center of the apartment. Added in 1984, Rag Apple, an orange New Hampshire stray kitten found barefoot and pregnant by the side of the highway. After a nasty bout with parenthood Rag Apple became huge and Rudi's special companion, more like a person than a cat. Immortalized by Bill Bolcom in a Rag after a visit to Gilmanton.

Out on the street walking the dog one day early in 1981 Rudi and I ran into Wolf Kahn, yet another gifted handsome dashing Abstract Expressionisto in the Village. He had warm words for Rudi and inquired about daughter Hilary. Hmmm I thought. Why didn't she choose him? Another time working as an Art photographer in 1982 I got to visit with another 1950s Art semi-legend, Michael Ponce de Leon. While I was shooting his work he asked my name and a visible light bulb went off over his head. You are Hilary's son! Suddenly a dim memory... of a sublet my mother had found and this guy, the tenant landlord climbing in the skylight, later to be fought off by my mother and our first maid Hattie. The odd thing was Mr. Ponce de Leon didn't look any older then in the 1980s than he had back in the 1950s. Could it be? I began to realise how scenes like these had shaped my world view, making me forever favor the female side even when that might be futile. Anyway, these somewhat repressed memories did little to help in the complex three way relationship between Rudi, my mother and me. I'd run away for good this time.

When Rudi and I played cards (Rummy) in NYC I would smoke a bit and he would sip Vermouth. Although we had smoked marijuana together a few times starting even when I was a teenager, it really wasn't his thing. Rudi told me stories about the Jazz musicians he knew however and their pot habits. The Mezz, for instance, whose autobiography <u>Really the Blues</u> on the shelf he recommended to me. Rudi said the word "roach" came from the fact that musicians would keep their personal puffers on the water pipes downstairs in the Jazz clubs where they would resemble cockroaches walking about. Don't mess with that one, it belongs to so and so. Certain musicians had marijuana reputations. Pee Wee Russell was always being joked about by Eddie Condon, for example, probably the origin for a lot of this. I once had heard someone from the Original Dixieland Jazz Band supposedly had gone insane from too much pot smoking (a cautionary tale) and of course Gene Krupa, the White teenage Jazz drumming sensation from the 1940s (with the Bennie Goodman Band) had been busted (set up - Krupa said, when Rudi interviewed him for <u>Combo USA</u>) by the Feds to make an example of Jazz musicians. But too late? I saw The Gene Krupa Story with Sal Mineo at the American Embassy theatre in Rome, definitely my first exposure.

One related story I remember from the period when Rudi and I lived together was the time we tried to change a few light bulbs. It probably wasn't a good idea to have shared a joint before this operation because before long it was obvious the gods were not with us. For one thing, the new bulbs didn't seem to work at all. Part of the problem was that Rudi hated to throw the old bulbs away when they burned out. They still looked fine. Maybe they would somehow come back to life. I think they call that magical thinking. You never knew what you were pulling out of the cardboard sleeve, a new bulb or one of Rudi's mummy bulbs. Suddenly there were no bulbs that would work but the old bulb that we were replacing now seemed okay. Maybe we should try this some other time Rudi. At other times when I set out (in a similar condition) to rearrange the location of various paintings on the wall our different operating styles came into play. Rudi, ever the gallery man had complex formulae, measuring the painting and the display area for finding the exact location of the nail on the wall, while I relied on guesswork, imagining where the nail might sit behind the painting. I don't remember if it was me or my grandfather who came up with the name for my technique -- machine gunning the wall.

Rudi's domestic specialty was defrosting the truly ancient refrigerator, itself also perhaps a relic from the Ragtime era. I say defrosting but of course Rudi was way too impatient for that. After about 45 minutes of boiling water treatment (all processes measured by the Circle Records stopwatch), Rudi would boil over himself and revert to the hammer method, getting back at technology (the Keaton Machine) and the world in general. The poor fridge looked like it had been through an auto wreck. A series of them. Rudi also held a real grudge against plastic: "The triumph of modern packaging" he would say, "the unopenable product". Its a wonder he didn't injure himself attacking some of these items in a frenzy with a knife.

Other times Rudi's hurry up nature would get the best of him in public. You wouldn't want to with him in a supermarket check out line for example. The impatience of youth I used to call it, usually to try to assuage the beleaguered check out person. You would have also done well to avoid being with Rudi at check out time in an unfamiliar restaurant, especially if they refused to take his check. Better to stick to Sing Wu where we were like family. Another time, I heard from Ethel Baziotes my grandfather had gotten impatient with some people who were blocking their way to Hansi's grave. Turns out these were the wrong type of Italian people to get vocal with because Rudi ended up getting punched in the face through the open car window, breaking his glasses. A sudden run in with the Mob. Most of the time, Rudi was the soul of patience and gentility. As the Jazz world had once experienced however, he got ornery when riled.

Rudi was a 78s man. When we got down to do some serious listening it was always stacks of heavy fragile shellac. Circle sides, Bessie Smith, Louis Armstrong, Jelly Roll Morton, Fats Waller, Lonnie Johnson, Django Rhinehardt, Billie Holiday, Lester Young, even Bennie Goodman had to be sampled in their original form. Rudi's record player at home was a funny looking Zenith with speakers that resembled wastebaskets. I used to make fun of Rudi's set up because I was from Massachusetts, home of KLH, AR, and other more snobby stereo manufacturers, but actually

148

even today those classic Zeniths are held in somewhat high esteem, for what they are. The only problem was that being a 78s man, Rudi was rough on vinyl. He never liked having to search for cuts in a crowded record side so he tended to slide into his favorite tracks. Rip! This was much worsened by the stack of change he used to weigh down the pick up, a situation that was only bettered when I stole the dimes. The worst experience of all (for me) was to look down at the rig while some classic LP was spinning, Rudi's mono copy of A Love Supreme, for example, and see the over invested needle set for 78. Ouch!

Once a week Rudi had me budgeted in for a dinner on him at his favorite (only) restaurant, Sing Wu on Second Avenue. I say only restaurant, but in truth there were times, once or twice during the summer when I was able to convince him to go with me to get borscht and peroghies at the Kiev on Second Avenue. This was just down the the block from Sing Wu so Rudi would insist we sit in back so none of the Sing Wu waiters would see him when they went out to feed the meters. He did love borscht. Hansi had made borscht in New Hampshire, along with schav, a lemongrass soup she cooked from wild plants picked at the farm. Rudi himself even made borscht for me once, the only time I ever saw him make anything other than instant coffee, an English muffin or a boiled egg in NYC. Rudi used to say that Sing Wu would go out of business if he didn't eat there as often as he did. It was also where he cashed his checks so that was important. (note: Sing Wu closed in 1985.)

There were other times Rudi skipped going to Sing Wu on Second Avenue. Sometimes he would subject himself to my cooking, for example. Spaghetti, in other words. As Rudi would say: there is al dente and then there's al cemente. When McDonald's opened on First Avenue I found it easy as a vegetarian to grab him a fast burger on my way home. Once I remember we had a bit of fun with the Black kids working at the Kentucky Fried Chicken outlet on Fourteenth Street. As a child I'd thought my grandfather was also secretly Burl Ives, but Rudi's resemblence to Colonel Sanders was even more remarkable at times and in this context, devastating. You should have seen those homies jump when I asked Rudi, I mean the Colonel what he thought of this establishment. He just shook his head. I don't know...

One night Rudi kept bugging me to take him with me when I went out. That was kind of unique and I wasn't sure I really wanted him along. But he kept asking so I said okay. The first stop for me was the pot shop on East ninth street. These innocuous looking establishments usually had a container of dishwashing liquid in the window Ivory Snow or something like that, as if that was what they sold there. Going in there was a bare room with a video game machine. A man usually sat in a little ticket booth. Maybe he was there to provide change for the arcade machine. It you slipped him a five dollar bill the weed in a small packet appeared. Tre bags were smaller. Once I'd gone in there and the place had been trashed. The guy in the booth was out trying to lift the booth back up off the floor. He was bleeding from the mouth. "Be with you in a minute..." Somebody had forgotten to pay the police off that week. Meanwhile the night I'm describing, outside Rudi was waiting for me when I left the dishwashing liquid store. Pot, huh? He was no fool. Next I took him to Dan Lynch where we both had a beer. Bill Dicey was at the peak of his powers that night channeling the Mississippi delta right through Chicago onto Second Avenue. Rudi was enthralled. Then Bill Dicey sang a song directly to Rudi, a personal performance. Who knows, maybe he knew who he was because the song Bill did was a pounding Blues version of St. James Infirmary. Way to go. A night to remember.

Sometimes Rudi and I would go up to the Dakota Apartments to visit with Mary Jane Grossman. By then Hansi's brother Botsy had passed away. Their big passion with Rudi had been playing dominoes, and so that's what we did, sipping sherry if I remember correctly. Mary Jane was a tough Old Irish New Yorker, what I like to call a real Knickerbocker Girl. She'd been Eugene's nurse when he'd gotten sick as a young man. He'd married her and as different as they might have been, they had a wonderful marriage.

Despite or perhaps because of his father having been a physician, Rudi didn't think much of doctors. Except for the psychiatric specialists he went to on the advice of Ethel Baziotes, I don't think Rudi went to a doctor once when I lived with him. The shrinks were a self serving lot in my estimation. Never once did any of them question my grandfather about his drinking, obviously one of the big contributors to his depression. Duh. Rudi told me at one point in the early 1970s he'd had a growth, a skin bubble on his hand that he didn't know what to do about. Going to the NYU physician he was informed the operation to remove it would cost hundreds of dollars. Returning to his classes at Queens a student noticed the lump and Rudi told her what had happened. She had Rudi visit her father, a retired country doctor living in the city.

Looking at the growth the old MD smiled. "We used to call those things 'Bible Banes', but I don't have a Bible here so this old medical book will do," taking the book and whacking my grandfather's wrist, he told Rudi it should be gone in a few days. No charge. It soon disappeared like he said.

Back home off the Bowery Rudi was mostly down. He didn't do much. I'd asked him why he didn't read a book at least. He'd look at me and say: "I'm a writer, not a reader." Got me there. Deep into his depression Rudi would sleep all day, get up make a cup of coffee and go back to sleep. A man from the Smithsonian Institute, a certain Tibor Arbolino came to the apartment to collect Rudi's furniture blueprints and design work drawings from the 1930/40s for their permanent collection. Rudi wouldn't get up, he said he was too old. I pointed out to him that the gentleman who'd come to visit was well into his nineties. That was my role, getting Rudi to do something. Other times I would dump most of his vodka down the sink and refill it 3/4 full of water. A necessary precaution. When friends came over there was an album I'd made of old pictures for Rudi to look at and explain. People would call my grandfather on the phone, the old number Grammercy 3-4227. One time somebody called to tell Rudi he was on TV, as part of a Scott Joplin biography show. "I don't have a television, God Damn It!" Rudi screamed, hanging up on them, whoever they were. The man from the previous century.

Before his depression and general funk took over Rudi had undertaken and completed several important Ragtime related projects in the 1970s. One pivotal publication he edited was The Ragtime Current, an important collection of (Rudi selected) contemporary Ragtime compositions that came out in 1976. He also did the notes for The Complete Works of Scott Joplin for the New York Public Library (1971), for which he was nominated for a Grammy. And also: the Ragtime folio book Classic Piano Rags, Selected, and with Introduction by Rudi Blesh in 1973.

So how did Rudi feel about Ragtime and Jazz at this point? When he was interviewed by John Edward Hasse of the Music Division of the Smithsonian institute in Gilmanton, NH in July of 1978, my grandfather had these observations, late in the game:

"...to me ... there [is] this interconnection between ragtime, which really is the music of the art nouveau period, and the whole subject of [that] period, ...the glorification of women. And jazz to me is just the opposite. It's the glorification of the male, that sort of thing..." "in other words, ragtime wasn't seeking to startle anybody, to frighten them, to harm them, or anything, it was aimed to cajole and to seduce and to flirt with you... (laughter)."

"Jazz is a much different sort of bag, of course, than ragtime. But I would think, for example, that jazz would be a... very hard thing on the players because it calls for... the maximum of original creativity at every moment they're playing."

"[Ragtime composers] begin to make most jazz.. just happenstance and chancey... sloppy almost... you know, the usual jam thing. You could get some little pianist sitting down and just playing Scott Joplin as he saw it from the score, and it came out better than those jam sessions. (laughter)"

Ragtimer Max Morath and his family were simply wonderful to Rudi, bringing him out to their house in Woodcliff Lake New Jersey on a regular basis, making him really a member of the family. It was Max and Norma Morath who finally convinced Rudi to accept me living with him. Now that was great. Another time, back in the 1970s while touring in England, Max had gone to a Ragtime production put on by a major London Ballet company. Shocked to find it mostly plagiarized from They All Played Ragtime, Max engaged a lawyer and got Rudi some much needed cash from the settlement, a repeat performance if you will. Max is what you'd call a solid friend. And of course over the many years, the mainstay of the modern Ragtime world.

Rudi's buddy Donald Ashwander also seemed to have a steady stream of work for Rudi, liner notes for Donald's various LP recording projects. Contemporary Ragtime. This was Rudi's most vital cause at this point in his later life, a field of music he and Hansi had created almost by accident when they rediscovered Joe Lamb. But at this point Rudi's depression often prevented him from completing these commissions. Donald probably never realized it but I ended up writing some of those liner notes, more great exercise for me in learning to copy Rudi's style of writing.

Soon after I moved in with Rudi, Donald's niece Sharon Moore showed up from Texas. A Blues/Rock belting bar singer a bit like Janis Joplin or Bonnie Bramlett, Sharon had the urge to do something sophisticated and arty with her unique uncle in the Village. Donald had written a series of Art Songs, classical pieces in the modern Ragtime mode, mostly little twisted Southern stories along the lines of Tennessee Williams or Cole Porter. Sharon could sing hard Rock and Blues but for this project she drew on a lighter resonant Classical/Jazz voice I'm not sure she knew she had. I got the job of photographing Donald and her for the LP cover. Alas, suddenly Mr. Ashwander's lovely niece Sharon was back off to Texas without much more than that.

Just to be plain about this, Donald Ashwander, the model of Southern graciousness, was of course, somewhat secretly... but still, Gay in that Southern discreet (but inevitably repressed) way. I would work on fix up projects at his apartment on First Avenue and there was a subtle pressure, a sad longing which I chose to ignore. He was a brilliant composer though a bit insecure. One of those kind of pianists who might flub up performances of his own work if he felt self conscious. But of course, a gem. He joined the Paper Bag Players, a well known NYC children's stage show as pianist and musical director. Actually what he played on stage was an electronic harpsichord. Listen to the music from the old Nintendo Games if you want to get some idea because it sure sounds like most of it was taken from Donald Ashwander. A very sweet man and a dear friend of Rudi's and mine.

When not in the Village, Donald would be out touring the world with the Paper Bag Players. Founded by Remy Charlip (another associate of John Cage / Merce Cunningham), the Bags were loads of fun for pre-video game idled children. Using recycling as their theme they made all their props from paper bags and cardboard boxes and by 1983 were major players in the children's musical theatre world. When Donald came back from his trips abroad he brought back loads of records and new fangled cassettes of old time performers, foreign collectors editions and Jazz/Vocal bootlegs manufactured in non-copyright honoring countries like Italy and Hong Kong. Let the listening begin!

I remember many nights running the turntable at 38 E 4 for Rudi and Donald while they called out old song titles, reminiscences. You couldn't get a better musical education. Scott Joplin, Joseph Lamb, Artie Matthews, Cole Porter, Hoagy Carmichael, Ruth Etting, Libby Holman, Fanny Brice, Helen Morgan, Cleo Brown, Sister Rosetta Tharpe, Ethel Waters, Mildred Bailey, the Boswell Sisters, Lil Green, and of course Eubie Blake.

Take me back...

Ragtime Stars

In the last days of the Ragtime era (1910-1920) there were people working hard to help Ragtime evolve into something else. Some of them are still well known names today (Jelly Roll Morton, WC Handy), others toiled away in obscurity still effecting things locally, or secretly perhaps. Black people served in the American Armed Forces during World War 1 and they had done very well. With their high style Ragtime marching bands they were the toast of France. Returning to the USA many of individuals of color in those bands had no intention of returning to subservience or second class citizenship. Some of them had already been stars before the War.

Bert Williams was one of those who didn't serve, having preached pacificism before (and even during) the great war. Many were imprisoned for that in the USA but Bert got away with it because he was such a big star. Bert Williams was a man of color, a dancer orator and singer once revered, but oddly now mostly reviled and forgotten for his blackface comedy tradition. But no one, no one ever did more to change American tastes in music and comedy. First in his early Ragtime era Cakewalk Dance show as part of the Williams and Walker team. This was the high class Ragtime that toured England and Europe. Then Bert Williams took to the stage as a solo act, creating a monologue comedy style totally his own. It started with the stereotype that most like to stick him with now, but it subtly evolved during each performance into analysis of current events, universal human truths, deep Caribbean wit and wisdom, philosophy and ridiculous surrealist humor. Example: folks expected blackface comedians to make fun of Black people eating chicken. So Bert Williams came out dressed as a chicken. Wicked. What most people don't realise is that Bert Williams hi-jacked blackface minstrelsy and used it to invent stand up comedy. Who knows, he could even have been the original inspiration behind the dada idea, he certainly pre-dates it.

Despite being Black Bert was the biggest star at the Ziegfeld Follies, itself the biggest show on Broadway. His proteges (who mostly imitated him) were Will Rogers, Eddie Cantor and W.C. Fields. His hip (Ragtime) point of view is inside all of us today though strangely few can even remember who he was.

from They All Played Ragtime:

154

"Bert Williams, apparently shuffling and loose-jointed, and with the gift of perfect timing and incredibly understated satire, and George W. Walker, the uppity dandy, immaculately dressed in high style, but, as was expected of him in his first days on the stage, groaning and rubbing his lightly shod feet, characterized to perfection the dual Negro portrait of minstrelsy. It might be well to remember a cold and bitter fact of the 1890's: namely, that no Negro, however divinely gifted, could then walk well-dressed onto a white American stage. Walker's insignificant, minimum gesture was a masterpiece of efficacy. Williams and Walker must be credited, too, first with reducing the whole minstrel show to a two-man vaudeville act that got them on the leading stages of America; then with proceeding to full-fledged shows of the most phenomenal success. Simple logic can perceive that the very possibility of subsequent triumphs hinged on these first steps.

Bert Williams in demonstrating his own genius demonstrated the unique genius of his race. His shows with Walker were such that the leading white critics wrote in this tenor: 'This 'colored show' stands with the foremost of musical entertainments... the piece comes very close to opera comique'; or, in unqualified words, of Bert himself: 'Bert Williams is a genius' There is not even the prejudice of faint condescension in these encomiums. It was a man of his own race, Booker T. Washington, a fighter in his day though he would not be militant enough for today's [1949] developments, who said of Bert: 'He has done more for our race than I have. He has smiled his way into people's hearts; I have been obliged to fight my way.'"

"The Dahomaeans [From the 1893 Chicago Worlds Fair] were not quickly forgotten. In 1902 Bert Williams and George Walker followed the Negro intellectuals of the day in an interest in things African and produced their smash hit *In Dahomey*. In the general confusion as to where the real values lay, they professed to desert ragtime, a music of genuine African rhythm, in the attempt, commendable in itself, to throw off the coon stereotype. Walker is quoted in the *Theatre* of August 1906 as saying: 'At that stage we saw that the colored performer would have to get away from the ragtime limitation of the 'darky.'"

from Nobody by Ann Charters:

"The blackface role that Williams inherited had come out of the minstrel show, one of the earliest, hardiest, and most irrepressible entertainments on the American popular stage. Williams started his career when the comic theater was still a theater of types, caricatures without specific or individual identity. Using grotesque costumes and mannerisms, comedians noisily burlesqued not only nationalities like the stock figures of the Dutch, Irish and Italians who had settled in America, but also religions and races like the Jew and Negro. Williams could do little to change the situation; he found he had to conform to the prevailing image of the stage Negro. Because audiences would have ignored or hooted down a light skinned colored man presumptuous enough to perform without a heavy Southern accent, it was out of the question for a Negro to act in serious drama. For an entertainer who took on the stereotyped role, however, the situation had become so favorable that, as one old performer put it, 'A colored man with a banjo would draw almost as big a crowd as an elephant in a circus.'"

from Jazz Dance by Marshall Stearns:

"In 1963 seventy-eight-year-old Harland Dixon could vividly recall the performers he saw as an eager youngster in 1906-1912, when vaudeville was taking the place of minstrelsy."

"Dixon remembers only one Negro dancer from those days: Bert Williams. He saw him in a white show, the Follies. 'He had a beautiful speaking voice and a trick step that I'll never forget-- he'd raise one knee waist high with his foot back underneath him, and then hitch the other foot up to it, traveling across the stage...'"

Stearns: "As far as the general public was concerned, the Negro performer had never appeared on stage, and his white imitator in blackface disappeared with minstrelsy, with a few scarcely understood exceptions like Al Jolson [another Williams imitator]. It was almost as if nobody knew that the Negro could be a fine entertainer and an even finer dancer, so that when the Negro appeared on Broadway around 1900 in the persons of Williams and Walker, he seemed like a delightful discovery. The Cakewalk was soon to ignite a new and more general interest in Negro-rooted dance, and it was followed by a series of social dances, launched at first with the aid of Vernon and Irene Castle, which were to sweep the ballrooms of this country."

from Man on the Flying Trapese The Life and Times of W. C. Fields by Simon Louvish:

156

"Many say Bert Williams was the best of them all. He had been in vaudeville longer than Fields, with his partner George Walker, who died in 1911. Following such pioneers as Ernest Hogan ('The Unbleached American' [a Rudi/Hansi informant]), Williams and Walker worked their way through medicine shows and small time to arrive at Koster and Bial's Music Hall in the 1890s. They appeared together in such variety shows as *A Lucky Coon, The Sons of Ham, In Dahoumey, Abyssinia* and *Bandana Land*, which crossed over from black to white audiences. *Bandana Land* introduced Williams' most famous number, the song 'Nobody', which became his anthem. Williams said:

'Nearly all of my successful songs have been based on the idea that I am getting the worst of it. I am the 'Jonah Man,' the man who, even if it rained soup would be found with a fork in his hand and no spoon in sight, the man whose fighting relatives come to visit and whose head is always dented by the furniture they throw at each other... Troubles are only funny when you pin them to one particular individual. And that individual, the fellow who is the goat, must be the man who is singing the song or telling the story...'

These truisms of comedy were clearly being absorbed by Fields as he watched his fellow comics perform. The melancholy lessons of the black American experience were conveyed on stage by Williams with an elegance which transceded the discomfort of the black man guying himself for the whites. Fields paid him tribute in a rare quote in a book about the great black star, from 1923:

'My good friend, Williams, met with so many unpleasantly limiting conditions... he would occasionally say, 'Well, there is no way for me to know this or that thing, which you say is going on - I'm just relegated - I don't belong.' It was not said in a bitter tone, but it did sound sadly hopeless and it did seem a pity that any artist who contributed so much that was of the best to our theatre, should be denied even the common comforts of living when on the road in cities like St. Louis or Cincinnati.'"

from Nobody by Ann Charters:

"Williams never stopped encountering racial prejudice, but only rarely did his impatience break through. Eddie Cantor told the story of Bert in a St. Louis bar, ordering gin from a bartender reluctant to serve a Negro. The man behind the counter frowned at Williams and said, 'I'll give you a gin, but it's $50 a glass.'

Without hesitation Bert took out his wallet and produced a $500 bill. 'Give me ten of them.' he said.

Although at the top of his profession, earning a greater yearly salary than the President of the United States, Williams faced the same prejudice encountered by any colored man in the country. Social attitudes toward racial discrimination changed slowly, and while the First World War hastened the process of integration in some situations, it did not bring the significant changes many people hoped for."

"Once discussing his attitudes about social equality with Lester Walton of the *Age*, Williams said:

'Since I have been with the Follies of 1910, I am more and more convinced that each member of the race must take it upon himself to solve the Negro question. I believe that the Negro is bound to get on top eventually, but it will be by pursuing a conservative policy.'"

"It was only in private that he discussed the matter, as in a letter to a friend in 1922:

'I was thinking about all the honors that are showered on me in the theater, how everyone wishes to shake my hand or get an autograph, a real hero you'd naturally think. However, when I reach a hotel, I am refused permission to ride on the passenger elevator. I cannot enter the dining room for my meals, and am Jim Crowed generally. But I am not complaining, particularly since I know this to be an unbelievable custom, I am just wondering. I would like to know when (my prediction) the ultimate changes come, if the new human beings will believe such persons as I am writing about actually lived?'"

finally, a story from <u>They All Played Ragtime</u>:

"It was in 1911, while he was in St. Louis, that Jelly Roll [Morton] wrote one of his outstanding ragtime numbers, *Bert Williams*. The great Negro comedian heard Jelly playing it and was greatly taken by the dancelike qualities of its themes. As the result of his praise, the number bears his name."

Bert Williams lyrics:

Nobody Bert Williams 1905 (words by Alex Rogers)

When life seems full of clouds and rain
And I am filled with naught but pain
Who soothes my thumping bumping brain?
Nobody

When winter comes with snow and sleet
And me with hunger and cold feet
Who says "Here's two bits, go and eat?"
Nobody

I ain't never done nothin' to Nobody
I ain't never got nothin' from Nobody no time
And until I get somethin' from somebody sometime
I don't intend to do nothin' for Nobody no time

When summer comes all cool and clear
And friends they see me drawing near
Who says "Come in and have a beer?"
Nobody

I had a steak some time ago
With sauce I sprinkled it all Oh!
Who said "That sauce is Tabasco?"
Nobody

When I try hard, and scheme and plan
To look as good as ever I can
Who says "Look at that handsome man?"
Nobody

Let it Alone Bert Williams 1907

In going through this pig iron world
it's sometimes asked of you
to give advice at certain times
and just - tell folks what to do

Now at these times I'm going to tell you
what I think's the wisest plan

when comes to mixing in with things
that you just don't understand

Let it alone
If it don't concern you why let it alone
Don't go four flushin' and puttin' on airs
sticking your face in other people's affairs
'cause if you don't know - why say so
Go on about your business and let it alone

You see two people fussin'
...well a man and a woman let's say
You just don't think it's right that
they should act and carry on that way

You think to yourself
well - I'm going to stop that row
but just as you draw nigh
the lady swats the gentleman
with a poker across his eyes ungh!!

Let it alone Let it alone
You don't know the people so let it alone
They know their business right all right
Why they practice that way every night
You go buttin' in and then they'll bust your chin
You better mind your own business and let it alone

(I'm going to dance some now... that's my glide)

You Can't Get Away From It Bert Williams 1907

When the silvery moon is rising
Mr. Rag goes burglarizing
comes a peeping slyly creeping
in the room where you are sleeping

In the day when you get silly
he's around it makes you dizzy
When he finds you he reminds you
No use hiding away

Syncopation rules the nation
you can't get away from it Aw...

160

It causes a sensation
You can't get away from it
Lawyers and physicians
even men on high positions
great big politicians all pal around
with the Rag musicians

They buy it Don't deny it
You can't get away from it Aw...
On Sunday same as Monday
You can't get away from it Aw...
Even poor old village preachers
have engaged their Tango teachers
Get away from it Get away from it
You can't get away from it at all No sir!

All the fishes in the ocean
swim around with a Raggy motion
Biscuit bakers even Quakers
are among the shoulder shakers
Soldier boys and men of letters
Chorus girls and suffrigetters
Aviators even waiters
No one ever escapes!

from: **Somebody Else, Not Me** Burt Williams 1917

Great moments come to everyman
Situations where he can
attain such fame - that folks acclaim
the very mention of his name...

(Modernism starts here. Bert Williams CDs - from Archeophone)

Another Black star of the early teens was James Reese Europe, a
fellow member of Bert Williams' Black Aristophelian theatrical
guild, The Frogs. Thanks to the tireless efforts of White socialites
Vernon and Irene Castle, it was Europe's Ragtime Band that
helped them introduce the Ragtime animal dances like the
Foxtrot to wealthy society folks. And in case you didn't know, just
about every Pop and Jazz song in the book, right up until Boogie
Woogie / Rock and Roll, was a Foxtrot. The Foxtrot was easy to
dance and the steady 4/4 time gave musicians plenty of space to
fool around, the basis for Jazz. Ragtime was turning into Jazz,

losing it's marching band origins, becoming a simplified dance music. The Castles, like Fred Astaire and his sister were an upper class dancing act. No other woman did more to shape the upcoming 1920s fashions than stylish Irene Castle with her short skirts, bobbed hair and Jazzy new (inter-racial) dance styles. Later, in the 1920s Ziegfeld chorus girl/actress Louise Brooks took the short bobbed haircut to its greatest heights but it really started with Irene. Vernon and Irene Castle, the original White Jazz Babies. Both volunteered early for World War 1 and Vernon, a Brit, was soon killed. It was said that Vernon Castle's favorite pastime was working out on the drum set from the James Reese Europe band. How many millions of us have followed in their footsteps - literally, or in those of the great Bert Williams? The Ragtime era is with us still. It's all in <u>They All Played Ragtime</u>.

After any war, people are always different. After World War 1, no one wanted to hear Ragtime anymore. That innocence was gone forever. The same thing happened after World War 2 when the big Swing Bands died, giving way to small Skiffle, vocal groups, R&B / Rock and Roll combos. After Vietnam there was not much more of that sweet Soul Music. After World War 1 the James Reese Europe band returned (from Europe) in triumph. What they played was not really Jazz, more like a sped up Ragtime (Maple Leaf Rag) with heavy synchopated parade drumming. James Reese Europe would have been a major player in the development of Jazz but his overworked drummer stabbed him to death on stage in 1918. End of story.

One Black stage act that was associated with the Europe band was Sissle and Blake, a brilliant pair of Ragtime songwriter performers. Like many Black performers Eubie Blake started out in Vaudeville and before that playing for parties as a child. He and Noble wrote hit songs. They created a hit show in 1921, Shuffle Along, that helped bring Black Music back to Broadway. The last previous show had been Williams and Walker appearing in In Dahoumey (1903), a revue inspired by the African village on display at the 1893 Chicago World's Fair and before that, an earlier show that showcased the talents of Harlem composer Will Marion Cook and Harlem poet Paul Lawrence Dunbar. That 1898 show, Clorindy, The Origin of the Cakewalk had itself been inspired by Williams and Walker, Cakewalk and Ragtime show originators. And so with that, after Shuffle Along closed, the brief Black renaissance on Broadway was put on hold for years. One of the songs Eubie and Noble wrote was I'm Just Wild About Harry, which worked for presidential candidate Harry Truman in 1948. What wasn't working anymore for Eubie in the late 1940s was his stage act. He'd retired in his fifties. A few years after Rudi and Hansi started Circle they rediscovered him living in Brooklyn. Rudi cut some records and managed to get Eubie some gigs. Eubie Blake was officially out of retirement.

One of the new recordings Eubie made was for Rudi's Circle label in 1951. The Jamming at Rudi's sides were recorded right in the East 4th Street apartment with Eubie playing on Rudi's old Steinweig square grand piano - actually right in the same exact place, in the same room, in the same apartment where Donald Ashwander, Rudi and I would be replaying that very recording on the record player in 1983 or 1984, over thirty years later. Now that's local resonance!

Eubie would also appear fairly regularly to surprise Rudi's classes at NYU and Queens College with a little first hand Ragtime history lesson. Eubie Blake took on proteges, Terry Waldo and Mike Lipskin being among the best known today. Also originally, hard working Ragtime Bob Darch, instrumental in relaunching Eubie's career in the early 1950s. Eubie and his wife Marion were friends with Max Morath and his wife Norma. The real Ragtime society. And at least <u>one</u> of Eubie's many birthdays was celebrated during the 1960s in the back room of Rudi's favorite (only) restaurant, Sing Wu on Second Avenue. Stinger Mr. Rudi?

Eubie Blake didn't hit the big time again however until 1969 when celebrated Columbia Records producer John Hammond recorded The Eighty Six Years of Eubie Blake which became a big seller. Hammond invited Rudi to the studio recording session so Eubie would have an old friend around. Sampling the various pianos in the studio, Eubie was unimpressed. You got anything else? Looking through the glass at a separate studio Eubie asked: What about that one? That is Vladimir Horowitz's personal instrument, Eubie. Let's try that one. So that was the piano he used.

The Eubie thing grew and grew all through the 1970s-1980s Ragtime Revival years. Sure there was Scott Joplin but here was someone who knew Scott Joplin and was still around and kicking. Rudi once asked Eubie the secret of his energy and longevity. Eubie leaned over and whispered. "I got a lot of exercise jumping in and out of beds". Another time Eubie had confided to Donald Ashwander what it was that future star (in France) Josefine Baker

163

had been doing when he discovered her and took her "off the street" to be in one of his shows. We all have to start somewhere. Eubiemania finally reached its climax, culminating in a live television show, Saturday Night Live which Eubie did in 1979 with tap dancer Gregory Hines. There was some question of whether Eubie could pull it off. After all, he was over ninety years old. But Eubie had been through playing in bawdy houses, rent parties, vaudeville... live television was really a piece of cake, a cakewalk if you will. They didn't have to worry.

I was present at Eubie's ninety ninth birthday party, held way downtown at the Selzer Sound recording studio on East Broadway. Eubie looked frail. They told me he'd eaten nothing but hard candy for the last year or so. When he wanted to get around he leaned on my arm and hopped like a rabbit. He and Rudi were so happy to see each other. I took some pictures. They looked like the shots Skippy Adelman had taken back in the 40s of Rudi with James P. Johnson, another great pair of old friends. Max Morath and his wife Norma were also there to celebrate. Modern Jazz pianist McCoy Tyner, from John Coltrane's old group, also present for Eubie's birthday was asked to play. He confided in me: "I don't know how to play Ragtime". McCoy played a typical chromatic composition. Then Eubie sat at the piano. He looked at if for a second like he had no idea what to do. Then the huge hands started darting around the keyboard like giant spiders and Memories of You came out sparkling just like he'd just written it yesterday. Memories of Eubie.

A year later Eubie Blake passed away at age 100. Even if he did allegedly backdate his age a bit, that's still musician's timing, real showmanship. At the memorial at Reverend Gensel's Midtown Jazz Church I sat between Grampa Rudi and producer John Hammond, brilliant man behind so many music careers.

A very good place to be.

from They All Played Ragtime:

"Eubie was not one to fall for the lure of the red-light Bohemia. In a year he was fixing his sights on a goal that then seemed more easily attainable for the Negro, that of an equal participation with white in the theatrical world. And, as near as any Negro in America has ever been able to reach that goal, Eubie attained it.

Eubie was one of the first of the Eastern Negro ragtimers to get his instrumental pieces published, though his junior, Luckey Roberts, beat him by one year with his *Junk Man Rag*."

from Reminiscing With Sissle and Blake by Robert Kimball and William Bolcom:

"Musical comedy had its greatest flowering during the twenties. As an entertainment form, it was a poly-glot embracing many kinds of expression. Perhaps the most all-around successful of all the genres was the revue, as spectacularly produced by Florenz Ziegfeld, George White, Earl Carroll, and the Shubert brothers. The revue traced its origins at least as far back as the minstrel show.

Beginning as an absurd white parody of black artistry, the minstrel show had evolved into a full-fledged variety show replete with all kinds of novelty acts--singers, dancers, jugglers, contortionists, ventriloquists and animal acts. Its early headquarters was the saloon, but by the late 1860s the minstrel show had become a 'clean' family-type entertainment, ensconced in 'opera houses' and given a dignified name: Vaudeville."

"There was a time around the turn of the century when the dominant white culture of America appeared ready to accept black artistry on its own terms. black artists had waged a long, determined struggle even since Emancipation to break the shackles that had virtually forced them into the ludicrous postion of imitating the white man's grotesque parody of themselves. During the 1890s black artists gradually cast off the bonds of minstrelsy and moved slowly toward the presentation of genuine Negro musicals on Broadway. The custom of applying burnt cork to Negro faces began to be discarded, women were introduced into productions and black musicals entered a new era." [Things went downhill after WW1.]

"Here then was the [anti-black] situation in the theater when Sissle and Blake teamed with Miller and Lyles in 1921 to write and produce *Shuffle Along* and to restore authentic black artistry to Broadway. More even than Cole and Johnson or Cook and Dunbar, Miller, Lyles, Sissle and Blake were to establish, on the Broadway stage, the humor and music of the American Negro in a pure form. For while there are intimations of ragtime in the work of the earlier men, the overlay of operetta was much stronger there than was to be found in *Shuffle Along*. Eubie Blake had already won fame as one of the principal composers of ragtime, that special American blend of European dance forms and African rhythm that would influence the entire spectrum of American theatrical and popular music. Ragtime's principal feature is the pitting of complex African syncopation against a strong, implacable basic beat. Blake was to accompany and abet the rise of this music from the bordellos of America to the vaudeville stage, and with Noble Sissle he would gain theatrical experience on the boards that would prepare them both for the arduous job of constructing a viable theatre piece. [Shuffle Along lead actors] Miller and Lyle can be credited with the successful launching of authentic Negro folk humor onto the nation's stage, and the fusion of these two vaudeville teams would result in not only a triumphant return of the black man to Broadway, but also an epoch-making stage work without which much that has been individual, original and viable in American muscial theatre would probably never have happened." (end of quotes)

And let us not forget the first Ragtime star of the Bowery, the runaway Southern White (? *11) boy who introduced the lowdown Blues to New York City in the 1890s, leading to all kinds of havoc when this explosive secret sauce also filtered into Jewish theatres on Second Avenue about the same time. Ben Harney.

from They All Played Ragtime:

"How remarkable a pioneer Ben Harney was is forcefully pointed up by... his famous 1896 Witmark hit, *You've Been a Good Old Wagon but You've Done Broke Down...*"

"Besides the patent fact that the words of this song are in definite blues imagery, the piano accompaniment and the concluding instrumental 'dance' section are bona fide, if elementary ragtime. It must be borne in mind that in the early 1890's the best of the coon songs had only a measure or two of ragtime and that the scoring of this syncopation was an art not mastered by arrangers until 1897. These facts establish Harney's unassailable priority as a pioneer of printed ragtime--if one disregards a mere matter of nomenclature or titling--and amply explain his own staunch conviction that he 'originated ragtime.'"

*11 - Eubie Blake maintained Ben Harney had some Black blood.

Sedalia

One day in 1983 Rudi got a call and then he told me we were
going to Sedalia for the Ragtime Festival. For months he'd laid
around and now it was off to the races. Sedalia Missouri was
where Scott Joplin got his musical start in the 1880s, studying at
the local Black music college, playing trumpet with his band
under the gazebo in the park, picking up the Ragtime licks from
banjo players in the Folk idiom. When they had these modern
events to commemorate Scott Joplin Rudi was often chosen to be
a headliner. The Guest of Honor, just like the title to Joplin's lost
first opera. Arriving in Sedalia in the late evening after two
exhausting flights my grandfather and I came upon a pool party at
the motel like you wouldn't believe. Uncle Max was there, along
with Missouri Ragtime legend Trebor Tichenor, former Rock and
Roll Star Ian Whitcomb and others including a Swedish Ragtime
piano prodigy who looked exactly like Peter Frampton. They were
all taking turns banging out Rags on an upright piano next to the
swimming pool. The party really took off once Rudi got there.
Every song deserved a toast and before long we were all toasted.
About 4 am people started falling out, but of course there were
those who just had to talk to Rudi. Sometime later we made it to
our bedroom.

A few minutes later it was 6 am and there was a banging at the
door. I crawled over and open it up and there were reporters
there including two camera people from the local TV stations
aiming lights at us. Rudi, there are some people here who want to
talk to you. Give me a minute. I'll be right out. To my
amazement he was already getting ready. No one had to coach
Rudi on how to promote Ragtime music. He and Hansi had
invented the school. Here he was at eighty four in the thick of a
culture that was once given up for dead. All through the day there
were seminars, concerts, debates, a US Post Office Scott Joplin
commerative stamp first day of issue to postmark. Rudi never
even blinked. He was gracious, witty, disarming, instructive,
authoritative, charming. The Ragtime man.

There always seems to be a divide between the arm chair critics
(like Rudi) and the player/performer critics, be it in Ragtime or in
Jazz. At one point my grandfather was matched up in a
discussion group before a large audience with one of his arch
rivals (at that time) in the Ragtime field. This person has spent a
lifetime trying to disprove everything, anything Rudi and Hansi

had ever written on the subject. If there was one fact in doubt then all of <u>They All Played Ragtime</u> was invalid and every one should read one of his books instead. But of course this person's books (whatever they might be) were written in the 1960s and 1970s and not in 1949 and of course relied on the interviews and other facts gathered in TAPR without which there wouldn't even be a forum for him to try to discredit Rudi. My grandfather never bothered with disputing the little details that obsessed this person. In Sedalia when his critic took a break from expounding on the defects of <u>They All Played Ragtime</u>, Rudi had a reply. Why didn't he return the notes he'd borrowed from Rudi? It seems that in his zeal this person had glommed onto Hansi's hand written records from 1949 as the Holy Grail of lost Ragtime scholarship. Unfortunately Hansi's original shorthand was pretty much indecipherable. As the crowd glowered in condemnation Rudi's critic promised to send them back. Still waiting. Then he made the comment that it was impossible to make a living playing Ragtime in 1983 and Rudi brought the house down when he replied: "ever heard of Max Morath?" Rudi's Nemesis, who resembles no one more than Bluto in the Popeye cartoons turned red as a beet. Even his beard.

Another performer who seemed to be managing or at least getting by in Ragtime used to do Rock and Roll before that. Starting out in Skiffle in the late 1950s, by the early 1960s Ian Whitcomb was an undergrad at Trinity College in Dublin when his band Blues Incorporated hit USA top ten in 1965 with his throwaway "You Turn Me On", a bit of R&B fluff based on a Marvin Gaye piano riff (Can I Get a Witness). It was also his long shaggy hair, and a certain resemblence to Mick Jagger (or was it Peter Noone?). An early model for Austin Powers perhaps. On tour in America in '65 Whitcomb got put down on the tour bus by the Byrds (probably David Crosby) for being bubblegum, which of course he was. So he turned to his other love, Ragtime and early 1920s commercial White Jazz. The Vo-De Oh-Do stuff you know. He visited Rudi at 38 East 4th Street around 1966, had read Rudi and Hansi's book and ultimately wrote his own musical memoir <u>After The Ball</u> that incorporated / interpreted some of that same history plus scenes from his own history in the music business for a younger audience. So in Sedalia 1983 Whitcomb sang novelty songs at the piano or plinking on his ukelele. So they do all still play Ragtime.

Another professional Ragtimer who seemed to be doing okay in his field was Trebor Tichenor. The epitome of the nineteenth century piano professor Treb puts on a period show on the Mississippi Riverboats still in use in St. Louis. Bowler hat, striped shirt, arm garters, Trebor has a nice touch in playing the old Rags. His name dervives from the fact that he disliked his father Robert for whom he was named. Trebor (Robert spelled backwards) also wrote his own Rags and Ragtime books, sometimes in conjunction with David Jason. Here in Sedalia he was accompanied by his young teenage daughter.

The Swedish Ragtime whiz. Kjell Waltman, was as close to a real Rock Star (not counting the older Ian Whitcomb) as you're going to get at a Ragtime Festival at that time. Kjell was really good on the keys but was intent on maintaining his Rock and Roll bad boy (or is it Ragtime) bottle on the piano image. His hero seems to have been Ragtime Bob Darch for whom he wrote an elligy: Jack Daniels #7, (A Lament). Actually the kid was really funny. He'd been playing on the ferry boats running between Sweden and Copenhagen and this, despite his excellent English was his first trip to the USA. Much to the consternation of Mr. Trebor Tichenor, whose pretty young daughter fell big time in no time for the long haired Ragtime star from Sweden. That demon Ragtime!

To save on cabfare while in Sedalia I'd walk to the day's events from our motel by the side of the highway, a couple of miles. It was an excellent education in middle period middle America for someone who'd lived the past few years in New York City. Car dealerships, fast food restaurants, furniture outlets, motel after motel, drive in churches, convenience stores. Suddenly a Cadillac screeched to a halt and the back door opened. "Ain't you Blesh's kid?" Grandkid. "Get in I'll give you a f*%#ing ride". What the hell. The back seat floor was filled up to my knees with flask bottles. Jack Daniels #7. "You must be Ragtime Bob Darch" "How'd ya know?" he asked pulling from a new one while puffing a big cigar. Then we were at the hotel and he said "Get out". Next day I saw Bob Darch playing in one of the pavilion tents downtown. He played Rags like he was trying to get through them the fastest. At the end he'd hop up and and turn around to the audence with that cigar in his mouth like he'd just set a new world's record. Ragtime Bob Darch the quickest draw in the West. And yet also, over the years, Ragtime's original greatest exponent. The exception that proves the rule?

Max Morath's showcase was in the large theatre. Alas he was no longer doing the full Max Morath Turn of the Century multi media show but the gist of it was still there. Plus, he's just a heck of a performer. That night in Sedalia Max was in fine form, although he had some problem with his newfangled wireless microphone. Bring out the megaphone. Later that night at a party he saw that I'd managed to associate myself with a young lady at the festival. He gave me a wink. What little I might know I learned from a master.

At the motel bar I tried to order a foreign beer and I got the hate stare. At the bar was a young State Policeman in his uniform. "I don't see why we gotta pay respect to an ignorant n____ who was a pimp and who died from venereal disease" he spit as he was looking right at me. Hey on second thought, skip that beer. At least I could take some comfort in the fact that all those "facts" however distorted, did come from <u>They All Played Ragtime</u>. Lottie Joplin did allow streetwalkers to use the Joplin Hotel in Harlem for their business. It was usually the only business she could get. Scott Joplin did probably work in bordellos, it was usually the only work a Black piano player could get at the time. Scott Joplin did more than anyone to take his music from the whorehouse to the conservatory, he just didn't quite make it all the way. Walking around Harlem with his opera under his arm, slowly going mad. It's all in the book. Oh and lots of people died of syphillis back then even including probably some of that punk cop's relatives. There was no penicillin.

On the flight back to New York Rudi and I walked through the TWA lounge in Kansas City to get to the plane . As we passed someone pushed a coffee table out and Rudi hit it square on the shin. He broke the tabletop right off the legs with the force of his leg. I look at his shin and it was all swollen and black and blue. I looked around the TWA lounge and all the employees who'd been there a second or so ago had suddenly disappeared. This didn't look good. Rudi looked at me and said. "I'm alright" and got up and calmly walked to the plane. Ragtime made him unstoppable.

Rudi Blesh, from the 1978 John Hasse interviews:

"[Ragtime] just didn't seem that important to me [while writing <u>Shining Trumpets</u>]. It seemed like something from my childhood. And I didn't think it was that important a part of ...jazz. ...Now ragtime seems much more important to me than jazz, because it's classical in a fixed form--it is there forever."

Although I was taking thousands of photographs in New York City in that period (1980-1984) I had pretty much struck out as a photographer. The galleries just laughed at the show of South Carolina pictures I had worked on for years. Articles with pictures I submitted to the Village Voice were rejected. It would be years before they would start covering the things I was interested in: street performers, street vendors, bicycle activism, animal rights demonstrations. After a while I pretty much gave up trying to get a break in that field. I did put on slide shows at the tiny East Fourth Street Gallery while another beatnik guy played a homemade instrument called a Gitler. I also put on slideshows of my photographs as part of the All Species Circle totem animal rights group I had joined. The shows were in the Central Park Dairy, magic - for the mask making workshops we did there every week. Our hope was to inspire everyone to respect animals by making animal mask wearing a new fashion statement. We ended up being a free babysitting service for Central Park joggers. One day some Black kids, foundlings from an uptown school made masks. One lad who didn't say much made a perfect representation of a deer in papier mache, complete with antlers from a nearby bush. It's a goat, he informed us. Anything you say man, you obviously got it straight from the source. The All Species Circle would also sometimes go down to West Broadway dressed as animals and try to engage the rich arty sophisticates there at play. Perhaps you saw me with my grey corduroy wolf mask and grey corduroy suit, speaking for the Canus Lupus/Aureus people. Woof!

The All Species Circle were a bunch of odd birds. My initial contact was through two adorable funny furry hippie types George L (from Alabama) and Bennie F (from Queens). Soon I met the others and a little later the founder of the group, Ponderosa Pine (Keith Lampe) a California Mr. Natural type character who resembled more than a little bit Adam Purple (David Wilkie), our local NYC Garden of Eden creator. There I've blown everyone's cover. When Ponderosa came to NYC he refused to wear shoes. He made a strange inaudible sound that hypnotised my cats. Pine traveled around the world advocating for the animals and that worked for me. This was a (ridiculous) guru I could handle. We made masks, we chanted, we invoked the species mind. I wrote poems and songs. We planned a giant rally in Central Park but were barred from the park by officials as we entered. So we went

171

to a restaurant instead. The uptown branch of the organization had always been a bit weird. At one workshop way out on Seventh Avenue it suddenly dawned on us (George L. and I) that the reason JR and the other uptown girls kept leaving and coming back was that those ladies were actually making a living in the next room. Ah, that heart of gold... But despite that or perhaps because of it, this was as pure as anything I had ever done. Pretty soon I too had a female escort as an all species girlfriend. I too walked barefoot on the filthy pavement washing my feet when I got home. Just like Niki and Ponderosa Pine. Now I knew.

In the summer of 1982 I met a beautiful woman on the island of Monhegan and I resolved to spend the summer with her and her two wild children. Of course that meant leaving Rudi alone for the Summer months driving and all. He was in his eighties and this was going to be a high risk strategy. The Moraths helped by staying up in New Hampshire with him for a while as did Bill Bolcom with his wife, singer Joan Morris. Simply wonderful people. I worried about my grandfather and spent time calling on the short wave radio telephone from the island but I was determined to stay. Monhegan was just too wild and wonderful and I might never get another chance. Just this one Summer. I got back to New York in the Fall and it was obvious, what had I been thinking? Rudi needed me, I had a home here. Had I really been ready to chuck all that to live on a magical island with a beautiful woman and her children? Unanswerable question. Rudi seemed glad to see me. He'd gotten through the summer okay mostly alone in NH, but just barely.

During this period I continued to see my aunt and uncle, Paul and Ethel Hultberg, living in Pomona, just north of New York City. Their somewhat improbable marriage, he a tall Western Swede, she a short NYC Jew turned into the only stability, the only constant in our web of families torn every which way. The amazing thing to me was that Paul and Ethel had friends forever, all kinds of friends, White, Jewish, Black, Gay, young, old... they're people people and for some of us perhaps the only solidity in a melting world. Some years later Paul and Ethel had their Fiftieth Wedding Anniversary in NYC. All kinds of people from all over the world came to celebrate, every one of them still a precious personal memory in Paul and Ethel's heart. How many of us can say we have even a fraction of that?

But in the scale of things artworldistic my father John Hultberg was always the real money, the big cheese. His big paintings (when he was painting) went for thousands of dollars and he did hundreds of them. His wife Lynne Drexler had started as a monotonous amateur but that was changing fast by 1984. When I moved out of the Broome Street loft Lynne took over my darkroom, teaching herself photography with a Rollei twin lens reflex. That camera changed everything for Lynne Drexler. With a composition to copy, suddenly depth and perspective entered her work. It was still made up of little circles but with a composition she was now an... Impressionist! And a damn good one. So it happened that after John and Lynne began living on Monhegan it was her paintings that began selling like hotcakes while John's recent efforts, his poems, plays and novels all added up to a pile of crusty unfinished manuscripts. The fortunes of artistic fate were changing and I doubt the old man was ready for it.

The big change John and Lynne had to deal with was that at some point, David Anderson, Martha Jackson's son, their benefactor, was finally going to pull the plug. After paying for everything for decades now they were going to have to go cold turkey. No more 2500 sq ft loft, free art supplies, all bills paid. From then on it would be self service, cash and carry. When this happened in 1985 obviously the only asset they had between them was the house on Monhegan, so I packed them up in a big truck and drove all their stuff up to Port Clyde and then by ferry out to the island. Exodus. Out on Monhegan, Lynne was in her element. A small town girl from the Virginia Shore she fit right in with the year round Island crowd. The cold didn't seem to bother her, at least here she had a community. Her paintings were a sensation in the local press and on exhibition in the house and it seemed as if Lynne was finally out from behind John Hultberg's shadow.

My father was less thrilled. He ran the Trail Committee for a while but did nothing. The Grump. Later that year John returned to NYC. Monhegan was not for him after all. He'd found a new art dealer who was going to support him again. Good for him. But it wasn't long before he was cheating on this woman with whom he was cheating on his wife, dealing his artwork out the side door in violation of his contract with her gallery, then known as Arbitrage. What a bad choice for a name of an art establishment. At one point John Hultberg sabotaged one of his own openings on Spring Street by painting all the canvases grey the night before. People were calling me up. Please get your father under control. Wrong number pal. John's new dealer on the side was unique even by Art World standards and it would have to be said that in her my father finally met his match for bottom of the barrel low down rotten behavior.

But of course by then there were other players in the Hultberg art sweepstakes. Brother Paul for example. While not as famous as John, Paul certainly had made a name for himself as an enamelist and also as a teacher in the SUNY university system. With shows in Rockland County, NYC, and at least one commission paying hundreds of thousands of dollars for his Japanese influenced work. Paul has an interesting history. Like John he grew up in California. Being younger he got into World War 2 a bit later, as an enlisted man, part of the first wave of American troops to occupy defeated Japan. Something happened though and Paul ended up totally disoriented heading into the mainland all alone. He said it was like an LSD trip. After days of roaming lost he collapsed into an irrigation ditch where the local farmers found him. They took him home and nursed him back to health, even dressing him as one of them and giving him a samarai sword. When the US troops finally got to that location they were ready to start helping people build new housing. Not to worry, Paul Hultberg had been trained as a carpenter by his father and he was already there doing exactly that. They didn't know whether to courtmartial him or give him a medal. Anyway, the upshot was that Paul was always very Zen, cool, a gentle person at heart.

Oddly enough, Paul met Ethel back in 1949 while working at Rudi's Circle Records store flattening warped 78 rpm records with a screw press. The teenage Ethel had breezed in on the arm of a Jazz musician (Coleman Hawkins?) and their glances met. Boom! A singer herself, my Aunt Ethel told me Rudi had taught her so much at that young age - about Art and Music. Too bad her kids used her Bessie Smith records for skeet shooting target practice.

One day in 1983 I got an invitation to attend an opening for the art works of the artist known as eSky. Add another Hultberg artist to the list. Ethel also painted now. She borrowed a technique used by Paul and other painters (Norman Rockwell for example), projecting photographs on canvas and then painting them. So I drove Rudi's car out to the Hamptons to go to my aunt Ethel's art show, which she was sharing with another wild woman artist, Johanna Vanderbeek. The show was interesting. Ethel's abstractions were perhaps actually tracings of maps taken from space. Cosmic. On the other side of the gallery Ms. Vanderbeek displayed tribal art, animal skulls with feathers beads and things. Her son Max played drums and his band entertained at the opening reception. I gave him and a couple of the other musicians rides back to NYC. I also met Johanna's daughter, A at that time. Again the month was August I believe.

Back in the City the Vanderbeek girl stayed in my mind. Her family and the Paul Hultbergs went back to the early 1950s when they all had lived together in the artists community known as the Gate Hill Coop, aka "the Land" in Stony Point, Rockland County, north of the city. Kind of almost a commune back in those days, but not quite. People in this group included my uncle Paul Hultberg and family, composer John Cage, dancer Merce Cunningham and later Shari Dienes a creator of the NYC Ear Inn. Also, Vanderbeeks. A's father Stan Vanderbeek had first used the term "underground cinema". Actually started a bunch of things. Allan Kaprow may very well have stolen "happenings" from Stan and Merce Cunningham for example. Monty Python took Stan's big fist crushing things from above animation trick. Vanderbeek made movies from found footage on big themes like nukes early in the 1950s. Daughter A had grown up in Stan's multi-media dome home environment: the moviedrome, where art was life and everyone explained their dreams each morning. How did I find these things out? Well, about a week later she called me from her apartment (convenently on East 7th Street) asking if I would cut down the legs of her bed to make it lower. And easier to get into as well I suppose.

I was off on a rocket ship ride. I'm not sure I'd ever felt this way about a girl before. It was the whole package, the bohemian background of our families not the least of it. When Rudi and Stan got together with us at the Dojo restaurant on St. Marks it all made sense. A had gone to Cambridge School just like me for just her senior year. She had run away from the insecurities in her proto hippie home life and enrolled herself. This girl had gumption. But of course in this case there was always competition. Always. What I noticed was the similarities in our backgrounds. What I didn't notice was that even though we might seem in the same place, we were headed in opposite directions. Me rocketing back from the marginal middle class to blessed bohemia and she away from the insecurities of her bohemian childhood to the middle class. Like my mother, A had no real respect for the world of art and music. They had only gotten hurt there. What they both craved was security, anonymity, conformity, respect, a normal American identity. Was it any coincidence that they were both enrolled in programs to become Doctors of Psychology? Now that's the ultimate control trip.

Still the rocket sped on. We spent time out with her mother in Amagansett, out in the Hamptons on Long Island. Johanna had a converted farmhouse and chicken coop that was her artist's refuge. She even took Rudi out there and showed him a great time while A and I got away to do bicycle touring. While out at Amagansett Rudi hooked up with his old friend local sculptor Roger Wilcox, drinking and reminiscing about building flying saucers when they used to hang out together in the early Hamptons art scene in the 1950s.

One day in 1984, back in New York City I read in the paper that Jimmy Ernst was having an opening up on 57th Street. With some difficulty A and I managed to get Rudi up to go. Come on Rudi, the guy worked for you for years. Jimmy Ernst, son of the world famous Max Ernst had gone on to be a fairly successful artist himself in the Southwest, using American Indian themes (those Kachina dolls again). At the gallery we found the place stuffed with people. Folks on all sides were laughing and joking, drinking and hob-nobbing in front of Jimmy's latest canvases. There was no place to sit down and no sign of Jimmy. Finally we went into a side room where a seat for Rudi might be found. In there we found Jimmy Ernst's wife, Dallas and daughter Emily, also making merry. Rudi asked about his old protege and got this startled reply: "Oh you didn't hear? Jimmy died yesterday. Charles Kuralt was coming to interview him for 60 Minutes and Jimmy had a heart attack right before they arrived. Oh well... the show must go on!" She toasted the sky with her champagne. Of course everyone was happy. This was the NYC Art world and Jimmy's work was all going to be worth a lot more money now that he'd kicked off. Happy happy happy.

Another time in 1984 Johanna Vanderbeek took us all to see the Gil Evans Orchestra at Fat Tuesdays. During one of those beautiful, impossible tuba solos by Howard Johnson of a Jimi Hendrix number, Up From the Skies, blasting a few feet way... I looked over at Rudi. He had his sly smile on. He'd never heard the song, but never missed a trick. "Jimi" he said, nodding to me.

This was almost as good as Slugs.

176

Gilmanton

During the years I took care of Rudi (or was is it Rudi taking care of me?), we still managed to spend a few weeks each year (not the whole summer) in New Hampshire, in Gilmanton, at the old farmhouse writer's retreat. While up in New Hampshire Rudi would take on his country persona. Years later I was with a friend in Gillmanton helping somebody named Doc Watson get some firewood. The old osteopath said he remembered Rudi. "A bit of a ladies' man" he said with a look of jealousy perhaps. That might have been true in as much as Rudi was well known, well liked and sought after as a dinner guest. There was only one widow in town who was seriously after him as far as I knew. When Rudi and I stayed up in New Hampshire I would usually sleep in a tent up the hill. As a kid I'd slept in the barn and watched the porcupines walk above on the rafters. Rudi wasn't much of an outdoorsman. He'd gotten lost on a mushroom hunt once with his old neighbor Joe Avisa back in the 1950s and he would always warn me about the dangers lurking in the woods. Another time he and Hansi had been picking apples in the Avisa's orchard when one of the neighbor's bulls had charged at Rudi knocking the the ladder away stranding him in the tree. The dangers of the New Hampshire countryside. I spent as much time out in the local woods as I could recharging my tree battery before our inevitable return to New York City aka civilization. Reading Rudi's 1800s copies of the Last of the Mohegans, Deerslayer, Walden, Emerson and other classics, writing poetry, taking photographs of mushrooms, smoking in the woods getting eaten alive by the ferocious Gilmanton mosquitoes.

Sometimes my sister Steffi would come up. One summer in the 1960s she and I took a canoe far out into the center of Loon Pond. Out there in the middle of the lake in a leaky little tin skiff, neither of us blissful hippies even had a life preserver on. Suddenly a small plane seemed to be circling overhead. Sure enough they were quickly beginning a descent and an approach to land on the lake. Exactly on top of us. Seeing us at the absolute last minute their roared overhead all but overturning the canoe. We got to shore and it seemed like just a laugh. Later, in the 1980s after she'd joined the Maharaji's and had her son Nahum she also came up, even taking care of Rudi for a few days so my friend Danny A and I could climb Mount Chocorua in 1983. Danny and I camped up near the summit, making a fire to keep warm. Later that night I climbed the rock at the top of the mountain once again. Naked barefoot and alone standing on the very spot where the native Chocorua was said to have lost his life in the legend, in the howling wind facing the Presidentials in the moonlight on one side and the rest of New Hampshire to the South I made my own sacred pledge to this wonderful rugged country.

Rudi's routine in New Hampshire was all dictated by the weather. If it was rainy we sat around, played cards, listened to records, then went to Laconia to the Spa to get the paper. If it was sunny we went swimming or drove to the store to get the paper, then sat around, played cards and listened to records. Needless to say there was no television. The records we played ranged from Fats Waller to Bix Biederbecke to Donald Lambert to Max Morath and Bill Bolcom and then back to Louis Armstrong. And of course Robert Johnson and the The Wind Cries Mary. Somewhere I have Rudi's mono copy of Jimi's first album, mint except for that one cut totally worn out. Rudi had this annoying habit of destroying record grooves. He liked to slide into the songs he liked which often made the previous song unlistenable. It didn't matter anyway his solution to all turntable related problems was to add more change to the head of tonearm. Rudi was an absolutist about listening to records. There was no easy listening. Being an old 78 singles man he would only played the cut he wanted on any one side of an LP. There was no talking during a listening session and there would be questions afterwards. For example: which of these versions of a selected tune was performed by the composer? That was easy. The one with the mistakes in it. If you got the answer right like the full name of Fats Waller's lyricist (Andria-manantena Razafinkarefo aka Andy Rasaf) - another gold star.

As kids Rudi would have us count the eagles in the room. In the paintings in the prints in the wallpaper in the sculptures and lamp designs in the ashtrays in the quilts, throw rugs, you get the idea. The place was an antiques museum. As young kids we each started out sleeping in the low rope strung bed with the hard tick mattress. That little room decorated with old 4th of July post cards Rudi had framed. A little older and we got to use the little single bed above the stairs in the open hallway where Rudi had used a sponge to create the cloud like accenting on the deep indigo blues in the moldings up by the ceiling. As a young adult or whatever we got to have the old farm hand's room at the end with a full four post bed and plain barn board panelled walls with the pencil markings on the wall of the childrens' heights from the real old days. The next room over was rarely used, a more ornate

178

Victorian style bedroom with lots of curtain frou frous and that sort of thing. On the other side was the master bedroom with dark paneling, it's own fireplace and tiger rugs. Rudi and Hansi's dream house full of period pieces, old precious everything, antique toys -- perfect for kids -- please don't touch anything.

The big obsession in New Hampshire was Rummy. Rummy 500 that turned into Rummy 50,000 the summer it rained every day (Steffi ultimately won that series). We'd play Rummy every day and Rudi had his own language to describe the different cards and bad hands he got dealt. Most of the things he said were from the Our Boarding House comic strips, the Colonel I believe: Brfffsk! Egad! My Word! Fap! all took on new meanings depending how deep he was bluffing. We never told Rudi we could read his cards in his glasses, even so he managed to win occasionally. When my little sister Genny came up she and Rudi had their own special game Zomberini, the rules for which I have somewhere in a scrapbook. By the mid 1980s none of these routines had changed much. Rudi collected stones from the driveway to place on all the window sills as an art exhibit. We still played Rummy and I still mostly slept outside. The old house was falling apart and neither Rudi nor I had any money. I did hack plumbing work and tried to patch the roof with tar from the inside.

One of my favorite walks in the woods in Gilmanton was down to the Smith Meeting House Pond, a peaceful spot where you might see a loon or even a blue heron on occasion. I would take the dog Nikita down there every chance I would get, sometimes just to get away from Rudi. On one first trip of the season going to the pond down the old Boston Road (now more of a trail) in the summer in 1983 I noticed that someone had started to build a log cabin by the edge of the Meeting House field. A summer later I was suprised to see a fully finished log house and another dog on my usual walk. A few minutes of interaction with the young people living there and come to find out she, D, was actually the god daughter of Creole Jazz star Muggsy Spannier. Of course she knew who Rudi Blesh was. A few weeks later I introduced Rudi to her large logger boyfriend. Rudi looked up in fear. He'd been robbed by the locals before and was somewhat suspicious. Despite all this I became good friends with R and D, wonderful folks, depending on them time and time again in the future when I needed a New Hampshire solution. The neighbors.

Rudi's relationship with the local people was complicated by the fact that he was a "Summer Person". Coming up to New Hampshire each year, our first job was to assess the damage done by hunters over the winter. Broken windows, forced door, beer cans strewn around, unflushed toilets. One year a break in artist ripped one of the ancient American Indian arrowheads out of Rudi's antique display. Look what I found out in the woods honey. Mostly the hunters just wanted a place to stay and didn't take any of the priceless antiques since they probably had no idea what they were. What they would take would be hammers, saws, woodworking devices. As Rudi used to say, they only steal tools so they can earn an honest living. Sounds like his father's humor to me. One year back in the 1960s, a tiny elderly woman came up during a thaw in the winter to the house from the deserted old road below in a horse drawn wagon. She had with her a young boy, a teenage runaway and between the two of them they pretty much cleaned the place out. After the robbery, the Belknap County Sheriff took an interest in the case and personally drove Rudi around to all the antiques dealers they knew in New Hampshire, Vermont and Western Massachusetts. Rudi got almost everything back.

By the time he reached his mid-eighties Rudi's driving up in New Hampshire had become somewhat erratic. He had his own little car, a little white Mazda station wagon, but he'd never really learned to use an automatic shifter so he rode the brake mercilessly like it was a clutch pedal, driving around with his brakes lights on. He would point out things by the road in Gilmanton: "that's the house up there on the hill where, you know... from Peyton Place...". By that time we were usually in the other lane or almost in the ditch. Finally in 1984 Rudi went in for his license renewal. No one was going to tell him when he had to stop driving. He'd been driving for 70 years. Behind his back I was gesticulating frantically to the DMV personnel. Don't give it to him! The man behind the counter asked Rudi to identify the letters on the eye chart. What eye chart? I had to comiserate with my grandfather as I drove us back to the farm. Those Motor Vehicle people sure were unfair Rudi.

Another time in 1984 while Rudi Niki and I were up in NH my mother announced she would be visiting with her husband, Ron. Hilary had married Ron Michaud a guidance counseler in Marblehead and was now on her way to getting her own advanced degree in counselling and psychology. She told Rudi she'd only have time for a 45 minute visit. That just made me mad. She hadn't come up in years and now she only had three quarters of an hour for us? Screw that. I headed down for the pond with the dog just before she was scheduled to arrive. I'd left my pipe by the pond and maybe she wouldn't mind waiting. Getting down to the pond I noticed the sky was getting darker. By the time I got down to the trees by the edge of the water it was worse and the second I put my hand on my illicit smoking device all hell broke loose. The wind was churning down from above pushing the trees against themselves. Tree limbs and whole trees crashed down right before our eyes and we had to jump because the ground rose up with the roots. The dog and I fought our way up the hill with giant hailstones pelting us all the way. By the time we got up to the Meeting House it was raining and by the time be got back to the farmhouse we were almost dry. Hilary and Ron were just getting ready to leave and didn't have much interest in my story. A week or so later I was walking down by the pond again. Twisted trees lay all about down by the shore. I told the elderly cemetery custodian, Mr. Paige what I had seen and gone through over there. "Oh you mean the tornado, stopped first down by Loon Pond, then it skipped up right to here. Took out the very trees this man wanted removed to make a view" he said pointing down to the grave he was digging. "What do you make of that?"

Up in Gilmanton, the Morath family, and sometimes the MacAgy's would visit but somehow our paths rarely crossed. Once I saw some artwork my grandfather had done, a cartoon about a "Bumpto Boy" whose job it was to turn off the refrigerator light when the door was shut, in the kitchen in New Hampshire. A pang of jealousy ran through me when I realized that Rudi had had these special moments with other people's kids. But with us back in the 1950s it had always been Oogie Oogie Wah-Wah, the old Indian Chief and his lovely daughter Snoorie Snoorie Boom-Boom. So you see we all had our shared treasures.

The one luxury Rudi afforded himself on his meager fixed income was a membership in the Loon Pond Association, the little lake club down Rte 106 from the Gilmanton farmhouse. It was there that all us grandkids had learned to swim, across the water from Peyton Place author Grace Metaleus's trailer, at least in the early 1950s. Where Steffi and I snuck out with the other members' canoes. Rudi loved that little lake beach club and got on well with the other folks there. Part of his regular Gilmanton social circle. The Loon Pond people.

Down by the lake it wasn't uncommon to see sandpipers and in
the distance of course, sometimes loons. One day in 1983 I
believe, I was looking for tracks on the sandy beach when I came
across some truly strange footprints. They looked like maybe they
came from some sort of Sasquatch, but suddenly I realized they
were Rudi's. Over the years he'd neglected to cut his toenails and
now he had claws. What kind of care was I taking of the old gent?
I quickly whipped out my Swiss Army knife and did some field
surgery, returning my grandfather to the family of man.

Other times when the tiny wavelets would come in on the dark
sandy beach around dusk Rudi would sit in one of the deck chairs
and recite a Yeats poem he loved from memory.

Lake Isle of Innisfree

I will arise and go now, and go to Innisfree,
And a small cabin build there, of clay and wattles made:
Nine bean-rows will I have there, a hive for the honey-bee,
And live alone in the bee-loud glade.

And I shall have some peace there, for peace comes dropping slow
Dropping from the veils of the morning to where the cricket sings;
There midnight's all a glimmer, and noon a purple glow,
And evening full of the linnet's wings.

I will arise and go now, for always night and day
I hear lake water lapping with low sounds by the shore;
While I stand on the roadway, or on the pavements grey,
I hear it in the deep heart's core.

The Greens

Asphodel, That Greeny Flower (William Carlos Williams)

> It is difficult
> to get the news from poems
> yet men die miserably every day
> for lack
> of what is found there.

(one of Rudi's favorites)

Around this time (1984) I had a new obsession. Following a dream that told me about a certain "spiritpolitik" (in German), I discovered there really was a similar kind of political group starting out in Germany, die Grunen. I went regularly to certain reading rooms and read steadily in the Christian Science Monitor, the only paper really covering the story, and started to make plans to start a similar group in New York. The name? The Greens. Before long Danny and I were putting out a little newsletter called GreenSpeak, Voices From the New York Greens. I went to seen a presentation by a Hopi elder (them again!) Thomas Banyacya. Out in the lobby a woman had a table with literature from her group, The New York Greens. I showed her my material and after a few minutes we both figured out we each only had one other member in our group. Why not join forces? The lady's name was Lorna Salzman and in another one of those amazing (non) coincidences, it turned out that she and her husband Eric Salzman had been instrumental in pushing Joshua Rifkin to perform Ragtime. "We created the Ragtime Revival" Lorna proudly told me one day. No, I said that would be my grandfather. And who pray tell who might your grandfather be? Rudi Blesh. Oh.

So began the story of the New York Greens. Lorna or others might dispute who created the New York Greens group but the truth is obvious. It was the two of us. The potential of course was and remains immeasurable, but of course like so many other good things in America, blocked. The first meeting of the consolidated New York Greens brought in a number of new people, a composer friend of Lorna's Michael Sahl, the wunderkind creator of the Learning Annex, WBAI radio personality Paul McIsaac and members of Murray Bookchin's School of Social Ecology. The second meeting of the New York Greens drew 120 people including Adam Purple, forager/herbologist Wildman Steve Brill, songwriter Michelle Shocked and also: Julian Beck and Judith Malina, creators of the Living Theatre. The legendary Living Theatre couple came up to me, clasped my hands and told me: "thanks for starting this". My City of Enlightenment Dream came true for me at that moment. By the end of that same second meeting it was decided we would model ourselves on the German Greens, using their fundamental principles or pillars as they were called: Ecology, Social Justice, Grassroots Democracy and Peace as our starting point. As we left the meeting to go back downtown I saw Adam Purple on his purple bicycle towing Michelle Shocked on her skateboard. Now that was some human powered energy!

Also in attendence at these early meetings was Lorna Salzman associate Kirkpatrick Sale. I got to meet this gentleman early in the game at the 1985 Whole Life Expo. I had a table there for the Greens that I was sharing with another fledgling organization, the Learning Alliance. Kirk took the Learning Alliance's David Levine to task for his lackadaisical arrangement of materials at the table while commending my artful display. If I'd known who Kirk Sale really was I'd have been mucho intimidated, but since I didn't I played the card. Because you see, Kirkpatrick Sale was the old Village hipster who'd introduced Dick Farina, his school buddy from Cornell to Buddy Holly, to Carolyn Hester herself. The Man in other words. Lucky I never figured that out until much later.

Later that year the Yippies staged a Green teach-in in Philadelphia which I attended along with Kirk Sale, Abbie Hoffman and others. Some of us rode down in Jimmy Two Feathers old Green Turtle hippy bus. At that conference I snuck out with a guy named John the Communist on bicycles and stood guard while he graffitied the Philly Move reconstruction site, just weeks after the bombing. Back at the conference I scored points with Mr. Sale by referring repeatedly to his mentor, Leopold Kohr, author of The Breakdown of Nations, the starting point for the E.F. Schumaker small-is-beautiful crowd. When the aged Mr. Kohr had come from Austria to the Village to speak earlier in 1985 I'd attended the event, put on by Kirk Sale. Kirk's wife came wearing a fur coat which of course I called her on. An omen.

Because before long the squabbling began. The out and out Leftists of which I would include all of the Bookchinites were already jockeying for position and power. McIsaac and Lorna were starting to flatter themselves as potential candidates for political office. Their only disagreement was which of them should run for Congress and which for City Council. Someone got up at the group meeting and denounced our newsletter, Greenspeak, saying that "It states on here plainly: 'The Voice of the New York Greens'" He should have learned how to read. The cover said: "Voices From the New York Greens". The division down the center of the New York Greens group was apparent right from the start. Since the recent collapse of the Soviet Empire had made socialism unpopular, Leftist power grabbers now wanted to use the Greens as a front to fashion an electorial machine to get themselves elected. On the other side were the anti-nukes people, peaceniks, communitarians, animal rights activists, cyclists, squatters, vegetarians, food coopers who wanted garden projects, recycling and bicycle activism among other things.

Obviously I figured in this latter group.

I also found myself getting involved in the struggle to save the Garden of Eden, a circular earthwork created by Adam Purple down on Eldridge Street. Turns out the old coot I'd seen collecting Central Park horsepoop had had a garden all along. He'd built it piece by piece, out of the rubble from the tenements being abandoned and destroyed around that section of the Lower East Side. As a neighborhood survivor and the superintendent of one such building Adam had had a revelation sometime during the 1970s, after reading a book called Soil and Civilization. Human fate was all in the dirt and it was time to get our shit together. Literally. Adam made soil out of brick dust and compost. He also composted his own (vegetarian) night soil but never actually got to use it in soil production. The next step. He built a round garden with ever enlarging concentric circles surrounding a yin yang protected by a beautiful curved stone wall built from window lintels he'd lugged and positioned by hand. A fast growing Chinese Empress tree which seeded itself out of the horse manure shaded the center circles. Another side of the garden was protected by piles of bedsprings which had rotted away creating a impenetrable springy maze Adam had seeded with black raspberry bushes. A work of art in other words. Ecology out of the trash. And everything he did without using motor vehicles, fossil fuels or electricity. Human power.

Climbing up the tiny rickety ladder up the side of the six story tenement building in the next lot over you got a great shot of the circular garden below and the World Trade Center in the background. That's what I did and that's what the photographer from National Geographic magazine did as well. Purple had become somewhat of an international celebrity by then. Back when he was the super he'd decided to speed the process of ecological community soil production. He tore the plumbing out of the building. With no landlord left the tenants left as well and Adam soon had a six story apartment built as temporary housing in circa 1911 all to himself. In one apartment he put bicycles he collected abandoned from off the street. In other rooms he stored thousands of books, records, magazines and other freebees he'd ordered (with the cooperation of the mailman) to fictitious names in his building. On another floor planks and other wood was stored across the bare floor joists. He lived in the ground floor apartment facing his garden, heating with wood, lighting with candles, eating sprouts, rice and tofu, hauling water up by hand from the basement, cashing in deposit bottles for beer. And shitting in a bucket, each layer separated by a newspaper (presumably the same one he just got finished reading and putting to other good use.) A neat system he hoped to export to the world. Chinese agriculture retooled for the modern western world. His companion had been named Eve (you've read the original story?) She'd been his first convert and for her he built the garden, like the Taj Mahal, piece by piece. As a green fundamentalist it was hard not to be impressed with the Garden of Eden. This wasn't some ecological theory, this was it. Or at least an interesting step in the right direction. An exemplary lifestyle and an ongoing social experiment that was surely green.

For the theorists, the radio personality "experts" in the Greens and the Murray Bookchin cultists from the School for Social Ecology this was clearly unacceptable. How could anything be ecological if it hadn't come from one of their heroes? Anyway the word was out. The City was going to destroy the Garden of Eden. The Koch administration had cut a deal with the local (corrupt) housing advocacy groups and it was a done deal as they say. Defending a lost cause would be a waste of everyone's precious time. So now we had the same dichotomy as the German Greens, the Realos (realists) who favored working with the system and the Fundi (fundamentalists) who believed in upholding principles. Of course in real life you have to do a little of both but if you admit to that how are you going to have a bitter debate? A few months later when German Greens luminaries Petra Kelly and Gert Bastion came to town, NYC Green activists like me were effectively boxed out from meeting them by the theorist power trippers.

I managed to get a few words in with the couple and give them the literature created by the group at large (Appendix #5). Petra Kelly told me, don't worry, all the German Greens did was fight amongst themselves and look they still got elected. Don't worry.

Of course in New York City there was a wild card, in the form of Dana Beal and his disreputable neo-Yippies. No longer the democratic youth movement of the 1960s that I had been part of, not even the Jerry and Abbie ego media show, the Yippies had become the private preserve of this one unsavory warlord character. From his filthy fort on Bleecker off the Bowery across from CBGBs Dana controlled various networks of hash smuggling, sexual exploitation of runaway minors, the annual Fifth Avenue Pot (legalization) Parade, the ridiculous US Rock Against Racism front and the sporatic publication of Overthrow magazine. Not exactly the kind of person you'd want to get involved with even if he did have a Compugraphic typesetting machine, the equivalent of a home computer word processor back in 1985. Well... maybe we'll use it just this once. It was so seductive and only three blocks away. Dana offered money, chicks, pot. I took nothing but I did use that typesetting machine. How could we keep Dana out anyway if the Greens were an inclusive democratic open door organization? Still you had to wonder, with all those resources, never getting busted... who was he working for?

As the group continued to meet we developed two more principles (pillars), Community Based Economics and Supportive Human Relations. Sometime girlfriend A took the lead role in SHR group putting her Psych PHD studies to work. We could have been quite the power couple within the group but the little wild one seemed to have different ideas. As the group devolved down from the peak of the second meeting into acrimony I settled into creating Bicycling and Recycling intitiatives that might actually go beyond theory and posturing. The summer was fast approaching and the richniks in the group like Lorna were going away to their summer houses for the whole season. The Bookchinites went to their bootcamp in Vermont where only they knew the secrets of the true deep social ecology. These people numbered around fifteen but they always acted like they owned the group. Put to a vote, the motion to suspend the group for the summer lost by a large margin. Those who remained after the would-be politicos left voted to support the Garden of Eden in it's struggle to survive. The Green Meanies (as they were known) have contended ever since that the "Action Faction" of the New York Greens stole their group but the truth is that their contingent simply lost the vote and then they left town.

Just at the start of the summer of 1985, on two separate occasions, I brought someone with me to contemplate in the peaceful circular Garden of Eden on Eldridge Street, each time walking all the way to get there from the Village. The first time it was with my father John Hultberg and the next time it was with Grampa Rudi Blesh. The power of circles.

All this time, starting with the All Species Circle and then with the Greens, Rudi had been taking an interest in my eco-political work. He'd take phone messages, offer positive comments. He even sat in on a couple of meetings at the apartment, notre eminence grise.

Rudi knew what some of us were trying to do. He'd thrown his rifle away as a kid to start a pet cemetery. He'd seen the Indian in the dog cage. Stood through Wagner's Ring Cycle in it's entirety. Gone to see the Original Dixieland Jazz Band in person in 1917.

Rudi had brought Scott Joplin and his animal dance ballet from Treemonisha back. Released Jelly Roll Morton doing the Animule Ball. Presented Louis Armstrong's teacher Bunk Johnson in the museum. Promoted Leadbelly. Rediscovered living legends of Ragtime. Wrote that poem for Bluesman Robert Johnson in Shining Trumpets. Knew the Lion and the Lamb ...as well as Joseph Lamb. Hung out with the Mezz.

Rudi was onto the secret of Buster Keaton and the animals

...and the real "skiffle" spirit.

I know the Greens meant something to him as well.

Finale

My sister Steffi had resurfaced in my life in 1984. After being the apex of the holier than thou Guru Maharaji part of the family she had come down a few pegs. She had broken with husband Chris the giant when he started becoming dangerously delusional. What's the difference in being dangerously delusional and believing you have magic words given to you by the Lord of the Universe? I got my sister back together with her father John Hultberg whom she hadn't seen since she was a toddler. Steffi was eager to visit in NYC and with her young son Nahum she showed up more than once without a cent. Despite being a brilliant artist like her father, at this point Steffi had rejected that identity and was living in Barry Massachusetts, near Worcester, working as an occupational therapist.

A couple years later, in 1987 she and I went out to Monhegan with her son for a few weeks in the summer, so yes, at last John Hultberg could say he'd used the Maine property as it was bestowed to him by Martha Jackson, to be with his children. Steffi's son Nahum was about seven and during that summer he was deeply into his capitalist phase. He was the kind of kid (like me) who played Monopoly keeping the money in his pocket. Out on Monhegan nephew Nahum quickly scoped out the local Spa, run by a retired dancing teacher from the Portland Arthur Murray School, Zimmie Brackett. Zimmie was a flambouyant character but he wasn't there at that point in the summer so the store was being managed by Jamie Wyeth of the famous painting Wyeth family. Nahum had it figured out that the penny candy at the Spa was underpriced. Using his allowance and some money he scrounged he went into the Spa and bought up a pretty good supply, then opened up his own penny candy (nickel candy?) store on a cardboard box right outside Zimmie's store. For some reason Jamie Wyeth was not amused and nephew Nahum's entrepreneurial venture was shut down. Grandfather John then put Nahum in charge of another (potential) family business enterprise, counting and appraising the value of the hundreds of used lobster traps stored on the property.

A precious family moment. Too bad they were so few.

I was two summers before that however, in 1985, that Steffi had announced that she and Nahum would be going up to New Hampshire with Rudi and me. I don't think I was really up for her

189

coming along. On the drive up she and I squabbled incessantly. I could see in the mirror this was causing Rudi stress. When we got up to the house and I got it opened up Grampa said he needed to rest. Steffi's son Nahum was five at that time and he was playing outside. He came up to me and told me to bring Rudi to the first floor window, he had something to show him from outside, a little trick. I told Rudi to go ahead and humor the child. As Rudi and I approached the glass Nahum was outside, with a sly smile as he held a piece of paper. He opened it up. It was a picture of a skull.

Rudi looked at me like he had just seen a ghost. He had, his own.

After that we took Rudi upstairs to lie down. A bit later he called me in. He told me how difficult it was for him to be there so old. He said he was the last leaf on the tree. All his friends were gone. "It's hard for me--especially for me." he said. Usually I would have argued this with him but that afternoon somehow I knew he was right. He was so vital, so independent, always in motion. A hummingbird, I thought, with music/art as his nectar. Except for his depression he had never been infirmed, incapacitated, down, ever. It wasn't in his nature. He told me he wanted to see Hansi and his mother. I could see suddenly that if my grandfather was still there it was because I was keeping him for my own selfish reasons. I had to let him go. As it got later in the evening it was obvious that Rudi was getting ready to leave us. I stayed with him on into the evening. "All I can say is that I feel devitalized" he said. A short time later with Steffi there he passed away in my arms, his essence making a clear ascent, a discernable diminishing white funnel cloud fading upward that lifted and disappeared above us. "Go to the best place!" Steffi offered up to the spirit as a blessing. Rudi Blesh the man was gone.

At the funeral, the surviving family members: my mother and us kids formed a small circle around the plot in the Smith Meeting House cemetery in Gilmanton, NH. In addition, there was Mr. George Paige, the cemetery custodian, the gentleman with whom I'd discussed the tornado a year or so earlier. For some reason an open space was left in the family circle and I could have sworn we had a visitor there for a few fleeting seconds. My suspicions were soon confirmed when Mr. Paige commented afterwards that he would always remember this as "the hummingbird funeral".

not really the end

appendix #1

Cast of characters :

<u>Harriet Janis</u>: too much could never be written about the effect
Hansi Janis had on Rudi Blesh, or on American culture. It was
her inspirations, her discipline, at least half her aesthetic and of
course her family's money that made Circle and all it's ancillaries
happen for Rudi. Although Mrs. Janis started out in the footsteps
of Peggy Guggenheim, in the end she accomplished far more with
her broad interest in the American Arts at large and Black culture
in particular. The tastemaker of the century in many quiet ways.
My grandfather was pugnacious, predisposed to pick fights,
dispute, but he was broadened and mellowed -- given additional
dimensions by this wonderful lady with the birdlike voice. My
memories of Hansi from childhood are all infused with that
wonderful musical sound. And of course no one deserves a
biography of her own more than Harriet Janis. Rudi mourned the
rest of his life after Hansi's passing. He kept his yarmulke from
her funeral in a special place in his dresser. Kaddish.

<u>Jimmy Ernst</u>: son of Max, I seem to remember Jimmy had been
some sort of swimming star in Germany before World War 2. I
also once thought Hansi had had a hand in getting Jimmy out of
Germany during the war (with a job guarantee), but Rudi and
Hansi sponsored a young woman from Europe with a position at
the Circle record store on East 3rd Street so perhaps the stories
crossed. Jimmy Ernst did all the quirky moody Circle Records
artwork, usually by cutting and pasting photos, combining them
with his own abstract art designs. Jimmy was also the director at
Peggy Guggenheim's Art of this Century gallery, pretty obviously
the reason my grandfather got the show there. When my father
John Hultberg got to meet Max Ernst at the 1954 Venice Biennale
he thought he'd impress the master with his acquaintance with
Jimmy. "Oh him... the son I don't like." was the surrealist's icey
reply. So much for name dropping. Years later in the 1980s we
tried to reunite Rudi with his former art director at a show but
somehow Jimmy had vanished before we could get there.

<u>Robert Alan Aurthur</u>: as a young man lived in NYC and wrote
liner notes for certain 1940s Circle releases. In many ways Rudi's
leading protege at the time. Aurthur's father had been one of the
Keystone Cops alongside the young Roscoe Arbuckle. After
writing for Circle for a few years R.A. Aurthur went to Hollywood

himself where he worked as a writer and aside from one article (excerpted above), never seems to have looked back much.

Julius "Skippy" Adelman: armed with the typical 1940s Speed Graphic large format flash camera, Skippy took most of the black and white pictures for Circle Records. A press photographer along the lines of WeeGee, Adelman's work conveyed the sponteneity, and the real love between the Jazz men and the Circle crew. Skippy also went to Hollywood eventually, like R.A. Aurthur to work on the Rifleman TV series. A step up?

Dan Burley: one of Rudi and Hansi's first Harlem connections. From Dan came a whole list of Black contacts who Rudi and Hansi were able to interview, record and/or retrieve essential manuscripts, photographs and other documents from. But of course there was so much more to Dan Burley, whose artistic instincts eventually resounded around the world. Burley of course gave us Skiffle, and through Lionel Hampton (Benny Goodman) Boogie Woogie (aka Rock and Roll), as well as influencing a whole generation of White Jazz fanatics with his essential hipster bible: Dan Burley's Guide to Authentic Harlem Jive. You get a sense of how much Rudi felt he owed Burley in my grandfather's over the top description of Burley's piano playing skills, a bit of an overstatement perhaps. Burley repaid the compliments in his inscription: "To Rudi Blesh - A Guy rich in folklore and square dealing sentiment and principle. Who should be to Jazz what Lincoln was to the slave, what Washington was at Valley Forge..." These guys really knew how to lay it on. So maybe Rudi fudged on the piano genius part but there is no doubt Burley's and Rudi's ecstatic enthusiasm for Skiffle was sincere. And it was the honest nature of the bond between these two men that reflected so brightly in the original Circle recordings and on the This is Jazz radio show broadcast in Europe. And it was the sincerity of that bond -- so contagious, that caused Skiffle, a totally unknown quantity to catch on and spread like wildfire in England. The origin of the "real 'skiffle spirit'" Dan Burley.

George Buck: a young man when Rudi gave him his first crack at being a record producer in the late 1940s. Mr. Buck repaid the favor after Circle went bust, buying up the Circle material and rescuing if from the bankruptcy of Riverside Records in the 1960s. You can still purchase many Circle titles through George's Jazzology label, including the complete This is Jazz radio show series. But not, as yet, the recordings Rudi made of Stride piano

192

genius Donald Lambert. George Buck got his start as the number one fan of the This is Jazz radio show. After the show was cancelled for lack of a sponsor, George went to radio station WWOD in Virginia, starting his own show that kept the Trad wave going, playing records over the air. His career was set for life. For years George operated out of Columbia, South Carolina, cuing up old Trad Jazz recordings and shouting into the microphone. A unique style. Years later in the 1990s I rediscovered Circle/Jazzology titles in the window of a restaurant in New Orleans. Ringing the bell outside in back a shutter opened above and a lady asked who I was. Rudi Blesh's grandson got me inside where I found Mr. Buck running his non-profit Jazz foundation operation. Almost blind at that time Mr. Buck had no trouble running his fingers down the spines of racks and racks of LPs and CDs, weighing me down with titles to take home. I asked him how he managed to fund all this, the mail order business, the record transfers (done by expatriate English Jazzman/historian Barry Martyn), the huge catalog of in print archaic Trad Jazz titles. Mr. Buck motioned for me to move closer as he whispered in my ear: "My wife owns Christian radio stations... the Lord provides."

Conrad Janis: Hansi's older son. The movie star of the family. As a teenager, Conrad picked up my mother's discarded trombone and taught himself the Dixieland "Tailgate" style in a few weeks. A few weeks later he had his own records out. On Circle, of course, his mother's label. And they're not bad. Teenagers having fun bashing out the old New Orleans standards. Not unlike the Beatles. Years later you could see Connie as the stentorian father of the female lead in Mork and Mindy, the television show that introduced Robin Williams to the world. You could also hear Conrad Janis play trombone with fellow Hollywood Trad Jazz fanatics like Woody Allen and George Segal. Hard Core Traddies.

Carroll Janis: Sidney and Hansi's younger son. Once, as a teenager, Carroll drove me up to New Hampshire in his brand new 1956 Volkswagen. I was six. Things got off to a bad start when he missed the entrance to the West Side Highway and did a U turn, right in front of a NYPD cruiser. Later I found a way to torment him by waving the dollar bill (probably the first one I'd ever had - for the Automat) out the vent window like a flag. It sure looked neat out there. Don't expect me to replace that if you lose it was Carroll's comment. With that I let go of the bill and it sailed away behind us. Well the joke was on me. When we got to the fancy roadside restaurant with the chromium plated coin operated doors holding all sorts of goodies I didn't even bother to go in. I just hung out at the gas pumps where, wouldn't you know it... I found a dollar bill. That was a great moment and for better, but mostly for worse I don't think I've worried about money since. Carroll went on to run the Janis Gallery. Once in 1981 I had lunch with Carroll Janis, passing down through stairwells filled with George Segal white plaster ghost people to get to the street. Of course when I recounted the dollar bill story Carroll was not amused. A pioneer in Fine Arts Graffiti. Gallery Man.

Eugene "Botsy" Grossman: Hansi's brother and number one (only?) investor in Circle Records. Ran a successful antiques store in Manhattan, for which Rudi and Hansi spent time collecting old country pieces in New Hampshire, Pennsylvania and other places. One thing that both Rudi and Botsy knew well was period furniture. Botsy, wife Mary Jane and daughter Mittie all lived high up in the Dakota Apartments. When I first applied to NYU I stayed with the Grossmans when I came down to be interviewed, sleeping in a tiny back room filled with books on Abraham Lincoln, Botsy's historical specialty. I remember sitting alone in their unused formal living room underneath one of the original Peaceable Kingdom paintings by Edward Hopper between two huge flowing Tiffany tree lamps. During that visit I also went to the top of the Empire State Building with Mittie (my only time - the first 25 stories by stair), hit 65 mph in the taxicab racing up Central Park West and saw children's star host Soupy Sales getting into a cab. Wow. Rudi, Eugene and Mary Jane's passion was dominoes, a tradition Rudi and I continued after Botsy passed away on visits with Mary Jane in the 1980s.

Bunk Johnson: it all started with a conversation in 1943. Bill Russell, or Dave Stuart asked Louis Armstrong if he'd ever known Buddy Bolden and the answer was no, his teacher was Bunk Johnson. Who? Is he still alive? Louis answered he'd just seen Bunk two weeks ago working as a laborer out at the New Iberia plantation. So the search began in New Orleans with Rudi raising money in San Francisco to bring him out West. Finally a star.

Bob Wilber: another Trad Jazz teen who got his start during the 1940s Revival playing on Circle and This is Jazz who is still playing, thrilling people with the hot New Orleans style Jazz clarinet today. America's last living connection with the genius of Sidney Bechet. Nobody does it better.

Dick Wellstood: yet another talented sprout who got a break playing Trad (piano) for Circle. Always looked ridiculously young in 1940s photos. Grew mustache to try to disguise youthfulness. Played Ragtime as well. Recently passed, sadly.

Sam and Ann Charters: around Rudi in the 1950s/1960s. Ann did indispensible work playing Rags for the second edition of They All Played Ragtime. Sam, also a musician, sang and performed in the Village on guitar, and did an early acoustic Rag/Blues/Skiffle revival LP with a teenage Danny Kalb (later of the NYC Blues Project) as the New Strangers in 1964. Sam also produced field recordings for Folkways, one of which, a visit to Ragtime composer Joe Lamb at home in 1959 shows him following closely in Rudi and Hansi's footsteps. Sam Charters is best known today for having created the first real book on Blues history, the hugely influential The Country Blues, in 1959. Sam Charters also helped rediscovered Lightning Hopkins, researched into Bahamanian Music (Joseph Spence), and produced Chicago the Blues Today, a showcase of young Black urban (electric) talent, a promo copy of which Rudi fed to me making me joe cool at prep school for a few weeks early in 1966. In addition, Sam Charters produced (among other things) The Holy Modal Rounders and Country Joe and the Fish, some truly serious Psych/Skiffle. Basically you could say what Sam got from Rudi, Mo Asch, Frederick Ramsey became the "60s" - at least musically. A prolific writer herself Ann Charters wrote a biography of Bert Williams, Nobody, that sadly nobody seems to have read. She is perhaps best known these days as the chronicler of the Beat poets. Sam and Ann Charters constitute a real power couple when it comes to our (Afro) American / Hipster cultural heritage. Not very much mention of Rudi's influence in their later work that I can find however. Oh well.

Donald Ashwander: Ragtime composer and close friend of Rudi Blesh from the 1960s on. With Rudi's encouragement Donald wrote many lovely Rags and also Ragtime Art songs. Donald helped Rudi by transcribing Rags for publication in later editions of They All Played Ragtime, for which he was paid in antique marble dust pictures. My younger sisters Genevieve and Alison grew up with Donald's records and on occasional trips to NYC, appearances of the Paper Bag Players. I'm sure they can still sing the songs he wrote for those shows. Hot feet on the city street! But especially invaluable in the long run for our family were our personal associations with Donald, a Gay man. The unspoken understandings that underlie all acceptance and love. Tragically,

Donald Ashwander passed away suddenly in 1994 from a heart attack. His sister in Texas continues to preserve his memory with a website and CD of her gifted brother's work performed by Nurit Tilles. She also got Donald's copyrights back from the Paper Bag Players. Donald Ashwander taught me so much about music.

Max Morath: one of the first and really the greatest performer of the Ragtime Revival. Hard working showman criss crossing the country in his classic Mercedes "Benz", hitting colleges, fairs, radio/TV shows, clubs, concert halls, other venues with his old time Ragtime razzamattazz. Taught by his mother who played in the Colorado silent movie houses, Max is a born humorist and crack piano player, really a Vaudevillian out of a time warp. A close friend of Rudi's (the Moraths were really my grandfather's other family) and of course my honorary uncle. The man who taught me to drink beer. Right up there with The Wind Cries Mary and Hellhound on my Trail for Rudi would have been Willy the Weeper by Max Morath off the Jonah Man: A Tribute to Bert Williams LP. Max was just about the only recording artist to break the unspoken ban on all things Bert Williams (blackface you know). The other exception, a bit of Ry Cooder's Jazz album, but he probably got it from Max. Max Morath. The man who gave us the definitive version of Willie the Weeper is also the modern master of Living a Ragtime Life, my only true natural ambition, obviously the meaning of all existence. Rag on Uncle Max.

Terry Waldo: another one man Ragtime show who can also often be seen and heard with a full Ragtime orchestra. Terry has produced radio shows on Ragtime music for NPR and played countless solo Ragtime piano gigs. He has also written a great book on the subject, titled (appropriately): This is Ragtime (1976 - still in print). I remember taking Rudi to see Terry's full band play in NYC (Fat Tuesdays?) in the 1980s. That was hot. At that event Rudi kept reminding me of the heritage (Ralph Waldo Emerson). Therein lies the source of the magic was my grandfather's inference I guess. My favorite sections of This is Ragtime are: the story Terry heard from his mentor Eubie Blake about a concert Rudi organized at Carnegie Hall in 1962. Apparently neither Eubie nor fellow Ragtime/Stride performer Willie the Lion Smith had ever heard the third pianist scheduled to play that night, the obscure Donald Lambert. True to form Eubie was cautious and The Lion brash, walking up to Lambert and calling him a "punk". What followed of course was that the quiet man from New Jersey wiped the stage with both of them.

196

The other section of <u>This is Ragtime</u> that really speaks to me is the conclusion of the book where Terry defines Ragtime by it's diversity. A fitting finale and a welcome breath of fresh air in what are often rather stuffy academic discussions regarding this ever lively music. Appearing this week at different locations in New York City. Check it out. The real thing from the Ragtime King. Rag on Terry Waldo.

<u>Mike Lipskin</u>: one of the biggest thrills of my eighteen year old life in 1968 while working as Rudi's assistant at NYU was the night I blew out the fuses in the Music Building plugging Rudi's portable KLH record player into the ancient 12 volt feed. No actually the biggest thrill was as the evening class ended, just before folks started to get up to leave, Rudi did one of his characteristic vaudeville tricks, pulling young Michael Lipskin, hotshot Trad/ Stride piano player out from behind a curtain to show the class, now extended, the various styles on the piano right there in the room. Another protege of Eubie Blake, Mike had the biggest Jewish Afro I had ever seen at that time. He played like all get out and even more amazing, was a major producer of the RCA records Vintage series, really about the only big label source for early Blues/Jazz at that time. And to pay for that project Mike did some side work for RCA, stuff he wasn't so hepped up on. Producing the Jefferson Airplane, for instance.

<u>Ralph Sutton</u>: a magnificent piano player, one Rudi said that other musician's all loved to work with. As a fantastic sight reader, Sutton did invaluable work for the first edition of <u>They All Played Ragtime</u>, playing then unknown scores for Rudi and Hansi to evaluate. Ralph also cannot deny he played a just about perfect version of Dill Pickles on the This is Jazz radio program in 1947, despite having fought with Rudi over the tempo right before the show. For all these things he was eulogized as a great Ragtime pianist, a sore point later when Stride players like Sutton (and Mike Lipskin) didn't want to have to get stung playing The Entertainer every night. Still one of Rudi's greatest (Jazz) discoveries. Stride on Ralph Sutton.

<u>Mezz Mezzrow</u>: occasional Rudi associate in the 1940s was a celebrity beyond just being a clarinetist. Played on the premiere This is Jazz radio show, when it was still a part of For Your Approval. The Mezz was Rudi's go to guy on smoking clarinet for that crucial first shot. As an author Mezz's autobiography <u>Really the Blues</u> 1946 plumbed the depths of the White hipster universe

of that time, a place the Mezz had largely invented having turned rising White Jazz stars Bix Beiderbecke, Gene Krupa and others onto real (Black) Jazz (and other things) as teenagers back in the 1920s. Mostly Mezz was known as one of the best marijuana dealers around in the 30s, the Reefer Madness era. The man who sold to Fats Waller and Louis Armstrong. If it was good, it was the Mezz. This became "The Nazz" when 1950s Jazz hipster poet comedian Lord Buckley went to eulogize and send up JC (decades before Life of Brian). From there The Nazz are Blue became first a Yardbirds flip side, and then as The Nazz, Todd Rundgren's late 60s proto-Glam Rock and Roll band. I don't think Rudi bought weed from the Mezz back in the 1940s. Mostly they just went to Harlem to buy used records together after Mezzrow was released from serving time (in the Black wing even though he was Jewish). The Mezz passed (for Black). As a clarinetist Mezz was immersed in the Blues and he tried hard to imitate Sidney Bechet. Not necessarily a genius on that instrument or on the saxophone, the Mezz made up in spirit what he might have lacked in pure talent. But it's the Mezz man! "Talk about a reefer five feet long, the real Mezz but not too strong..." (If You're a Viper - Stuff Smith 1936).

Baby Dodds: the man who many claim invented Jazz drumming. Rudi's drummer in the All Star Stompers and also his roommate at 38 East 4th Street. It was Dodd's practice sessions that inspired Hansi to create Circle if for nothing else, to record those marvelous exercises. Baby Dodds also provided important information for Rudi and Hansi, helping them rediscover almost lost Black talent like Montana Taylor and Bertha Chippie Hill. Dodds may have also given Rudi the original idea for the This Is Jazz radio show. In his autobiography The Baby Dodds Story, Baby describes being fired from that program (temporarily) by Rudi for drinking. Rudi had Dodds's best interests at heart, it was alcohol that brought the drummer's career to a virtual halt shortly thereafter. Somehow Rudi Hansi Hilary and Baby all managed to live/stay in that five room East Village apartment with no hallway. Just your average 1940s mixed race inter-generational cohabitation arrangement. Still, perhaps a bit hard to explain to your high school friends, even if this was the Village. My mother said she did notice as a teenager that Baby wasn't always necessarily faithful to his wife when she went home to New Orleans. Ah the life of the entertainer. Baby was worshipped by hordes of teenage Trad fanatics in the Village who'd line up outside the pad for the honor of carrying his drums from gig to gig. My mom said what she cherished most from her teenage years was her friendship with Baby Dodds. The Talking Drums.

<u>Pops Foster</u>: the other half of Rudi's crack rhythm section in The All Star Stompers. The man who first slapped the bass also played soulful mournful music with a bow. Sample Dusty Bottom from South Side Shake, Dan Burley's Skiffle sessions (Jazzology CD). Pops Foster took the bass fiddle and created the bass, the basis for all subsequent Jazz. It must have been excruciating for Rudi to have all this talent in New York and to have the scene stall while Trad fought it out with Modern Jazz (and lost). I recall finding the Union cards of some of the various Black musicians Rudi had brought up from New Orleans and invariably the profession listed was "painter" "wall paper hanger" "plasterer". This was the work they'd done in New Orleans despite some of them being the best in the music business, the inventors really of the entire Jazz/Pop style and scene, and this is what they had to look forward to if they returned to the Crescent City, where being a musician--even a great originator like Pops Foster--was still a side line.

<u>Wild Bill Davison</u>: another one of those larger-than-life Jazz characters. Not that being able to play sweet as Louis (sweeter in some estimates) wasn't enough. Wild Bill also had a brash side to his playing (and life). George Buck's all time favorite and the man he got to produce as a young man with Rudi's assistance. Wild Bill hung around the East 4th Street pad when not playing in the West Village at Eddie Condon's or Nick's. Somewhat of a prankster or troublemaker perhaps but unassailable on the cornet. Many recordings still available from Jazzology New Orleans. Hot.

<u>Georg(e) Bruni(e)s</u>: another New Orleans originator. Started out with the New Orleans Rhythm Kings in the 1920s, later with Muggsy Spannier. In the 1940s he lived and played in New York. Another clown prince Brunis had a bizarre sense of humor. Liked to outplay other trombonists while using his foot and laying on the floor while encouraging people to sit on him. Dropped the e from the end of his first and last name on the advice of a numerologist... you know, one of those. For some reason Brunis and Blesh had a falling out part way through the This is Jazz radio show resulting in one program in July 1947 going out without any trombonist at all. According to Jazz historian Barry Martyn, Rudi maintained he'd always thought it was something he might have said regarding the Nazis in Europe. What could he have said? Brunis later denied the rift but none the less suddenly George

Brunis was gone, soon replaced by Jimmy Archey who then had a brand new career in the Revival himself. Crazy man.

Jack Teagarden: yet another New Orleans immortal. Once said Jazz was children trying to play Ragtime. He should have known he was one of those kids in the "Second Line". Tea wasn't shy about singing about marijuana either. In fact, his wise, somewhat sarcastic style, like that of Eddie Condon, pervades our modern ethos -- through people like Frank Sinatra. Never a tailgater, an originator. Blues man. Rudi said he saw Tea out in his shirtsleeves in the sub zero whipping Chicago wind in 1964 in front of a club and knew he wasn't long for this world. Somewhat embittered by the music business but still, The Tea. Actually made great records in the Stereo Trad era (early 60s), a music category usually worth avoiding. And, like Louis Armstrong, Jack Teagarden was tremendously influential as a Jazz vocalist.

Louis Armstrong: what more can be said? Except that Satch was the performer who brought Jazz into the world of true artistic endeavor, in much the same way as Charlie Chaplin, Roscoe Arbuckle and Buster Keaton worked to create comedic Art (Film) out of the peepshows. Louis Armstrong's Hot Five / Hot Seven recordings of 1925-1928 are the defining moment when Jazz went irrevocably over the edge, into the world of Art. Aided by his visionary first wife Lil Hardin Armstrong, (a Rudi and Hansi informant) Louis created the Jazz scene. The fact that Louis Armstrong became a world wide superstar constantly called upon to display his gifts as a soloist was the fly in the ointment for Rudi. Where had the lovely ego-less New Orleans ensemble style gone? This was as bad as opera. Still for the Trad Jazz crew Louis was it. Someone asked Pee Wee Russell if Jazz musicians were aetheists and he said no they all worshipped Louis. Not just for his music, but for his laid back (implicitly stoned) point of view. After the demise of Bert Williams, Hip restarts here. Louis' letters to Rudi, all in his characteristic green ink were signed "red beans and ricely yours" and a photo is autographed "to the man who has made us all happy" probably referring to Rudi's efforts to find work for Louis' old bandmates Pops Foster and Baby Dodds. Rudi was incredibly fortunate to have been in the position to see eye to eye with this great genius and wonderfully simple earthy human being. Louis Armstrong. The Man of the Century.

Thomas "Fats" Waller: along with Louis, the other huge Jazz Clown Prince of the 1930s-1940s. Of course they both smoked a lot of the Mezz's weed. Fats learned to play piano at the house of his mentor, the older James P. Johnson, putting his fingers where the player piano dropped the keys. Fats also spent many afternoons looking over the shoulder of the lady who played organ at the silent movie theatre, eventually becoming her substitute as a teenager. But mostly Thomas Waller and his best friend Andy Rasaf lucked out being the bicycle delivery boys for Connee's drugstore in Harlem. That's right, delivering balls of opium just like Rudi. When Prohibition struck, pharmacies were still allowed to dispense alcohol, kind of like medical marijuana. So Connee's quickly transformed itself into a nightclub as well giving their teenage delivery boys a chance to write show music. And write these kids did, often selling their work to unscrupulous White publishers for a flat fee. Fats was another one of those Swing/Pop music characters who Rudi the Jazz snob would put down but of course Rudi the Jazz fan totally loved. I grew up on The Spider and the Fly and Your Feet's Too Big. Check out the recordings made of the Beatles doing their stage act in Hamburg in 1962. It's right there in the set list: Your Feet's Too Big. Fats Waller was a giant in the Jazz world, like Cab Calloway who imitated him to a certain degree, poised between the Ragtime comedy attitude of Bert Williams, the source, and all the modern comedy, Jazz, R&B and Rock and Roll to come. It was Fats who first blurted out "Bebop" anyway, it was his concept to be sure. Fats died on a train of pneumonia in 1943 so he missed his chance to be on This is Jazz. Too bad he didn't live to be a unifying force of peace in the Jazz world. Well alright then!

Andy Rasaf: actually an exiled prince from Madagascar who grew up in Harlem. His mother... well it's a long story and young Andy started out with a long name: Andriamanantena Paul Razafinkarefo. Ten points up in New Hampshire if you got that one right. Andy and Fats Waller were the Harlem songwriting team to beat back in the day though they probably threw away as many songs as they ever published under their own names. Asked on his deathbed what was his favorite from his songs Rasaf whispered: I Can't Give You Anything But Love. Of course that's just one of many he and Fats sold for perhaps $100, the only alternative to being cheated out of royalties because they were Black. Ain't Misbehavin', In the Mood, Honeysuckle Rose, (What Did I Do) To Be So Black and Blue?

James P. Johnson: Fats Waller's Stride teacher. One of Rudi's favorite people on Earth. Simple and unassuming, a secret master behind the scenes as Ragtime morphed into Jazz. Played with Bessie Smith on Back Water Blues in 1927. Certainly, James P. Johnson's If I Could Be With You One Hour Tonight would have been one of Rudi's all time favorites, the song that probably most reminded him of Hansi. There's a great Skippy Adelman picture of Rudi and James P. at a Circle recording session in the 1940s that absolutely captures the love between these men. When Rudi rediscovered and recorded the great but seriously secluded Donald Lambert, the Stride pianist had insisted they call James P. Johnson on the phone to get permission before Lambert would record one of his tunes. Whether to acknowledge the originator or just to test the veracity of Rudi's connections it's hard to say. Rudi certainly had the connection.

Charles Luckeyeth Roberts: rarely recorded (except on Circle) Luckey Roberts was another one of the originators. Lucky enough to have the connections to play at upper class White society events, Roberts didn't waste much time recording, an often unfruitful enterprise for Black performer/composers at that time. He also had a restaurant/bar uptown in Harlem to fall back on. It was there that my mother and father had their wedding reception in 1949. Those family connections. Years later in the 1990s I was contacted by the granddaughter of Luckey Roberts and I was able to give her a family scrapbook that Rudi must have "borrowed". It was just as well because according to this young lady, another one of Luckey Roberts relatives had just destroyed a whole collection of archival material. Welcome to the complex world of the (White) Jazz historian.

Willie "the Lion" Smith: yet another Stride pianist who could lay claim to being an originator. Played on the first Blues record: Crazy Blues by Mamie Smith and her Jazz Hounds (1920). Willie claimed to have first heard Jazz in Haverstraw, New York (on the Hudson River, North of NYC) in the teens and thought it originated from contact with Caribbean or Georgia Sea Island musicians. Used to scare my teenage future mother half to death calling for Rudi on the GR3-4227 number and roaring into to the phone: "Tell him this is THE LION!". Willie had gotten his nickname and numerous decorations serving as an officer in a Black artillery regiment during WW1. The name suited him: a larger than life, somewhat chaotic piano player, a Black Rabbi, writer of his own autobiography, like the Mezz, a real character. An original as well as an originator.

Donald Lambert: one of the greats would have died a virtual unknown except that Rudi found out he was playing for drinks in an obscure bar in New Jersey. A retiring recluse and a really serious alcoholic this piano genius was content to live out the remainder of his life playing sentimental Irish songs and Show music for working class stiffs for small change. Coaxed into the studio one time Mr. Lambert produced perhaps the greatest Stride piano album ever made. Too bad it came out on Rudi's short lived Solo Art label in 1962 and strangely, despite it's historical importance it remains un-reissued by Jazzology. I guess the great Donald Lambert was just fated to be an obscurity. Some guys can never seem to cop a break.

Eubie Blake: here's where the Ragtime Revival picked up it's first living classic superstar in 1949. And he was still going strong thirty three years later. Eubie's energy and showmanship provided the experience, the vibrant example of the Ragtime life. His proteges, like Terry Waldo continue that experience today, an unbroken chain. Eubie was Ragtime in the flesh. To hear him play his Charleston Rag with all it's explosiveness or Rudi's favorite Memories of You with all it's honest emotion still at the heart was an experience of a lifetime. Eubie's autograph to my grandfather reads: "To Rudi Blesh... my benefactor, or should I say, one of my benefactors." What a classy guy.

Jimmy Archey: another Rudi and Hansi Trad Jazz rediscovery. Halfway through the run of This is Jazz on the radio George Brunis suddenly quit, leaving the (still unnamed) All Star Stompers without a trombonist. It was a tip from Pops Foster that led Rudi to another legendary player from the early big Jazz bands. Trombonist Jimmy Archey had played with King Oliver in 1929 and the Louis Russell/Louis Armstrong band during the 1930s. Though diminutive in size Archey was big in sound, and not just that smeary so-called "tailgate" style, a veteran of the big bands, Archey had a brilliant incisive rhythmic sense that really drove a Trad Jazz unit forward. So George Brunis, the "King of the Tailgate Trombonists" exited stage right and Archey took over as the main man blowing the low end for the 1947 Stompers on records and on the radio. Jimmy Archey was back.

Marcel Duchamp: legendary French Surrealist scenemaker sometimes hung out with Rudi and Hansi at the 38 East 4th Street residence. Once borrowed Rudi's George Brunis record That Dada Strain to exhibit as a readymade. Originally sold toilet to collector as "Fountain". Gave Rudi giant desk and antique Hopi Kachina dolls which Duchamp had inherited from Max Ernst and Dorothea Tanning. When I was getting ready to vacate the apartment in 2005 I was faced with the prospect of having to prove the provenence of these items. Undaunted I approached a descendent of Monsieur Duchamp, Jackie Matisse Monniere with my grandfather's version of the items' histories. Ms. Matisse Monniere was nice enough to answer my queries but had no information to offer about the desk or the dolls. But perhaps it had been Rudi who had introduced her grandfather to his idol Duke Ellington. Perhaps, I replied though I don't think my grandfather thought much of the Duke. In her final reply Jackie suggested I get in touch with Dorothea Tanning, Max Ernst's widow, still around in her 90s. I remembered the work of Ms. Tanning: crying naked little children in dreamscape halls. Terrifying. While I stalled suddenly a letter from Ms. Tanning appeared. Jackie Monniere had forwarded my questions to her. "Sorry to explode your theories..." the letter began, then went on to corroborate the whole story. The aquisition of the giant desk (named by her L'Elefante) from an antiques dealer under the El on the Bowery, the origins of the Hopi dolls from the Indian museum in Harlem. All in her beautiful but chilling script. So yes we were able to sell the Kachinas that had once belonged to the Hopi Indians, The Museum of the American Indian, Max Ernst, Dorothea Tanning, Marcel Duchamp (and Rudi Blesh). At one time I heard Patti Smith was interested in the desk but I ended up donating it to my cousin David Hultberg, a restorer of fine furniture on the West Coast. One more story: In the 1980s I went to The Sidney Janis Gallery as it was then, to see a retrospective of Duchamp's work. On display was another of his "Ready-mades", a set of bicycle handlebars set up to look like the horns of a mythical ancient sacred bull. Lifting the handlebars off their pedestal when no one was looking I saw they were of recent Japanese manufacture. So Marcel had indeed truly given Sidney a license to print money.

Huddie Ledbetter: aka Leadbelly pretty much embodied The Blues for my whole generation. Rudi featured Leadbelly on This is Jazz and promoted him whenever possible. I have one recording of Rudi showcasing Huddie at a 1949 concert at CCNY. In his introduction my grandfather said that Leadbelly would soon be setting off on his first tour in France. Unfortunately for the great Bluesman that didn't amount to much, nor did Huddie really gain very much from his enormous influence. After Huddie

204

passed away, Pete Seeger expended an incredible amount of energy in publicizing Leadbelly's work, resulting in the posthumous success of Goodnight Irene. But during Huddie's lifetime it had always been a struggle. When he first got out of prison in the 1930s he worked as the driver for John and Alan Lomax. Growing up in Connecticut in the 1940s, Eric Von Schmidt, later the founding father of the early 1960s Cambridge Folk Blues scene idolized Huddie Ledbetter, telling all his teenage buddies about this mythical character. "Oh you mean the guy who lives down the road, big old Black man with blue eyes and a big Stella 12 string guitar?" replied a younger kid nobody thought much of. After laughing at the joke it was a few months later that Von Schmidt learned that Huddie Ledbetter had indeed been a resident in his home town right up to his passing. Bringing it all back home. But not necessarily to the Ragtime Society. My mother said she didn't think Leadbelly was ever at the East 4th Street apartment, but I always thought that maybe just once, maybe when she was at school, perhaps Huddie Ledbetter and Marcel Duchamp might have rubbed elbows, or maybe just passed each other in the hall. Just a fantasy I suppose.

Bessie Smith: behind most great male genius "originators" there is usually a female creatrix. Behind Louis there was Lil Hardin, behind all White Jazz there's the foxtrotting Irene Castle and behind every Blues man or woman stands Bessie, a rare case where the creatrice was also pretty much the originator. The Blues flowed out of Bessie Smith like matriarchy flowed out of Africa. An unstoppable force of nature her identity is in every aspect of modern feminism, for better of worse. Bessie now imprints our DNA. Is that musical success?

Jelly Roll Morton: New Orleans Ragtime Jazz composer bandleader and all around paradoxical character. His Library of Congress recordings which Rudi and Hansi bravely released told the story of the music and also of the downsider culture that would inevitably accompany it, for better of for worse. Sociology. Like Pandora's Box the intoxication with the gritty Negro element would have all sorts of additional psycho-sexual implications in the long run. Perhaps none of it truly comprehensible to the aesthetically charged up Jazz critic championing, at least in his own mind, the cause of an entire race at that time. As Rudi would have said: Jelly was a genius, like Chopin, and a pimp. Get over it and learn to appreciate his unique gifts as a performer, arranger, composer, bandleader and raconteur. Another vital heavy link in

205

the Negro/White Hipster chain of American artistic and cultural inspiration. As Rudi often pointed out to me: "that Spanish Tinge...", and of course, The Animule Ball. Jelly!

<u>Tony Jackson</u>: New Orleans greatest Ragtime pianist. Probably the only man Jelly Roll Morton ever really feared. Luckily Jackson stayed in the Crescent City so Jelly was able to dominate out of town. Tony Jackson was the entertainer, never recorded, published rarely. Best remembered for Pretty Baby, still being sung by Ragtime era survivor Jimmy Durante in the 1950s, and later, the source of a period movie with all the original scandal attached. In old New Orleans, where Tony Jackson once ruled.

<u>Brownie and Sticks McGhee</u>: Rudi's choice for a rhythm section on Dan Burley's - South Side Shake - Skiffle recordings. The McGhee brothers performed only briefly together. Granville Stick(s) McGhee (recorded by Circle as "Globetrotter", probably for contractual reasons) also recorded for Atlantic in 1947 delivering a hit with Drinkin' Wine Spoddee Oddee before passing away early. He sang and played hot guitar. His brother Brownie had a long career performing (and fighting) in Folk clubs with blind harmonica genius Sonny Terry. The "real Skiffle Spirit".

<u>Frederic Ramsey, Jr.</u>: Rudi's predecessor and most serious competition in the Jazz Critic sweepstakes of the early 1940s. Of course Ramsey had already produced <u>JAZZMEN</u>, with Charles Edward Smith in 1939, a volume of varied opinions destined to be a much better selling book than <u>Shining Trumpets</u> would ever be. <u>JAZZMEN</u> featured articles written by different critics from around the country, including Bill Russell and Stephen W. Smith. By another strange coincidence in the 1980s I was friends with the sons of two of the other contributors to that volume: Roger Pryor Dodge (Pryor) and Wilder Hobson (Archie). Jazz Babies. In 1942 Ramsey collaborated with Charles E. Smith and Bill Russell again, this time with Charles Payne Rogers to create <u>The Jazz Record Book</u>. Fred Ramsey, record producer for Folkways and others, attended Jelly Roll Morton's last session, recorded Leadbelly's Last Sessions. A giant in other words.

<u>Art Hodes</u>: another one of Rudi's running buddies, one who just about matched him in the energy department. Russian heritage but steeped in the early Chicago Blues, Hodes lived the life of a rough and tumble low down Blues/Jazz pianist. Resided in NYC during the 1940s, appeared on This is Jazz radio show, and like

Rudi, had a Jazz radio show on WNYC during the 1940s-50s. But he also could edit and write. Hodes' book <u>Selections From the Gutter</u>, was taken from the magazine he published and wrote for in the late 1940s, The Jazz Record. Copies of which I could still be found hawking on the street in the early 1980s.

<u>Lenny Kunstadt</u>: a Jazz scholar and, in the early 1980s, New York City's last surviving 78 record auctioneer/dealer. His record trading magazine was called Record Research. I offered him the contents of Rudi's front room (thousands of warped copies of Mary Lou Williams doing Sposin') but could only get him to take half of them by adding in copies of The Saga of Mr. Jelly Lord, much to Rudi's horror. The hundreds of old shellac records nearly destroyed the springs in Lenny's old car as he drove away from 38 East 4th Street. Len Kunstadt, a White guy was also married to Black recording label owner (and former 1920s Blues singer) Victoria Spivey. Wow what a dude. Also wrote <u>Jazz A History of the New York Scene</u> with Sam Charters in 1962. Anyone want a free copy of Mary Lou Williams doing Sposin'?

<u>Ralph Berton</u>: little brother of well known Swing Jazz percussionist Vic Berton, Ralph is known for having idolized 1920s White Jazz cornetist Bix Beiderbecke and writing <u>Remembering Bix</u>. It is significant, that as much as Ralph loved Bix he still chose to use Rudi's send off from <u>Shining Trumpets</u> as one of the book's quotes: "Bix was neither a tragic nor a heroic character." Sometimes Ralph would call Rudi up when he'd had a few and harangue him on the Bix issue, as always the most important concern in the Jazz world. In 1985 after Rudi was gone Ralph called up again and was more than willing to talk my ear off about Bix as well. I liked that and began to think more highly of the doomed drunk cornetist who played with a softer style. I know Rudi prized In a Mist as one of his all time favorite recordings. In a Mist was done on the spot in the studio by Bix on the piano in 1929. Half Debussy and half Ragtime it might have passed, like some of Jelly Roll Morton's experimental pieces of that period, for "Modern Jazz". Whatever that is.

<u>Ahmet Ertegan</u>: started Atlantic records in the mid 1940s around the same time as Rudi and Hansi got Circle going. Also recorded Granville Sticks McGhee, resulting in Atlantic's first big R&B hit. Ertegan was originally attached to the Turkish Embassy in the 30s, helped rediscover Jelly Roll Morton, discovered Ray Charles. Otis Redding called Ertegan - Omelet. Ended up being a major

creator of Rock gods (Led Zeppelin). Like Rudi an avid art connoissieur, in later years Ertegan would send my grandfather a card at Christmas each year showing a different Renee Magritte Surrealist masterpiece, all from his personal collection of course. Not rubbing it in or anything. Ahmet's inscription to Rudi on a 1940s photo: "Don't forget to mess around!"

Lord and Lady Donegal: how often are authentic members of the British Royal family also raving insane Jazz nuts? Lord Don would visit Rudi in New York from time to time with the Lady and invariably insist on hitting every Jazz club in the Village. He also sent records to Rudi of himself playing along (very badly) with other records on a harmonica. One time the New York press was notified about the presence of the Royal couple (she an actual Stuart) at a nightclub in the Village. Rudi looked around the table for Don as he was known, but he'd just disappeared, only to reappear a few minutes later after the photographer had left. The Royal Gent had been on the floor under the table looking for a dime he'd dropped.

Eddie Condon: the other big Trad Jazz booster in the Village, Condon came in with a touch of Swing as well. Kind of an un-doomed Bix-like character with a big heart and tons of energy. And of course he'd played with Bix. Started out at Nicks but soon Eddie had his own West Village nightclub, radio shows, records, Town Hall Concert, best selling book - the Eddie Condon scene. Played mostly inaudible guitar and never soloed. None-the-less so popular he won the Downbeat Poll twice during the 1940s. An unstoppable jokester Condon never failed to have fun with the potheads in his band, especially clarinetist Pee Wee Russell whose reputation was sealed for eternity. Once when Eddie Condon was stuck in the hospital with severe stomach problems he quipped that he must have been given Fats Waller's blood during a transfusion because he was getting high. An upbeat Jazzer, Condon certainly carried the Trad/Swing Jazz banner through the 40s-50s with far more grace and diplomacy than my grandfather could ever muster. Hugely influential. Solid.

Albert Nicholas: brilliant New Orleans clarinetist and also probably the most disgruntled person Rudi ever worked with. Made a big fuss when he quit This is Jazz. From Downbeat (1947): "Rudi Blesh is the biggest, the wordiest and the broadest hunk of baloney ever to hit the music business... not only does the man know nothing about music, but he is out to get a monopoly of all the so-called New Orleans musicians." The bopster Downbeat writer then added some choice words of his own about my grandfather: "blunderingly dictatorial", "rates himself as king of the jazz aficionados.", even going as far as calling Rudi "an ex-interior decorator", a slur with definite connotations back then. Nicholas then complained about Blesh's "fantastic temperment" and that "...he was trying to shove that ancient stuff down the people's throat and I just couldn't stay with it any longer." Hey, it was a Trad Jazz revival and people were loving it. Sounds like sour grapes and perhaps also that Mr. Nicholas, for whatever (probably well-founded) reason, just couldn't trust Rudi as a White man. His dissatisfaction with Rudi as a potential manager and businessman of course would have been astute and completely understandable. Albert Nicholas went on to have an independent career in the despised Trad Jazz revival - as it was being swallowed up by Modern Jazz.

Max Kaminsky: another White Jazzman playing in the Village regularly. Came from Brockton Mass, unlike most of the rest of that set (Davison, Condon, etc.) who were from the Midwest. Didn't end up recording for Circle but still good friends with Rudi and Hansi. At one point, because of his Jewish heritage, jokes were made about a possible Hebrew Jazz record. Proposed titles: Blues Jumped a Rabbi, Bagel Call Rag and Just a Kosher Walk With Thee.

Douglas MacAgy: Rudi told interviewer John Hasse that after he'd lost his little brother Kelly Blesh, Doug MacAgy, the young director of the San Francisco Art Museum became a sort of substitute. As told in David Beasley's Douglas MacAgy and the Foundations of Modern Art Curatorship, together in 1943 Blesh and MacAgy hatched Jazz "Performance Art" conspiracies that still reverberate to this day. Previous to the This Is Jazz (band show) MacAgy had already begun breaking rules, by exhibiting Alexander Calder's (Clay Spohn inspired) circus mobiles, for example. Rudi was indeed lucky to have been able to work with at least a few people in his life who were his match in the field of artistic endeavor. Doug MacAgy was definitely of that class. The man who introduced Rudi to Hansi. A life long true friend.

Marshall Stearns: another lifelong friend, Marshall Stearns was also a neighbor, living off Washington Square Park. Seemingly pretty well off, Marshall seems to me to have started out like Rudi's understudy. Rudi Blesh wrote a book about Jazz. Then

Marshall Stearns wrote a book about Jazz. Then Stearns created the first major written work on the subject of Jazz Dance. Stearns also was able to fulfil one of Rudi's cherished dreams, creating an actual School of Jazz at a major university. Ultimately ending up at Rutgers out in New Jersey, Rudi had high hopes for the idea. In actuality, for Rudi it proved to be a disappointment. My grandfather told me he had seen sloppy handling of archival materials, things thrown away, pilpherage. After Rudi's passing I was faced with what to do with boxes of correspondence, pictures, tapes from Rudi's life. Weighing his words I decided to donate the stuff the Institute of Jazz Studies at Rutgers anyway. At the Institute I met briefly with Director Dan Morgenstern. I thought it odd that he never opened his eyes during the entire interview. The Jazz Brahmin. A few years passed and, well this is one time when the Old Indian was finally wrong. When I recently requested a copy of the Circle sessions list recently from IJS (on a Saturday), I got an answer on Sunday and the info (Appendix #4) on the way to me Monday. Thank you Marshall Stearns.

Lester Young: neither a Traddie nor a Bopper, Lester embodied it all. One of those seminal characters (like Bert Williams) whose personality/influence is too huge to measure. Lester epitomized hipness with his laconic saxophone delivery, late but never too late, laid back. Played back fast without feeling it's Be-Bop. Played right it's Lester. Destroyed in the Army Lester Young survived to haunt the 1950s. Billie as a horn. Rudi favorite.

Billie Holiday: once attacked by Rudi for being part of Swing, later vindicated in Combo USA, in a piece we wrote together. How do you deal with the greatest female singer since Bessie Smith? The driving force of fashion. The child prostitute. Jelly Roll Morton all over again. Beautiful in sound and feeling personified Billie Holiday still lives - and for many acceptance is now open.

Mary Lou Williams: one of Circle's last 78 releases was this brilliant lady's solo piano sides: Sposin' (by James P. Johnson) and Handy Eyes (a ML Williams original honoring WC Handy). Rudi also recorded some of Ms. Williams' unique vocal group arrangements though they remained unreleased. A distinctly beautiful and deeply spiritual person, Mary Lou had been a major Swing piano accompanist and most importantly a hugely influential arranger for Andy Kirk's Mighty Clouds of Joy in the 1930s. You probably also can trace some of the origins of Bebop to her musical insights. While working at the Institute of Jazz

Studies with my grandfather's material I got a chance to also peruse the large collection they were concentrating on at that time, that of Mary Lou Williams. While looking through the artifacts I came upon a paystub from a concert she'd given at NYU in the 1960s. On it she'd written "Sad Sack". I suddenly realized she'd jotted that down to describe the person who'd organised her appearance at the school. That would have been Rudi Blesh.

John Hammond: though not strictly a Jazz critic, Hammond did everything else, discovered talent, made historic recordings, started world changing nightclubs, set off giant Jazz crazes from his position at Columbia Records. From the 30s through the 70s, what didn't this man do? Undoubtedly it was John Hammond who turned Rudi on to Robert Johnson. And Billie Holiday, who Rudi said was the most beautifully radiant woman he had ever seen. Hammond also included Rudi at the recordings made in 1968 that became the 86 Years of Eubie Blake, an award winning record. In Jazz - this is the Man. Hammond also dabbled in other musical genres discovering people like Bob Dylan and Bruce Springsteen. Mr. Hammond signed Pete Seeger in the 1960s despite the blacklist, so Pete could make some wonderful records that set off the ecology movement. John Hammond: the benevolent wizard of Jazz, Boogie Woogie, etc..

Alan Lomax: Folklore giant not closely associated with Rudi but on a cooperative parallel track with the 1940s Folk revival, mostly Alan's own creation. A culture hero and an example for sure. In his book The Land Where Blues Began, Alan cites the Blues as the greatest music he'd ever experienced with the possible exception of real authentic New Orleans Dixieland Jazz. A tip of the hat for sure. Rudi's only critique of Alan Lomax was that Alan mixed business with pleasure with a few of his female client/performers, a debasement of the producer's role and a conflict of interest in Rudi's universe. Touched by the Blues perhaps.

Pete Seeger: Folk Music giant started as a Trad Jazz banjo fanatic. The one who most embodied Rudi's ideal: "Socialization of Music" - just by creating the Hootenanny. Although they never had much contact, Rudi said Pete had helped him and Hansi in the 1940s get around some union rules so they could put on concerts in New York City. As fellow Jazz mover and shaker John Hammond found out when he'd run out of money in 1938 trying to open Cafe Society in the West Village (NYC birthplace of Boogie Woogie), it was always useful to have friends in the Communist Party back then. Pete: American godfather of Folk, Peace and Ecology.

Stuart Davis: gentle gifted visionary at the start of the Modern Art revolution. Rudi loved that some painters like Stuart Davis, Evsa Modell, Bill Baziotes and also my father John Hultberg remained basically landscape artists throughout the Modern Art / Abstract Expressionist frenzy. Like the "numerical precisions" of Ragtime in music, landscape art somehow survived to reemerge later in Pop Art and eventually in Photo Realism. But no one did it with more pure style and poetic insight than Stuart Davis early on.

Bill De Kooning: the artist as astronaut, leading man, tortured genius and action hero all thrown into one. De Kooning's naked macho sexism seemed like some sort of refreshing honesty back in the early 1950s. After sixty years on the repeat button today I'm not sure what good that kind of honesty really does. One truly honest, and I would say constructive sexist soul bearer, and possibly a direct descendent of De Kooning is Robert Crumb, whose 1960s comic book fantasies truly opened doors of the male psyche. Again however, how many times does this experiment have to be repeated to be meaningful? De Kooning somehow survived his self promotional battles with Art and Woman to live to be 93. Maybe there is something to it after all.

Jacqueline Lamba: former wife of Andre Breton caused a big stir when she split from Surrealist originator. She ended up in the Hamptons where Rudi and Hansi met her in the late 40s early 50s while hanging out with rising Janis Gallery star Bill De Kooning and other future Modern Art greats out on Long Island at that time. The relationships between the Abstract Expressionists and their (often also artist) wives was the subtext behind the Modern Art (male genius) school in general. Witness top Surrealist Gorky who quickly unravelled when dumped by his young wife. Rudi and Hansi were supportive of Ms. Lamba, who Rudi said was also involved with Matta, who was also involved with wife of Gorky... you get the idea. The upshot was that Rudi had purchased a painting by Jacqueline Lamba, a gloomy dingy ugly thing, just black spray painty looking flowers on an otherwise blank canvas. I always hated it and with my mother, after Rudi's passing, put it up for sale. It was then that I read the title on the back: "Malgre tout, Printemps" 1943. Wow.

Abe Walkowitz: an artist friend of Rudi's and Hansi's, Mr. Walkowitz could lay claim to being one of the first, if not the first of the American Cubist painters back in the 1920s. Although never the subject of a Rudi bio (like Bill De Kooning and Stuart Davis), Abe was a buddy and perhaps because he didn't write about him, Rudi did accept some gift work. One time in the late 1980s I was after my mother to do something with her student art projects from the 1940s. Just throw it all away was her only wish. I disregarded that and brought the portfolio up for her to go through. I even slipped it into her car so she wouldn't just chuck it first. What do you think she found in there along with her own early work? Wonderful pencil sketches by Abraham Walkowitz, some of naked strong men, others of 1920s dancer Isadora Duncan, now framed by her front door.

Paul Hindemith, Ferruccio Busoni and Henry Cowell: three modern composers Rudi recorded work by for his Composers Workshop imprint in the 1950s. Paul Hindemith was a German composer who by the late 1940s had worked as a cultural ambassador for the Nazis and then emmigrated to the USA. He was reknown as a teacher of composition (at Yale), a "neo-classicist" with his own ideas about scales, etc. His Sonata for Trombone and Piano (1941) was recorded in 1951 by Rudi with Davis Shuman on trombone and Sam Raphling on piano. Also Morning Music by Hindemith, Five Miniatures For Brass by Robert Starer and another Hindemith piece for solo trombone and string quartet. Busoni had been an Italian prodigy known for his interpretations of Bach in the piano roll and Edison Cylinder days. His work was interpreted for Composers Workshop in 1952 by Edward Weiss with Richard Burgin on violin. Henry Cowell was an American Modernist, folklorist and musical associate of John Cage and Pete Seeger's father Charles. Cowell was also a Gay man who'd served serious time in the 1940s for a "morals charge". Cowell performed his own work for these sides. All sessions engineered by Peter Bartok. So totally obscure none of these releases is in any of the composers' discographies. So rare (Composers Workshop Label) - now also impossible to find.

Bill Bolcom: perhaps the composer/musician who contributed the most to and also gained the most from the 1960s-1970s Ragtime Revival. Bolcom was already favored as a growing talent but his association with Rudi at Queens College was certainly fortuitous and fruitful. In addition to becoming a major Modern Composer Bill also wrote Reminiscing With Sissle and Blake, a terrific history of Eubie's Ragtime era, with Robert Kimball. As if that weren't enough, he and his wife Joan Morris have done brilliant Ragtime period LPs and were also wonderful friends to Rudi in his later years. They even spelled me at least once in New Hampshire so I could go do some bicycle touring with my girlfriend. Now that's generosity. While up in Gilmanton Rudi would subject Bolcom and Morris to some of his usual routines. Waking everybody up for pancakes at 8 am with Sousa marches played full blast (by the Czech State Orchestra) was one of them. Bill returned the favor by writing Rags about Rudi (Raggin' Rudi) and about Rudi's pet cat (Rag Apple Rag). Rudi's Bolcom Rag favorites: Graceful Ghost, and also Lost Lady.

William Albright: another modern American composer who became enraptured with Ragtime, probably from contact with They All Played Ragtime. A brilliant Ragtime interpretor and also composer in his own right, Albright was unique in that he also was an organist, wrote hymns and most unusually, Rags for the organ. But of course Fats Waller also played the organ. William Albright taught for many years at the University of Michigan, passing away in 1998. Sweet Sixteenths.

Tom Turpin: who owned the saloon in St. Louis in 1895, perhaps even the one where Frankie and Johnnie... but more importantly Scott Joplin got a start. Turpin's Harlem Rag and Ragtime Nightmare predated Scott's Rags, much the way Roscoe Arbuckle (who Turpin somewhat resembled) predated (and also sponsored) Chaplin/Keaton in film. Both Turpin and Arbuckle quite literally larger than life. Big Tom Turpin. Here certainly is an authentic American character/setting for a great movie or historical novel.

Louis Chauvin: the classic doomed artist. His one surviving work, Heliotrope Bouquet, in collaboration with Joplin is quite simply the most beautiful Rag ever written. In a picture from Rudi's collection (also in They All Played Ragtime) that's Chauvin sitting between the hunting dogs and the shotguns at the Negro sporting club, a glimpse of this once vibrant 1800s middle class life with all it's aspirations and dreams. In his case destroyed by drugs. Extremely poorly depicted in the one Scott Joplin bio movie, Louis Chauvin deserves a real revival. He set the mold for the future that was for sure.

Scott Joplin: another one of those people it's impossible to feel neutral about. So obviously an artistic originator. He found a

214

way, like Stephen Foster to channel the Folk melodies into the copyright column but in so doing, created the lovely lilting piano music that will always be associated with his name. Ragtime. When Rudi and Hansi rescued his papers they only had four arms between them. Just think what we might have if they'd had more resources or time to get Scott's material into the safety zone. As it is, his legacy has stood the test of time. Folks acknowledge the advances of the other Ragtime composers, the modernist evolution from a dance music based on marches into the realm of the haunting modern Art Song. Composers like Joseph Lamb and Zez Comfrey right down to Bill Bolcom and Donald Ashwander in more recent times. Still you have to hand it to Scott Joplin, the perfector of the form. His were the Rags we remember the melodies to. Ragtime songs without words we play in our minds, and that is real genius at work.

James Scott: Scott Joplin's younger protege wrote independently of Joplin in a style that more closely prefigured Jazz arrangements to come. James Scott's compositions, like Climax Rag were favored by Jazz orchestrators like Jelly Roll Morton from the start for their friendly changes. What musicologist Thornton Hagert calls "inner voice parts" and "vanishing melody", the secrets of Jazz. James Scott, one of the Ragtime "Big Three" whose Rags remain perennial favorites to this day.

Artie Matthews: wrote brilliant Rags in his spare time, the bulk of which were discarded after being played a few times in weekly show performances at Tom Turpin's brother's local TOBA (Black vaudeville) circuit theatre in St. Louis. Matthews' Pastimes 1-6 (1913) are all that have survived today and they are counted among the most beautiful Rags of all time. Just think what he threw away. And what other composer/players there must have been at that time, actively just tossing things like this off. The richness of a Black culture we can only half imagine today.

Arthur Marshall: Scott Joplin's classmate at the George Smith School of Music in Sedalia and part of the extended family that included Scott Hayden. Arthur Marshall performed in Scott Joplin's productions of The Ragtime Dance and The Guest of Honor (lost). Marshall composed Rags with Joplin including some pencil written folios (Lily Queen) still in Rudi's collection. Rudi and Hansi rediscovered Mr. Marshall, an extremely valuable informant about Scott Joplin's early years and from that exposure Arthur Marshall published more Rags and did his first recordings.

<u>Scott Hayden</u>: another young Scott Joplin collaborator, student and protege. Some of Scott Joplin's sweetest Rags: Sunflower Slow Drag, Something Doing and Felicity were written together with this other Scott during a happy period in Joplin's life. Not to be confused with James Scott. Scott Joplin married Hayden's sister but it seems the marriage didn't work out. Unhappiness.

<u>John Stark</u>: Prairie visionary Sedalia/St. Louis, then NYC music publisher, tough Christian realist who signed a contract granting copyright royalties to a certain person of color, Scott Joplin in 1899. Also published James Scott, a Negro and subsequently, on Joplin's recommendation, the young White composer Joseph Lamb. The man who discovered, nurtured and originally publicized the Ragtime "Big Three" also treated them all with full respect and paid out based on straight bookkeeping. A unique event in the history of the Music Industry. Stark was an honest man with a messianic mission: Ragtime music. Stood by Joplin right up until the opera would have bankrupted both of them. A real human being. Rare. (Also hated Jazz.)

<u>Louis Moreau Gottschalk</u>: American "Classical" composer/performer from mid 19th century from New Orleans who incorporated Black elements and themes into his rollicking pieces. Souvenir of Puerto Rico, one of those compositions was a Rudi Blesh favorite. Of mixed Creole/Jewish ancestry, Gottschalk was a major commercial draw as a pianist performer across the United States during the years following the Civil War. His specialty: bravura Romantic showpieces, one of which had him playing Battle Hymn of the Republic with one hand and Dixie with the other. The Civil War on the piano. Rudi at one point was commissioned to write Gottschalk's biography but he balked when he learned one version of the circumstances of the pianist's death in Brazil (discovered by the emperor with his wife, captured, mutilated, died onstage doing his signature piece: Mort!). Romantic, but a bit gruesome.

<u>Brun Campbell (The Ragtime Kid)</u>: One of Rudi and Hansi's most fascinating Ragtime rediscoveries. Brun had apprenticed to Joplin himself in Kansas City when he was fifteen. Kind of your normal longhaired White kid enthralled with Black culture, you know the usual thing... in 1901 as Ragtime was blending with the Blues. Campbell gigged all over the Midwest, finally settling down to be a barber. A valuable informant about Scott Joplin and the

era as a whole, interviewed by Rudi and Hansi and then writing articles himself, Brun was a veritable goldmine for Ragtime scholarship, and also an inspiration for modern Ragtime composers. And still continuing in the literary vein: as Brun Campbell now figures in <u>A Ragtime Fool: A Ragtime Mystery</u>, a recent novel by Larry Karp. Campbell's rival (for some Joplin folios) in this made up mystery is none other than that shady protagonist named Rudi Blesh. Definitely stranger than non-fiction.

<u>Percy Wenrich (The Joplin Kid)</u>: another White Ragtime prodigy from the early years of the twentieth century who got rediscovered and written up in <u>They All Played Ragtime</u>, The Kid was named for Joplin Missouri not Scott, but when interviewed Wenrich said he wouldn't have minded having his nickname refer to Scott Joplin because he always wanted his Rags (like The Smiler, Peaches and Cream and Red Rose Rag) to be "real Negro". Wenrich went on to Tin Pan Alley and copyright heaven when he scored big with Put on Your Old Grey Bonnet, a sentimental song that sold millions (but definitely wasn't "real Negro"). A Rudi and Hansi informant, Wenrich also wrote the music to Moonlight Bay, another 1920s favorite that was revived by madcap Canadian Ragtime/Jazz/Blues revivalist Leon Redbone in the 1970s. (Before that, in 1963 The Beatles did a comedy sketch on English television where they wore straw hats and striped shirts and sang Moonlight Bay as a Ragtime barbershop quartet. No kidding.)

<u>Ben Harney</u>: Ragtime's first real star was this White man from Kentucky who appeared on the Bowery in the 1890s, oddly not far from where Rudi (and I) lived at 38 East 4th (up the block from CBGBs), also near the place where Williams and Walker, Bert Williams' original act hit about that same time--that resonance thing again. Harney's Ragtime songs and strict piano playing were a huge improvement over the derisive Minstrel Show--a real progressive amalgam of Black/White artistic/cultural elements. Loosely defined "Jig Piano" now becomes classic Ragtime, and the Blues gets introduced to White audiences at Tony Pastor's with Mister Johnson Turn Me Loose and You're a Good Old Wagon, but You Done Broke Down, still being performed by Bessie Smith in the 1920s. Harney was interesting because he seems to have been a young man from a good Southern family... who basically passed for Black. Ben Harney's story was an important part of <u>They All Played Ragtime</u>, because the guy set off a music culture fad that flowered on the Bowery in the 1890s and is still going... really. On nearby Second Avenue in the Jewish theatres a similar

Blues explosion went on concurrently with The Irwin Sisters and their tough Bully Song. Among the later Bowery Ragtime stars were Irving Berlin known for his many compositions (Alexander's Ragtime Band, America the Beautiful...), and Jimmy Durante who started on St. Marks Place in the 1900s, and then worked his way through Vaudeville, all the way onto LPs and early television. Once they all played Ragtime, now they just call it Show Business.

Bert Williams: ever the source for that high tone, classy Ragtime, the man who brought the Cakewalk to England, Bert Williams really created a point of view. A cool modern mentality so universal today that no one can remember the archaic way we all used to think before this brilliant Caribbean man retooled our minds. And because we all take his post racial point of view for granted, very few now can even remember the poor guy's name. W. C. Fields, the great 1930s film comedian got his start as a mime and a juggler. His role model: Bert Williams. Bert was literate, studied the classics, Aristophanes and much more. So Bill Fields got a trunk and filled it with books he read as he toured the world juggling in the 1890s. To improve his mind. Later when they were both in the follies Fields got to travel with Ragtime Blues star Fanny Brice (Funny Girl) and her gangster boyfriend Dutch Schultz, with Eddie Cantor in his early open sportscar. But all W.C. Fields could think about was poor Bert who couldn't travel with them in the car, and had to stay in "colored" accomodations. Like other geniuses caught between the races (Chuck Berry, Jimi Hendrix, Bob Marley, others): Nobody.

May Irwin: simultaneous to Ben Harney's letting the Blues loose on the Bowery in the 1890s was the dangerous Blues explosion in the Jewish theatres that lined Second Avenue in the East Village. (Later, in the 1960s one of these theatres became the Fillmore East). In the 1890s the highlight was May Irwin, loud, tough originating Yiddishe Mama from the Lower East Side. Her signature song: May Irwin's Bully Song was as rough a "Coon" song as ever was heard. To hear all that razor toting violence coming from a gal was a new kind of show. The Blues, obviously. Soon that was set as part of Show Business and a new generation of entertainers came in May Irwin's wake. Fanny Brice, Mae West, Sophie Tucker, many others. And a new style as well, sung by a masochistic gal, the "Torch Singer" in nightclubs still today.

Joe Lamb: the final result of Rudi's obsession with artistic evaluation and strict categorization. At the end of their travels in

1949 Rudi and Hansi still had not been able to locate the third of the "Ragtime Big Three". All over the country players and composers had offered opinions on the identity of the man known only as Jos. Lamb. Some Black players maintained he was Black, an unknown. Others claimed it was just a pseudonym of Scott Joplin himself. The authors were stymied until Rudi pulled out the Brooklyn phone book. Going down near Coney Island by subway they searched for the address. They stopped a young lady with a baby carriage and asked if she'd ever heard of a Joseph P. Lamb and she exclaimed: "Oh Grampa!" Getting to talk to Joe they found him, a poor White man home after laboring as a street worker in the garment district. The poor guy was so down-trodden he could only ask: "How much is it going to cost me to be in your book Mr. Blesh?" Disavowed of that notion Joe went on to help fill a chapter in They All Played Ragtime with his wonderful story. Predestined by his family for the priesthood, pre-ordained, Joseph had received surrepticious piano lessons from his older sisters. Sent off to a seminary in Toronto at fourteen he was soon expelled after they found him writing Rags. Back home in NYC he sought out Scott Joplin, as ever happy to help out young talent. Scott got Joe's Rag Sensation published nationally and after Scott's passing there were more, culminating in Lamb's last Classic Rags going out in 1919. After that Joe Lamb had settled back into the working class existence as Rudi and Hansi found him. His own family didn't even think much of him as a composer. But Rudi and Hansi sure did. Pretty soon Joe was enjoying some of the well deserved recognition his Rags had earned him. Never much of a player, Joe got to record his pieces for the first time for Sam Charters on Folkways and on the Jazzology LP They All Played Ragtime, and then, started composing new material. These new Rags were sparkling melodic creations brimming with modern musical ideas. A genius rediscovered and a new category for the record store bins (and modern composers): Contemporary Ragtime.

Milton Kaye: In 1973 Rudi discovered, or was actually discovered by a marvelous piano player who had the time, patience and definitely the talent and desire to really get down and explore some interesting Ragtime together with him. Working with Carnegie Hall soloist Milton Kaye, Rudi was there to help fine tune that sense of what a perfect Ragtime tempo might be, how much ornamentation, stomp... also an opportunity to present unpublished material like Scott Joplin's Dream, an unknown Joe Lamb Rag composed with Joplin himself. Never bestsellers, these

Golden Crest Records recordings: Ragtime at the Rosebud (Tom Turpin's St. Louis cafe), The Classic Rags of Joe Lamb 1 & 2 and You Tell Em Ivories, Milton Kaye Plays Zez Confrey are simply the best Ragtime Rudi ever produced himself.

Ian Whitcomb: Rockers into Raggers, a trend perhaps. In addition to Whitcomb, the late 60s saw a bit of a Trad revival as part of the campy Beatlesque scene. Maybe it started with Paul McCartney's When I'm Sixty Four. The Sopwith Camel did Hello Hello with a bit of vo de oh do and a group of studio musicians in the UK put out Winchester Cathedral, complete with megaphone effect vocal which went top ten. (Rudi loved both those songs.) Part of that crew that recorded Winchester Cathedral went on to be the Bonzo Doo Dah Dog Band, a Trad/Psych unit somewhat hooked up with the Beatles that pretty much defied categorization until Monty Python came along to continue the idea visually. Before that in 1964-65 it had been Herman's Hermits nicking Joey Brown's Henery the Eighth and Mrs. Brown You've Got a Lovely Daughter that had kept the aging turn of the century Music Hall Tradition, the English Vaudeville alive. Ian Whitcomb looked like Herman but he sang breathless Rock until he bottomed out in the American Northwest in the late 60s. A copy of They All Played Ragtime brought him to Rudi and a new angle. Ian also finished up his studies at Trinity College with a dissertation that became After the Ball, a great read on the subject of Ragtime/Jazz/Rock. In Sedalia I was squeezed into a cab with Whitcomb at one point listening to him complain about the emphasis on Scott Joplin. More to his liking it seems at the time the madcap White college oriented Pop Jazz bands of the 1920s with their bizarre song titles and frenetic dance floor tempoes. That evening in Missouri Ian performed songs like Where Did Robinson Crusoe Go With Friday on Saturday Night on vocals and ukelele with magician/pianist Dick Zimmerman to great effect.

Dick Hyman: another consumate Carnegie Hall pianist with an avid interest in Ragtime. Recorded The Complete Works of Scott Joplin for RCA, with notes by Rudi Blesh, yet another contender for the best Ragtime interpretations. Played at Rudi's 85th birthday party at Max Morath's NYC studio. Scott Joplin has been redeemed.

Ragtime Bob Darch: probably gets a bad rap from me for following the evil Ragtime stereotype to a certain degree but there was no one, and that includes Max Morath a little later who did more to get the Ragtime Revival off the ground right after he'd read They All Played Ragtime in the early 1950s. The spark plug. Darch was the authentic reproduction of a turn of the century piano Professor and a heck of an entertainer to boot. Not many recordings available. Shy in the studio perhaps? Sadly passed in 2002. Is there any Jack Daniels #7 in heaven?

David Jason: ruthless Ragtimer, and definitely a heavy when it comes to Rudi but none the less a hard working music scholar and historian. Jason's lists, articles and books (one with Trebor Tichenor) tend to be informative (based on TAPR), and the series of LP reissues David Jason did for Folkways did bring to light a great deal of commercial Ragtime and early Jazz from the 1920s and before. But still way too aggressive, and over the top trying to define himself in opposition to They All Played Ragtime, itself obviously only a founding work. The only bad thing I remember Rudi saying about Jason was that he wouldn't want to have to play a piano after Dave had finished with it. That guy had what you might call "a heavy touch". Ouch!

Trebor Tichenor: another serious contender in the world of the modern Ragtime revival. Trebor's specialty: Mississippi Valley Folk Ragtime, music from the original turn of the century circuit, as showcased nowadays on the riverboats at St. Louis. It doesn't get more authentic than that. Trebor holds his own in the field of Ragtime scholarship as well with a book Rags and Ragtime (with David Jason), television, radio interviews and articles to his credit. Mr. Tichenor's Mississippi Valley Ragtime LP was prized by Rudi for its accurate portrayal of the era. Scott Joplin, Arthur Marshall, Charles Hunter, Tom Turpin, Brun Campbell, Blind Boone, Jelly Rolly Morton, come alive in these recordings along with a couple of Trebor Tichenor's Brun Campbell influenced "Blue Rag" originals. Tichenor seems to always get it right and he adds fun and entertainment in for good measure. The original purpose of Ragtime I suspect. Rag on Treb.

John Edward Hasse: piano player/author/curator/Jazz historian connected to the Smithsonian Institute. Even handed dispenser of Jazz justice and thoughtful scholarly research. Very helpful regarding this present endeavor. Mr. Hasse had the prescience to record a great far ranging interview with Rudi up in New Hampshire in 1978. Now why didn't I think of that?

John Arpin: Ragtimer from Canada brought prodigious piano playing skills and a somewhat different perspective. A bit of the elegant candelabra, black suit and coat tails approach back in 1965. Effervescent. Rudi thought Arpin's interpretations of Joplin, Scott and Lamb to be right up there with the best.

Nurit Tilles: a young pianist in the 80s, and friend of Donald Ashwander worked hard to create her own LP of contemporary Ragtime by various composers. She wisely chose Raggin' Rudi by Bill Bolcom as one of her selections and Donald got Rudi to write some notes. It all took some time and improvisation but the finished product was well worth the effort. Nurit also came up to New Hampshire once (without her girlfriend) and got to experience my comical attempts at outrunning the NH police (for an out of date inspection sticker) and also sit in a tent. All parts of living a Ragtime Life. Nurit was also one of Steve Reich's dozens of talented pianists, recently recorded a CD of the work of Donald Ashwander, and more.

Mike Montgomery: another Rudi associate who worked on They All Played Ragtime, specifically the 1960s Grove Press/Oak edition with the most complete set of revisions and corrections. An astute historian and collector of Afro-American cultural artifacts Mike Montgomery is perhaps best remembered today as a pianist and expert on piano rolls, obscure Blues artists and an authority on the lives of Sippie Wallace and Hociel Thomas. Solid Blues/Jazz enthusiast scholar offshoot who just passed away in 2011. Roll on.

Eric Von Schmidt, Dave Van Ronk, Danny Kalb: Blues Ragtime guitar originators in the early 1960s. Dave Van Ronk and Danny Kalb were West Village based, tied up with Sam Charters as the Ragtime Jug Stompers in 1964 and with just Charters and Kalb as the New Strangers also in 1964. Before that it was Charters and Van Ronk as the Orange Blossom Jug Five doing "Skiffle in Stereo" in 1958. Charters of course ended up producing lots of people, Danny Kalb became an electric Blues guitarist and Dave Van Ronk kind of just stayed in the Village. Between the three of them they pretty much had it covered as far as the sixties were concerned. I would like to say all of them had some contact with my grandfather, but aside from Sam Charters... who knows? Eric Von Schmidt grew up in Connecticut, almost met Leadbelly as a kid and ended up kicking off the Cambridge Mass Folk Blues scene in the late 50s. He was also an illustrator, doing LP covers for many Folkies on Vanguard. Eric did the covers for some of Max Morath's best selling LPs on that label. And just as Elektra Nonesuch competed with Vanguard (Morath vs. Joshua Rifkin), Rifkin's Nonesuch LP covers were done by artist Saul Lambert in a style that was virtually indistinguishable from that of Eric Von Schmidt's. Nothing tougher than an independent record label.

Felix Pappalardi: not really a Rudi associate, but in Max Morath's first Ragtime band in the early 1960s, when Rudi and Max were just getting hooked up. Felix played mandolin in Max's unit, then went on to be a session musician on numerous Folk records, playing guitarron, a Spanish bass guitar. Later produced Rock, resurrecting the sputtering early Cream with the help of songwriter wife Gail who ultimately shot him in a domestic dispute in 1983. World of Pain, see also: Mountain.

Billy Taylor: one bop pianist who wasn't afraid of Trad or Ragtime even for that matter. Billy Taylor is best known for having written I Wish I Knew How it Would Feel to be Free, a Protest anthem in the 1960s, but he was also a well known educator and historian, working hard to keep the whole Jazz story alive. Fluent in any style he even wrote a book on Ragtime piano solos. Jazz master.

Hank Jones: another Bop pianist who embraced Ragtime, put out an LP This is Ragtime Now in 1964 recorded with bassist Milt Hinton. This was unique and the record is unique as well. As in hard to find. In his life Hank Jones was part of many all star Jazz ensembles. Sadly, both Ragster Bopster educators Hank Jones and Billy Taylor passed in 2010. Important figures as Jazz finally embraced its full diversity with inspired playing, fluency in and respect for all styles.

Jackie Byard: still another Modern Jazz piano stylist who played the archaic styles as well. In Jackie Byard's case he'd just throw the old Ragtime/Stride rhythms right into the middle of a Free Jazz piece. How free is that? Known for his work with Charlie Mingus who also used to visit the Jazz past. (Both artists' LPs - part of the secret Modern Jazz stash of Professor Rudi Blesh.) Jackie Byard was also an educator at the New England Conservatory and the New School. Ragtime Free Jazz Stride Bop - Jackie Byard never knew when to stop. Fluency with brilliant fluidity. Passed in 1999. Stride on.

<u>Bill Russell</u>: Rudi's counterpart in New Orleans searching for Louis Armstrong's teacher Bunk Johnson back in the early 1940s. Did some of the same Jazz things as Rudi, usually a little earlier. Also a Modern composer who influenced John Cage, but is mostly known for the recognition he brought to his adopted hometown New Orleans' Jazz history and the legacy of Jelly Roll Morton. He would crop up from time to time like when I got to photograph him and Rudi at a reunion in Sedalia in 1983. An immortal.

<u>Dr. Edmond Souchon</u>: part of the Six and Seven Eighths string band in the teens, Dr. Souchon went on to recreate that unit as a quartet performing with Bill Russell in the 1950-70s. Classic Jazz scholar he started the New Orleans Jazz Museum and National Jazz Institute. Corresponded regularly with Rudi. Sweet.

<u>Lu Watters/Turk Murphy</u>: in and out of the service in the early 1940s these two still managed to set off the Trad boom with their hot Jazz booming out of the Dawn Club on Annie Street in San Francisco. On hand to immortalise the proceedings, fledgling Jazz critic Rudi Blesh of the San Francisco Chronicle. A heady confluence of events that only became more momentous once Bunk Johnson had been brought out of retirement and up to San Francisco to play again. The scene.

<u>Wally Rose & Lonnie Donegan</u>: two intermission entertainers who set off revival crazes: Lonnie in Britain in the early 1950s with his do-it-yourself Skiffle inspiring 1960s stars and Wally with his Ragtime playing in the Jazz clubs of San Francisco in the early 40s, that revival coming in the 1970s. The common element: Rudi Blesh.

<u>Johnny Maddox</u>: commercial Ragtimer who crossed over into the Art zone in 1977 with Tres Moutarde LP collection of interesting rags done right. With notes by Rudi Blesh. That's doing it right.

<u>Barry Ulanov</u>: teenage Bop enthusiast/Jazz Critic at Metronome magazine in the 40s. Rudi's nemesis in certain Trad/Bop debates and mc for the Bopsters at the New York Herald Tribune's Bands for Bonds Battle of the Bands in 1948, also poster boy for the Jazz war's generation gap. In the 1990s I got to talk to Professor Ulanov briefly after attending one of his lectures on Carl Jung at the New School. The Bop Unconcious.

Leonard Feather - English Jazz critic, songwriter, producer, early Modern Jazz adopter--the leading critic to come out of the Bop experience. In the late 1940s the Modern Jazz fraternity closed ranks and pushed the Moldy Fig Traddies out of the clubs, the bibliographies and the record bins. From then at least until the 1970s Traditional Jazz went mostly unheard in the USA. The Blues was slowly reintroduced, but primarily as Folk/Rock, not a Jazz element. Certain names from the past were left unspoken, excluded from indexes. The love that dares not speak it's name. Feather in 52nd Street: "It was a very emotional period because we were embattled. There were many people who were violently opposed to everything Bop stood for--and incidentily, everything I stood for, because I was a strong proponent for the new music." "We were excoriated by critics whose idea of Jazz was, maybe, up to New Orleans and a little beyond. Articles were written--how did I dare to put up Art Tatum, Roy Eldridge or Oscar Pettiford as representing Jazz? Why didn't I present the *true* Jazz? and they'd name Jelly Roll Morton or Bunk Johnson. Everything was polarized, and a great deal of animosity was directed at me and Ulanov and the new musicians, who were supposed to be the enemies of the real Jazz." Gee I wonder who he's talking about.

Edward A. Berlin: one more Ragtime writer obsessed with the fore image of Rudi Blesh and Harriet Janis. Many references on the internet to his writings, almost all of them for facts originally sourced from They All Played Ragtime and uncredited. Visiting Mr. Berlin's website you find a homepage dedicated to supposed errata and left wing influences (?) in They All Played Ragtime. Mr. Berlin's claim is to have researched factual written evidence about various minor biographical details of Scott Joplin's life. These would have been from legal records, perhaps not too accurate when it came to the Black community back in the 1800s. Even so, what you have here are two histories, one in the case of Rudi and Hansi which was oral, taken from the actual Ragtimers themselves--people like Arthur Marshall and Brun Campbell, and the other perhaps official, differing only in a few details. Why does an addition to the historical record have to be a disproof and established authors discredited? Is a social history really a socialist plot? What is wrong with musical scholarship these days?

Virgil Thompson: believed in Rudi enough to bring him East to write for his paper. Right off the start Rudi must have come across as too radical and divisive, because his byline seems to have lasted about a week in the national/international edition of the NY Herald Tribune in 1946. After that he was strictly in the local edition. and there was rarely any mention of Black Jazz in the Trib at large. An occasional article by Paul Bowles. Even Virgil himself seems to have been cut back, and he rarely wrote about Jazz. Virgil Thompson's review of Shining Trumpets was also somewhat measured, a prediction it seems. Rudi, with his insistance on purity and Black artistry, as always a bit too early.

Danny Barker: the third (and mostly invisible) secret New Orleans element in Rudi's All Star Stompers rhythm section. Quiet unassuming guitarist was never flashy but perpetually solid. Wrote an autobiography: Bourbon Street Black, signed with some kind words for Rudi: "You have given so much energy to the Jazz and Ragtime Music. Telling, writing the history for better understanding and appreciation." Class Act.

Buster Keaton: I grew up thinking of Buster as some sort of god, a homegrown American Dada, the prairie surrealist. Deprived of access to his films for most of our youth we lived on the myth, the look, the man described in Rudi's book. The features in the photos of the man Orson Welles once described as one of the most beautiful human beings who ever existed. So then later, after Buster's films were re-released finally into VHS and subsequently on DVD, alongside the work of Charlie Chaplin and the other long lost 1920s silent movie comedian Harold Lloyd, how do the movies compare today? You'd have to say that after Arbuckle, the first Film genius was Charles Chaplin. His early movies (1914-1920) contain many long unedited shots of pure cinematic comedic perfection. Hard to beat. With Arbuckle out of the picture there came the rise of Harold Lloyd, a hard working heroic kind of all American kid whose round glasses became a 1920s fad (Rudi's younger brother Kelly was the spitting image of Lloyd). Harold Lloyd's gift was his normalness and then his death defying climbing and nearly falling stunts. Also hard to beat. So Keaton tried a narrative style that seemed to work best in The General. He also did stunts, mostly falling on his butt. But primarily it was his iconic image, haunting, sad, unsmiling yet somehow (like us?) destined to be successful. That unique face.

Rudi Blesh: someone who helped change the course of music history. Introduced Dixieland/Trad back into Jazz, Skiffle/Blues into Rock and Roll, and Ragtime into Modern Classical Music. The revivalist. Caused many worthy artists of all races, sexes and persuasions to become unforgotten. My grandfather.

Rudi's favorite recordings (NH box):

Jonah Man Songs of the Bert Williams Era - Max Morath
If I Could Be With You One Hour Tonight... - Donald Lambert
Really the Blues - Ray Bryant / Atlantic Recordings - Ray Charles
The Wind Cries Mary - The Jimi Hendrix Experience
Hellhound on my Trail (others) - Robert Johnson
Dizzy on the French Riviera - Dizzy Gillespie
Ragtime at the Rosebud / Classic Rags of Joe Lamb - Milton Kaye
Hot Five and Hot Seven Recordings / 78s - Louis Armstrong
Complete Columbia Recordings / 78s - Bessie Smith
Hot Peppers Recordings RCA Vintage / 78s - Jelly Roll Morton
Ragtime a New View / Sunshine and Shadow Donald Ashwander
Bolcom Plays His Own Rags / Heliotrope Bouquet... - Bill Bolcom
RCA Recordings Vintage / 78s - Fats Waller, other titles as well
Hot Club de Paris 78s - Django Rhinehardt and Stephan Grappelli
Jalousie - Stephan Grappelli and Yehudi Menuin
Scott Joplin's Rags / The Ragtime Women... - Max Morath
The Animule Ball - The Saga of Mr. Jelly Lord (Circle red vinyl)
Columbia Recordings - Count Basie/Lester Young/Billie Holiday
Atomic - Count Basie / The Eighty Six Years of Eubie Blake
A Love Supreme - John Coltrane / Frederick Delius 78s
Pinetop's Boogie Woogie 78 - Pinetop Smith/ also Cleo Brown 78
Smithsonian/Folkways Recordings / 78s - Leadbelly
South Side Shake 78s - Dan Burley and his Skiffle Boys
Tomorrow Night - Lonnie Johnson (1950s version w/ electric gtr)
Lonnie Johnson and Eddie Lang / In a Mist - Bix Beiderbecke 78
They All Played Ragtime - Max Morath, Donald Ashwander,
    Trebor Tichenor... (Jazzology LP - contemporary Ragtime)
Complete Piano Works of Scott Joplin RCA - Dick Hyman
Prairie Ragtime - Thomas Shea / Concert in Ragtime - John Arpin
Mississippi Valley Ragtime - Trebor Tichenor
Vaudeville, Songs of the Great Ladies of the Musical Stage /
        After the Ball... - Bill Bolcom and Joan Morris
Too Much Mustard - Johnny Maddox/Waldo's Ragtime Orchestra
Silks and Rags Dawn of the Century Orchestra /Jazzology releases
TJ Anderson / Gunther Schuller New England Ragtime Ensemble
Lu Watters / Turk Murphy / Original Zenith / Preservation Hall
Sidney Bechet with Mezz Mezzrow, Bob Wilber / Ralph Sutton
Aretha Franklin / Little Brother Montgomery / Jackie Byard...

Abraham Blesh

Rudolph Pickett Blesh

Dr. Blesh, Theo, Belle and Rudi 1899

Guthrie Oklahoma Territory 1890s

First Fliver at Fifteen

May 22, 1917.

Dartmouth bound, 1917

Remains of house in Berkeley 1923

Rudi at opening of Golden Gate Bridge

Belle Blesh, Berkeley

Editha

231

Harriet Janis 38 E 4th, behind her is Evsa Model painting
and door to Baby Dodd's room

Hansi on the go

With lobsters in the Hamptons

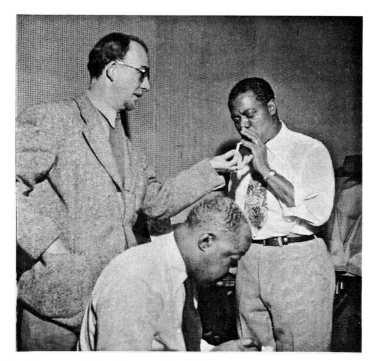

The Keepers of the Flame. Rudi, Baby Dodds, Louis Armstrong

Hansi, Rudi and R.A. Aurthur, This Is Jazz

Bertha Hill and Montana Taylor

Bunk Johnson

Dan Burley and His Skiffle Boys (collage by Jimmy Ernst)

Jamming at Rudi's, 1951, w/ Lips Page, Sonny Greer,
members of Duke Ellington Band

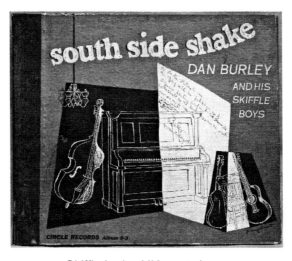

Skiffle in the UK starts here

238

Rudi and Hansi at the 38 East 4th Street apartment

the
saga
of
mr.
jelly
lord

the
jazz
piano
soloist

Vol. VI

JELLY ROLL MORTON

circle long playing

The "Delta Project"

239

Belle, HIlary and Rudi 1936

California

1945

New Hampshire 1951

First Birthday with John Hultberg and
Aunt Ethel

Brooklyn 1956

On tour with Rudi Holland 1957

Tivoli Gardens 1960

241

Peace Conference at Birdland

FM pioneer

Big Tom Turpin

Scott Joplin

Louis Chauvin

Williams and Walker

243

Old Friends: Rudi and James P. Johnson, 1946

Old Friends: Rudi and Eubie Blake, 1982

244

The greatest Stride
album of all time?

Donald Lambert playing for drinks in NJ

Memories of You

Max Morath at the Turn
of the Century in 1968

Ragtime Bob Darch

Uncle Max

246

Donald Ashwander and Sharon Moore

Rudi and Bill Bolcom

Eugene "Botsy" Grossman
with Mitty and me 1954

Rudi and Nikita at Loon Pond 1981

Hillforge, Gilmanton NH

Rudi on TV 1962

Collecting stones with
Bill Bolcom 1984

Last radio show WGBH 1984

No respect for art 1955

Christmas in Marblehead 1970

Rudi with Granddaughter Steffi and Great Grandson Nahum Marblehead 1984

Rudi with Granddaughters Alison and Genevieve 1984

251

That face

Buster and the animals

Buster and Rudi 1965

Sherlock Jr. - with father Joseph Keaton

The escape plan? 253

Buster on TV

Rudi and Granddaughter Genny at Union Square 1983

Village Green

This is Jazz List of artists and dates:

<u>For Your Approval</u> January 18, 1947 Punch Miller, tpt Max
Kaminsky, tpt Albert Nicholas, clt Mezz Mezzrow, clt George
Brunis, tbn Luckey Roberts, pno Wellman Braud, sbs Cy St. Clair,
tuba Baby Dodds, dms
1. **Program Introduction**
2. **High Society**
3. **Tiger Rag**
4. **Basin St. Blues** (Punch Miller, vcl)
5. **Dippermouth Blues**
6. **I Wish I Could Shimmy Like My Sister Kate** (Miller vcl)
7. **Ain't Misbehavin'**

<u>This is Jazz</u> February 8, 1947 Muggsy Spannier, cnt
Albert Nicholas, clt George Brunis, tbn Luckey Roberts, pno
Danny Barker, gtr Cy St. Clair, sbs & tuba Baby Dodds, dms
1. **Program Introduction**
2. **Muskrat Ramble**
3. **Tin Roof Blues** (George Brunis, vcl)
4. **Clarinet Marmalade**
5. **Rose Room**
6. **Ripples of the Nile**
7. **Lazy River**

<u>This is Jazz</u> February 15, 1947 Muggsy Spannier, cnt
Albert Nicholas, clt George Brunis, tbn Joe Sullivan, pno
Danny Barker, gtr Cy St. Clair, sbs & tuba Baby Dodds, dms
also: Coot Grant, vcl Kid Socks Wilson, pno & vcl
1. **Program Introduction**
2. **Bugle Call Rag**
3. **Don't Do That to Me** (Grant vcl, Wilson pno vcl)
4. **Royal Garden Blues**
5. **Hey Daddy** (Coot Grant vcl, Kid SocksWilson pno vcl)
6. **Squeeze Me** (Coot Grant vcl)
7. **Eccentric**

<u>This is Jazz</u> March 1, 1947 Muggsy Spannier, cnt
Albert Nicholas, clt George Brunis, tbn James P. Johnson, pno
Danny Barker, gtr Pops Foster, bs Baby Dodds, dms
also: Sydney Bechet, clt
1. **Program Introduction**

2. **That's a Plenty**
3. **Baby Please Come Home** (George Brunis, vcl)
4. **I Know That You Know**
5. **Original Improvised Blues**
6. **Caprice Rag**
7. **Charleston** (written by James P. Johnson)

This is Jazz March 8, 1947 Muggsy Spanier, tpt Albert Nicholas, clt George Brunis, tbn Charlie Queener, pno Danny Barker, gtr Pops Foster, sbs Baby Dodds, dms
1. **Program Introduction**
2. **At the Jazz Band Ball**
3. **Ja Da**
4. **Darktown Strutters Ball**
5. **Relaxin' at the Touro**
6. **Dinah V**(Georg Brunis, vcl)
7. **Me Pas Lemma Ca** (Albert Nicholas, vcl)
8. **Panama**

This is Jazz March 15, 1947 Muggsy Spanier, tpt Albert Nicholas, clt George Brunis, tbn Joe Sullivan, pno Danny Barker, gtr Pops Foster, sbs Baby Dodds, dms
1. **Program Introduction**
2. **That Da Da Strain**
3. **Riverside Blues**
4. **South Side Shake** (Dan Burley, pno)
5. **Some Day Sweetheart**
6. **Dusty Bottom** (Dan Burley, pno)
7. **Fidgety Feet**

This is Jazz March 24, 1947 Muggsy Spannier, cnt Albert Nicholas, clt George Brunis, tbn Art Hodes, pno Danny Barker, gtr Pops Foster, sbs Baby Dodds, dms also: Sydney Bechet sop
1. **Program Introduction**
2. **Sensation Rag** (Sydney Bechet soprono saxophone)
3. **You're Some Pretty Doll** (Sydney Bechet soprono sax G. Brunis vcl)
4. **Twelfth Street Rag**
5. **Buddy Bolden's Blues**
6. **Black and Blue** (Sydney Bechet soprono saxophone)
7. **Summertime** (Sydney Bechet soprono saxophone)
8. **Farewell Blues** (Sydney Bechet soprono saxophone)

<u>This is Jazz</u> March 31, 1947 Muggsy Spannier, cnt Albert Nicholas, clt George Brunis, tbn Joe Sullivan, pno Danny Barker, gtr Pops Foster, bs Baby Dodds, dms
1. **Program Introduction**
2. **The Sheik of Araby**
3. **Sweet Lorraine**
4. **At Sundown**
5. **Sweet Lovin' Man** (Georg Brunis, vcl)
6. **Little Rock Getaway**
7. **Ad Lib Blues**
8. **I Found a New Baby**

<u>This is Jazz</u> April 5, 1947 Muggsy Spanier, tpt Albert Nicholas, clt George Brunis, tbn Joe Sullivan, pno Danny Barker, gtr Pops Foster, sbs Baby Dodds, dms
1. **Program Introduction**
2. **Sweet Georgia Brown**
3. **A Good Man is Hard to Find** (G. Brunis, vcl)
4. **September in the Rain**
5. **Lonesome Road**
6. **Love is Just Around the Corner**
7. **I Used to Love You**

<u>This is Jazz</u> April 12, 1947 Muggsy Spannier, cnt Albert Nicholas, clt George Brunis, tbn Art Hodes, pno Danny Barker, gtr Pops Foster, sbs Baby Dodds, dms also: Brownie McGhee gtr vcl, Granville McGhee gtr
1. **Program Introduction**
2. **There'll Be Some Changes Made**
3. **Heartaches**
4. **My Honey's Lovin' Arms**
5. **I'm Leavin' in the Morning Blues** (B McGhee gtr vcl, G McGhee gtr)
6. **Tennessee Shuffle** (Brownie McGhee gtr vcl, Granville McGhee gtr)
7. **Ja Da**
8. **Organ Grinder Blues**
9. **Saints Go Marching In**

<u>This is Jazz</u> April 19, 1947 Wild Bill Davison, cnt Albert Nicholas, clt George Brunis, tbn James P Johnson, pno Danny Barker, gtr Pops Foster, sbs Baby Dodds, dms also: Sydney Bechet sop, Bob Wilbur clt
1. **Program Introduction**

258

2. **Maple Leaf Rag**
3. **Basin Street Blues**
4. **Polka Dot Stomp** (Sydney Bechet sop, Bob Wilbur clt)
5. **Kansas City Man** (Sydney Bechet sop, Bob Wilbur clt)
6. **Jazz Me Blues**
7. **Carolina Shout**
8. **Panama**

This is Jazz April 26, 1947 Wild Bill Davison, cnt Albert Nicholas, clt George Brunis, tbn Art Hodes, pno Danny Barker, gtr Pops Foster, bs Baby Dodds, dms also: Louis Armstrong cnt
1. **Program Introduction**
2. **Saints Go Marching In** (Louis Armstrong vcl)
3. **219 Blues** (Louis Armstrong vcl)
4. **Do You Know What it Means** (Louis Armstrong vcl)
5. **Dippermouth Blues**
6. **Basin Street Blues** (Louis Armstrong vcl)
7. **High Society**
8. **I'll Be Glad When You're Dead** (Louis Armstrong vcl)

This is Jazz May 3, 1947 Wild Bill Davison, cnt Albert Nicholas, clt George Brunis, tbn Joe Sullivan, pno Danny Barker, gtr Pops Foster, sbs Baby Dodds, dms also: Coot Grant, vcl Kid Socks Wilson, pno vcl
1. **Program Introduction**
2. **Everybody Loves My Baby**
3. **Rose Room** (Coot Grant vcl, Kid Socks Wilson pno vcl)
4. **Have Your Chill** (Coot Grant vcl)
5. **Yellow Dog Blues**
6. **Cherry** (Coot Grant, Kid Socks Wilson pno vcl)
7. **I'm a Dirty Cat**
8. **Clarinet Marmalade**

This is Jazz May 10, 1947 Wild Bill Davison, cnt Albert Nicholas, clt George Brunis, tbn Joe Sullivan, pno & celeste Danny Barker, gtr Pops Foster sbs Baby Dodds, dms also: Kirby Walker, pno vcl
1. **Program Introduction**
2. **St. Louis Blues**
3. **Tin Roof Blues** (George Brunis, vcl)
4. **Rampart St. Boogie**
5. **The Shout** (Kirby Walker pno)
6. **Oh, I'm Evil** (Kirby Walker pno vcl)
7. **Moonlight on the Ganges**
8. **Tiger Rag** (George Brunis, vcl)

This is Jazz May 17, 1947 Wild Bill Davison, cnt Albert Nicholas, clt George Brunis, tbn Art Hodes, pno Danny Barker, gtr Pops Foster, sbs Baby Dodds, dms also: Johnny Glasel, cnt
1. **Program Introduction**
2. **Original Dixieland One Step**
3. **I Ain't Got Nobody**
4. **Hotter Than That** (Johnny Glasel cnt)
5. **Shine**
6. **Memphis Blues**
7. **Yesterdays**
8. **King Porter Stomp**

This is Jazz May 24, 1947 Wild Bill Davison, cnt Albert Nicholas, clt George Brunis, tbn James P Johnson, pno Danny Barker, gtr Pops Foster, bs Baby Dodds, dms also: Sydney Bechet, sop
1. **Program Introduction**
2. **I'm Crazy 'Bout My Baby** (George Brunis, vcl)
3. **Wild Cat Blues**
4. **Squeeze Me** (George Brunis, vcl)
5. **Ain't Misbehavin'**
6. **Chocolate Bar** (George Brunis, vcl)
7. **Blue Turning Grey Over You**
8. **I've Got a Feeling I'm Falling**

This is Jazz May 31, 1947 Wild Bill Davison, tpt Albert Nicholas, clt Georg Brunis, tbn Joe Sullivan, pno Danny Barker, gtr Pops Foster, sbs Baby Dodds, dms also: Blu Lu Barker
1. **Program Introduction**
2. **Ostrich Walk**
3. **Don't Leave Me Daddy**
4. **After You're Gone** (BL Barker, vcl)
5. **Georgia Grind** (BL Barker, vcl)
6. **A Monday Date**
7. **If I Could Be With You One Hour Tonight**
8. **Strut Miss Lizzie**

This is Jazz June 7, 1947 Wild Bill Davison, cnt Albert Nicholas, clt no tbn James P. Johnson, pno Danny Barker, gtr Pops Foster, sbs Baby Dodds, dms also: Freddy Moore, washboard dms vcl
1. **Program Introduction**
2. **I Wish I Could Shimmy Like My Sister Kate**
(Freddy Moore vcl)

3. **Ad Lib Blues** (Freddy Moore vcl)
4. **Poor Butterfly**
5. **Snowy Morning Blues**
6. **Salee Dame** (Albert Nicholas, vcl)
7. **Confessin'**
8. **Big Butter and Egg Man** (Freddy Moore washboard)

This is Jazz June 14, 1947 Wild Bill Davison, cnt Albert Nicholas, clt Jimmy Archey, tbn James P. Johnson, pno Danny Barker, gtr Pops Foster, sbs Baby Dodds, dms also: Huddie Ledbetter, gtr vcl Momma Alberta Price vcl
1. **Program Introduction**
2. **Fidgety Feet**
3. **Ain't Gonna Give Nobody None Of My Jelly Roll**
   (A Price vcl)
4. **Green Corn** (Huddie Ledbetter gtr vcl)
5. **John Henry** (Huddie Ledbetter gtr vcl)
6. **Solo Drum Improvisation**
7. **Sugar**
8. **Muskrat Ramble**

This is Jazz June 21, 1947 Wild Bill Davison, cnt Albert Nicholas, clt Jimmy Archey, tbn James P. Johnson, pno Danny Barker, gtr Pops Foster, bs Baby Dodds, dms
1. **Program Introduction**
2. **Panama**
3. **Trombone Preaching Blues**
4. **Ain't Cha Got Music**
5. **Sensation Rag**
6. **When It's Sleepy Time Down South**
7. **St. Louis Blues**

This is Jazz June 28, 1947 Wild Bill Davison, tpt Albert Nicholas, clt Jimmy Archey, tbn Ralph Sutton, pno Danny Barker, gtr Pops Foster, sbs Baby Dodds, dms also: Montana Taylor, pno vcl
1. **Program Introduction**
2. **Shine**
3. **Black and Blue**
4. **The Five O'Clocks** (Montana Taylor, pno)
5. **I Can't Sleep** (Montana Taylor, pno vcl)
6. **Struttin' with Some Barbeque**
7. **Tishomingo Blues**
8. **I Found a New Baby**

This is Jazz July 5, 1947 Wild Bill Davison, cnt Albert Nicholas, clt Jimmy Archey, tbn, Ralph Sutton, pno Danny Barker, gtr Pops Foster, sbs Johnny Blowers, dms also: Bertha "Chippie" Hill vcl
1. **Program Introduction**
2. **Rosetta** (
3. **Save it Pretty Mama**
4. **How Long Blues** (Bertha Hill, vcl)
5. **Skeleton Jangle**
6. **Careless Love** (Bertha Hill, vcl)
7. **Dill Pickles**
8. **Shim-Me-Sha-Wabble**

This is Jazz July 12, 1947 Wild Bill Davison, cnt Albert Nicholas, clt Jimmy Archey, tbn Joe Sullivan, pno Danny Barker, gtr Pops Foster, sbs Baby Dodds, dms also: Sydney Bechet, sop
1. **Program Introduction**
2. **Alexander's Ragtime Band**
3. **Sugar** (Sydney Bechet, soprano saxophone)
4. **There'll Be Some Changes Made**
5. **Dear Old Southland** (Sydney Bechet, soprano saxophone)
6. **Margie**
7. **Albert's Blues**
8. **Clarinet Marmelade**

This is Jazz July 19, 1947 Wild Bill Davison, cnt Albert Nicholas, clt Jimmy Archey, tbn James P. Johnson, pno Danny Barker, gtr Pops Foster, bs Baby Dodds, dms also: Bertha Hill
1. **Program Introduction**
2. **Twelfth Street Rag**
3. **Darktown Strutters' Ball** (Bertha Hill, vcl)
4. **I'm Sorry I Made You Cry**
5. **Oh, Lady be Good**
6. **Whitewash Man**
7. **Lonesome Road** (Bertha Hill, vcl)
8. **Muskrat Ramble**

This is Jazz July 26, 1947 Wild Bill Davison, cnt Albert Nicholas, clt Jimmy Archey, tbn Ralph Sutton, pno Danny Barker, gtr Pops Foster, bs Baby Dodds, dms also: Bertha Hill
1. **Program Introduction**
2. **Eccentric**
3. **Tishomingo Blues**
4. **Hotter Than That**
5. **Don't Leave Me Daddy** (Bertha Hill, vcl)

262

6. **Big Butter and Egg Man**
7. **Baby Won't You Please Come Home** (Bertha Hill, vcl)
8. **Sensation Rag**

This is Jazz August 2, 1947 Wild Bill Davison, cnt Albert
Nicholas, clt Jimmy Archey, tbn Ralph Sutton, pno Danny
Barker, gtr Pops Foster, bs Baby Dodds, dms also: Sidney Bechet
1. **Program Introduction**
2. **I Never Knew I Could Love Anybody Like I'm Loving**
You
3. **Dardanella**
4. **China Boy**
5. **Love For Sale**
6. **Dear Old Girl**
7. **Wolverine Blues**
8. **California, Here I Come**

This is Jazz August 9, 1947 Andrew Blakeney, tpt Joe
Darensbourg, clt Kid Ory, tbn Buster Wilson, pno Bud Scott, gtr
Ed Garland, bs Minor Hall, dms
1. **Program Introduction**
2. **Oh Didn't He Ramble**
3. **Snag it** (Bud Scott, vcl)
4. **Maryland, My Maryland**
5. **Savoy Blues**
6. **Down Among the Sheltering Palms** (Bud Scott, vcl)
7. **C'est L'Autre Can Can** (Kid Ory, vcl)
8. **Weary Blues**

This is Jazz August 16, 1947 Lu Watters, tpt Bob Scobey, tpt Bob
Helm, clt Turk Murphy, tbn Wally Rose, pno Harry Mordecai,
bjo Dick Lammi, tuba & sbs Bill Dart, dms
1. **Program Introduction**
2. **Cakewalking Babies**
3. **Antigua Blues**
4. **Pineapple Rag**
5. **Beale Street Blues** (Turk Murphy, vcl)
6. **Chattanooga Stomp**
7. **Jazzin' Babies Blues**
8. **Snake Rag**

This is Jazz August 23, 1947 Wild Bill Davison, cnt Albert
Nicholas, clt Jimmy Archey, tbn Ralph Sutton, pno Danny
Barker, gtr Pops Foster, bs Baby Dodds, dms, vcl

1. **Program Introduction**
2. **Ballin' the Jack**
3. **Four or Five Times** (Baby Dodds, vcl)
4. **As Long As I Live**
5. **Trombone Preaching Blues**
6. **Mandy**
7. **Peg O' My Heart**
8. **Nobody's Sweetheart**

This is Jazz August 30, 1947 Wild Bill Davison, cnt Albert
Nicholas, clt Jimmy Archey, tbn James P. Johnson, pno Danny
Barker, gtr Pops Foster, bs Baby Dodds, dms also: Bertha Hill
1. **Program Introduction**
2. **At the Jazz Band Ball**
3. **Sometimes I'm Happy**
4. **Some of These Days** (Bertha Hill, vcl)
5. **Just a Gigolo**
6. **Put Your Arms Around Me, Honey**
7. **Improvised Blues** (Bertha Hill, vcl)
8. **The World is Waiting For the Sunrise**

This is Jazz September 6, 1947 Wild Bill Davison, cnt Edmond
Hall, clt Jimmy Archey, tbn James P. Johnson, pno Danny
Barker, gtr Pops Foster, bs Baby Dodds, dms
1. **Program Introduction**
2. **Clarinet Marmalade**
3. **Tishomingo Blues**
4. **S'Wonderful**
5. **Ol' Man River**
6. **Maple Leaf Rag**
7. **Georgia On My Mind**
8. **Bugle Call Rag**

This is Jazz September 13, 1947 Wild Bill Davison, cnt Edmond
Hall, clt Jimmy Archey, tbn James P. Johnson, pno Danny
Barker, gtr Pops Foster, bs Baby Dodds, dms
1. **Program Introduction**
2. **It's Right Here For You**
3. **I'm Not Gonna Give Nobody None of my Jelly Roll**
4. **I'm Coming, Virginia**
5. **Can't We Be Friends**
6. **Skeleton Jangle**
7. **The Blues**
8. **Muskrat Ramble**

264

<u>This is Jazz</u> September 20, 1947 Wild Bill Davison, cnt
Edmond Hall, clt Jimmy Archey, tbn James P. Johnson, pno
Danny Barker, gtr Pops Foster, bs Baby Dodds, dms
1. **Program Introduction**
2. **Indiana**
3. **Sunday**
4. **Liza**
5. **I Can't Believe You're in Love With Me**
6. **St. Louis Blues**
7. **All Of Me**
8. **Dippermouth Blues**

<u>This is Jazz</u> September 27, 1947 Wild Bill Davison, cnt Edmond
Hall, clt Jimmy Archey, tbn James P. Johnson, pno Danny
Barker, gtr Pops Foster, bs Baby Dodds, dms
1. **Program Introduction**
2. **Jazz Me Blues**
3. **Royal Garden Blues**
4. **Take Me Out To the Ball Game**
5. **Avalon**
6. **Wrap Your Troubles In Dreams**
7. **Swingin' Down the Lane**
8. **High Society**

<u>This is Jazz</u> October 4, 1947 Wild Bill Davison, cnt Albert
Nicholas, clt Jimmy Archey, tbn James P. Johnson, pno Danny
Barker, gtr Pops Foster, bs Baby Dodds, dms also: Sidney
Bechet, sop sax*
1. **Program Introduction**
2. **Sensation**
3. **Ja Da**
4. **St. Louis Blues** *
5. **Laura** *
6. **Big Butter and Egg Man**
7. **Sweet Lorraine** *
8. **Farewell Blues**

Farewell to This Is Jazz...

Entire series is available from Jazzology Records on CD.

from Rudi's Circle Master notebook:

LIST OF CIRCLE MASTERS, COMPLETE December 12, 1964

A,B, etc., following master number indicates take.
AC= Actate M= Metal Master either 78 r.p.m. or 33 1/3
microgroove MO= Metal Mother either 78 r.p.m. or 33 1/3
microgroove
CI= Circle RIV= Riverside (processed from Circle under license)
Where masters are on tape it is so indicated.
* indicates unissued master. NY= New York SF=San Francisco
SL= St. Louis LA= Los Angeles C= Chicago NO= New Orleans
R= Solo Art, 1938-39 [label purchased by Circle]

BABY DODDS TRIO: Albert Nicolas cl; Don Ewell, p; Baby
Dodds, dms, Jan 6, 1946
*NY-1 Wolverine Blues (trio) AC
NY-1A   "   "   "   AC AC M RIV tape 12-216 B
NY-2 Buddy Bolden's Blues AC AC M RIV tape 12-216 B
*NY-2A "   "   "
NY-3 Albert's Blues AC AC M RIV tape 12-216 B
NY-4 Drum Improvisation No. 1 (Dodds, dm solo) AC AC M MO
NY-5 Drum Improvisation No. 2   "   "   "   M MO MO
NY-6 Manhattan Stomp (Ewell p solo w/ Dodds) AC M MO

LUCKY ROBERTS, p solos   May 21, 1946
NY-7C Railroad Blues AC AC M
NY-8E Ripples of the Nile AC AC M
NY-9B Pork and Beans AC AC M
NY-10 Shy and Sly AC AC M
NY-11 Music Box Rag AC AC M
NY-12 Junkman Rag AC AC M

DAN BURLEY, p and v with Brownie and Sticks McGhee, guis,
and Pops Foster bs. June 11, 1946 Issued on CI 78 only,
pre-1953
NY-13A Big Cat, Little Cat (v) AC MO
NY-14A Shotgun House Rag [?] AC MO MO
NY-15A Lakefront Blues (v) AC M MO
*NY-16 Fishtail Blues AC M
NY-17 Three Flights Up AC MO
*NY-18 Hersal's Rocks AC? M

NY-19   Dusty Bottom (Burley + Foster <u>con arco</u>) AC M MO
*NY-20 31st Street Blues (v) AC M
*NY-21 Landlady's Night M
NY-22   South Side Shake

BROWNIE and STICKS MCGHEE, v and 2 guis   June 11, 1946
*NY-23c Movin' to Kansas City AC AC M
*NY-24   Railroad Bill AC M
*NY-25   Rocks in my Bed AC M
*NY-26   Tennessee Shuffle (instrumental, no v) AC M
NY-27A   Precious Lord Hold My Hand AC M
NY-28   If I Could Hear My Mother Pray Again AC M MO
(NY 27A and NY 28 issued on 78 rpm only, as by "The Tennessee
Gabriel"

JAMES P. JOHNSON, P solos June 5, 1947 never issued in the
USA
NY-29D Daintiness Rag AC M
NY-30   Mama and Papa Blues AC M
NY-31   Aincha Got Music? AC M
NY-32   Old Fashioned Love AC M
NY-33   I'm Crazy 'Bout My Baby AC M
NY-34   Wildcat Rag AC M
(see also NY-199/200)

NICK'S CREOLE SERENADERS (JAZZ A LA CREOLE): Nicholas
cl; Danny Barker gui and v; James P. Johnson p; Pops Foster bs.
June 12, 1947
NY-35B   Mo Pas Lemme Ca M MO   RIV tape 12-216B
NY-36   Salee Dame, Bon Jour M MO   "   "   "
NY-37C   Les Ognons AC? M MO   "   "   "
NY-38   Creole Blues M   "   "   "

BESSIE SMITH: sound track montage from 1929 film, with Hall
Johnson Choir, and orchestra featuring Joe Smith, Buster Bailey,
Big Green, Kaiser Marshall, James P. Johnson, and others.
NY-39   St. Louis Blues Pt. 1 M MO
NY-40   St. Louis Blues Pt. 2 M MO
NY-41   St. Louis Blues Pt. 3 M MO
NY-42   St. Louis Blues Pt. 4 M MO

ALL STAR STOMPERS (Airshots from radio series, THIS IS
JAZZ, 1947): Wild Bill Davison, tpt; Nicholas cl; Jimmy Archey,

trom; Danny Barker gui; Pops Foster bs; Ralph Sutton p; Chippie Hill v#
[also Baby Dodds]
NY-43   Eccentric AC M MO CL/4 M RIV tape 2514 A
NY-44   Tishomingo Blues AC M CL/3 M RIV tape 2514 A
NY-45   Hotter Than That AC M CL/4 M RIV tape 12-211 B
NY-46   Big Butter and Egg Man AC M CL/3 M
NY-47   Baby Won't You Please Come Home? # M MO MO CL/4 M
NY-48   Sensation M MO CL/3 M

TONY PARENTI and HIS RAGTIME BAND: Davison tpt; Parenti cl; Archey trom; Cy St. Clair tuba; Baby Dodds dms; Sutton p. November 22, 1947
NY-49   Grace and Beauty M MO RIV tape 12-205 A
NY-50   Hiawatha RIV tape 12-205 A
NY-51   Praline M MO RIV tape 12-205A
NY-52   Swipesy Cake Walk M MO RIV tape 12-205B
NY-53   Hysterics Rag RIV tape 12-205B
NY-54   Sunflower Slow Drag RIV tape 12-205B

ALL STAR STOMPERS (from This is Jazz 1947) Davison tpt; Ed Hall cl; Archey trom; Barker, Foster, Dodds, Sutton.
NY-55   Can't We Be Friends (Sutton, Hall) M MO RIV tape 2514 B
NY-56   Ain't Gonna Give Nobody None Of This [My?] Jellroll
                        (Hall, Sutton) M MO RIV tape 2514 B
NY-57   Avalon (Sutton, Hall) M RIV tape 12-211 A
NY-58   Swinging Down the Lane (Sutton, Hall) M RIV tape
                                    12-211B
NY-59 Clarinet Marmalade (Sutton, Hall) M MO RIV tape 2514 A
NY-60 It's Right Here For You (Sutton, Hall) M M MO   "   B

WILD BILL DAVISON (Davison Showcase): Davison; Archey; Garvin Bushell cl and bassoon; Sutton; Sid Weiss bs; Morey Feld dms. 12/27/47
NY-61B   Just a Gigolo CL/29 M RIV tape 12-211 A
NY-62   She's Funny That Way M MO CL/30 M MO RIV tape
                                    12-211A
NY-63 Ghost Of a Chance M MO CL/30 M MO RIV tape 12-211 A
NY-64   Yesterdays M CL/29 M RIV tape 12-211 A
NY-65   Why Was I Born M MO CL/29 M RIV tape 12-211 A
NY-66   When Your Lover Has Gone M CL/30 M MO   "

ALL STAR STOMPERS (This Is Jazz 1947): Davison tpt; Nicholas; Archey; Barker; Foster; Dodds; Sutton (except NY-69, James P. Johnson).
NY-67   As Long As I Live M MO RIV tape 12-211 B
NY-68   Lonesome Road (Chippie Hill, v) M MO
NY-69   St. Louis Blues M MO CL/4 M RIV tape 12-211 B
NY-70   I Never Knew I Could Love Anybody M M
NY-71   Shim E She Wabble M CL/3 M RIV tape 12-211 B
*NY-72 Mandy Make Up Your Mind M MO

TONY PARENTI: THE RAGTIMERS, Parenti cl; Sutton p; George Wettling dms. January 22, 1949
NY-73   Crawfish Crawl M MO RIV tape 12-205 A
NY-74   Entertainers Rag M MO RIV tape 12-205 A
NY-75   The Lily Rag M MO RIV tape 12-205 A
NY-76   Cataract Rag M MO RIV tape 12-205 B
NY-77   Nonsense Rag M MO RIV tape 12-205 B
NY-78   Redhead Rag M MO RIV tape 12-205 B

RALPH SUTTON piano solos January 22, 1949
NY-79-1 Dill Pickles M MO RIV tape 12-212 A
NY-79-2 "   "   "   "   "   "   "
NY-80-2 Whitewash Man M MO RIV tape 12-212 A
NY-81-2 Carolina In the Morning M MO RIV tape 12-212 A
NY-82-2 St. Louis Blues M RIV tape 12-212 A

SIDNEY BECHET and HIS CIRCLE SEVEN: Albert Snaer tpt; Buster Bailey cl; Bechet sop sax; Wilbur de Paris trom; Walter Page bs; James P. Johnson or James Toliver p; George Wettling dms and tympani January 27, 1949
NY-83   I Got Rhythm M MO RIV 139 virgin pressing (vinyl LP)
NY-84   September Song AC MO RIV virgin vinyl pressing
NY-85   Who AC MO RIV virgin vinyl pressing
NY-86   Song of the Medina (Toliver p) AC M

BOB WILBER and HIS JAZZ BAND: Wilber clar and sop sax; Henry Goodwin tpt; Jimmy Archey trom; Pops Foster bs; Dick Wellstood p; Tommy Benford dms. April 28, 1949
NY-87B   Sweet Georgia Brown M CL/31 M MO
NY-88   The Mooche M MO CL/31 M MO
NY-89B   Coal Black Shine M
NY-90   Limehouse Blues M CL/31 M MO
NY-91   Zig Zag M
NY-92   When the Saints Go Marching In M

SIDNEY BECHET with BOB WILBER and HIS JAZZ BAND (all Bechet compositions): personel as above.   June 9, 1949
NY-93C   I'm Through, Goodbye MO CL/31 M MO Riv vinyl
NY-94B Love Me With a Feeling (Bechet V) M MO Riv tape 139 A
NY-95B   Waste No Tears M MO RIV 139 vinyl pressing
NY-96E   Box Car Shorty (Duke of Iron v) M MO
NY-97F   The Broken Windmill M MO Riv 139 vinyl pressing
NY-98A   Without a Home (Bechet, Wilber cl) MO RIV 139 vinyl

MUGGSY SPANIER and The All Star Stompers (This is Jazz 1947):
Spanier cnt; Nicholas cl; George Brunies trom; Barker gui; Foster bs and Cy St. Clair bs and tuba; Luckey Roberts, Joe Sullivan or Charlie Queener p. 1947
NY-99   A Good Man Is Hard To Find (Brunies v) (Roberts, St. Clair) CL/57x M MO
NY-100   Eccentric (Foster, Sullivan) CL/57Z M MO
NY-101   Bugle Call Rag (Foster, Sullivan) Cl/58x M MO
NY-102   Tin Roof Blues (Brunies, v) (Roberts, St. Clair) CL/58x "
NY-103   Muskrat Ramble (Roberts, St. Clair) CL/57x M MO
NY-104   Jada (Foster, Queener) CL-58x M MO
NY-105   Panama CL/58x M MO
NY-106   Lonesome Road (Foster, Sullivan) CL/57x M MO
NY-107   That's a Plenty (Bechet added) CL/57 (track 1) M MO

CONRAD JANIS and HIS TAILGATE JAZZ BAND: R.C.H. Smith tpt; Tom Sharpsteen cl; Conrad Janis trom; Danny Barker gui; Foster bs; Freddie Moore dms; Bob Greene p. November 24, 1950
NY-108   Tiger Rag CL/11 M
NY-109   Yellow Dog Blues CL/11 M
NY-110   Bugle Boy March CL/12 M
NY-111   Kansas City Stomps CL/11 M
NY-112   Gettysburg March CL/12M
NY-113   1919 March CL/12 M
NY-114   Original Dixieland One-Step CL/12 M
NY-115   Oriental Man (Moore washboard) CL/12 M

JAMMING AT RUDI'S NO. 1: Smith, Janis, Sharpsteen, Barker, Foster, Moore, plus Bob Wilber ten sax; Eubie Blake and Ralph Sutton p. (see also NY-173/174, same date) January 7, 1951 (see also

NY-241/242)
*NY-116   Panama (4:36) CI tape
*NY-117   Weary Blues (4:32) CI tape
*NY-118   Maryland My Maryland (3:29) CI tape
NY-119   See See Rider (6:22) CI tape Riv tape 12-215 A
NY-120   High Society (6 min +) CI tape Riv tape 12-215 A
NY-121   That's a Plenty (6 min +) CI tape Riv tape 12-215 B

JAMMING AT RUDI'S NO. 2: Oran Lips Page tpt; Paul
Quinichette ten sax; Bernie Peacock alto sax; Tyree Glenn trom;
Barker gui; Ken Kersey and Dan Burley p; Sonny Greer dms.
February 10, 1951
*NY-122   Blues No. 1 CI tape
*NY-123   Blues No. 2 CI tape
*NY-124   Dan Carter Blues CI tape
NY-125   Skiffle Jam CL/49 M MO
NY-126   Moanin' Dan (Lips Page v) CL/49 M MO
NY-127   Sweet Sue CL/50 M MO
NY-128   Kersey's Boogie (Kersey p w/ rhythm) CL/50 M MO
NY-129   I Got the Upper Hand (Lips Page v) M
NY-130   Sunny Jungle (featuring Greer) CL/50 M MO
NY-131   Main Street (Lips Page v) M

FATS WALLER, p and v [from another source]
NY-132   You Can't Have Your Cake and Eat It MO
NY-133   Not There, Right There M

CONRAD JANIS and HIS TAILGATE JAZZ BAND: Smith tpt;
Sharpsteen cl; Janis trom; Moore dms; Barker bjo; E. Snoebel p.
(Recorded at Rudi Blesh apartment) May 8, 1951
NY-134   Willie the Weeper (3:18) MO RIV tape 12-215 B
NY-135   Eh La Bas! (Barker v) (3:34) RIV tape 12-215 B
NY-136   When You and I Were Young Maggie (2:48) MO RIV
                                              tape 12-215 B
NY-137   Down By the Riverside (Moore v) (3:00) MO
*NY-138   Blue Bells Goodbye (4;54) CI tape #1
*NY-139   Weary Way Blues (6:09) CI tape #1
*NY-140   Just a Closer Walk With Thee CI (3:06) tape #2
*NY-141   Creole Belles ((4;27) CI tape #2
*NY-142   Maryland, My Maryland (2:31) CI tape #3
*NY-142B   "   "   "   (2:34)   "
*NY-143   Alabamy Bound (P and Rhythm) (2:07) CI tape #3
*NY-143B   "   "   " "   "   (2:39)   "

*NY-144 Danny's Banjo Blues (Barker bjo solo) (4:41) CI tape #4
*NY-145 Mahogany Hall Stomp (3:03) CI tape #4
*NY-146 Over In Gloryland (3:59) CI tape #4
*NY-147 Ain't Gonna Give Nobody Any Of This Jelly Roll lost?
*NY-148 Snag it lost?
*NY-149 Sobbing Blues (4:43) CI tape #6
*NY-150 When You Gonna Pop the Question? (3:51) CI tape #6

MARY LOU WILLIAMS p with Skippy Williams bass cl; Billy
Taylor bs; de la Guerra bongoes; Al Walker dms; and Dave
Lambert and His Friends, v. June 15, 1951 add: The Great
Macbeth v, #
NY-151B Walking MO
NY-152B De Function # tape
NY-153C Cloudy tape
NY-154B I Won't Let It Bother Me tape

MARY LOU WILLIAMS p with Al Walker dms; Billy Taylor bs;
Sabu bongoes; June, 1951
NY-155A The Sheik of Araby M MO
Willie Correa in for Sabu June 11, 1951:
NY-156C When Dreams Come True CL/53-1 M MO
NY-157C Bobo CL/53-1 M MO
NY-158C Kool CL/53-1 M MO
NY-159E Lover Come Back To Me CL/54-1 M MO
NY-160 'Sposin CL/54-1 M MO
NY-161B Handy Eyes (St. Louis Blues) CL/53 M MO
NY-162B Tisherome CL/54-1 M MO

COLEMAN HAWKINS, ten sax solos with orchestra
[from another source]
NY-163 The Men I Love
NY-164 It's the Talk Of the Town

Probably MARY LOU WILLIAMS, to be identified:
*NY-165
*NY-166

MARY LOU WILLIAMS p with rhythm: 1951 or 1952
*NY-167 Lonely Moments M MO
NY-168 Unidentified missing

HUGH PORTER and DOCTOR COOK gospel singers with p and
organ 4/18/52

NY-169C   I Promised the Lord (2:30) M MO
*NY-170B   God's Amazing Grace (3:32) missing
NY-171B   Briny Tears (2:45) M MO
NY-172B   This Same Jesus missing

JAMMING AT RUDI'S NO. 1, additional master January 7, 1951
NY-173   When the Saints Go Marching In (Moore v) (6:35)
NY-174   (continuous performance) M MO RIV tape 12-215 A

RALPH SUTTON with George Wettling dms.   June 11, 1952
NY-175C   A Flat Dream CI CL/63 RIV tape 12-212 B Track 1
NY-176B   African Ripples CL/63 RIV tape 12-212 A
NY-177C   Drop Me Off In Harlem CL/64 M RIV tape 12-212 B
*NY-178   Lulu's Back in Town CI tape
NY-179   Fascination CL/63 RIB tape 12-212 A track 5
*NY-180   Ballin' the Jack CI tape
NY-181   Love Me Or Leave Me CL/64 M RIV tape 12-212 B
NY-182   I'm Coming Virginia CL/63 RIV tape 12-212 B
NY-183   Sugar Rose CL/64 M RIV tape 12-212 B
NY-184C   Bee's Knees CL/64 M   "   (this take 6/12/52)

ALL STAR STOMPERS WITH WILD BILL DAVISON (This is
Jazz 1947): Davison tpt; Archey trom; Nicholas and Ed Hall cl;
Barker gtr; Foster bs; Dodds dms; J.P. Johnson and Sutton p.
NY-185   Trombone Preaching Blues (Nicholas, Johnson) RIV
                                                tape 2514 A
NY-186   Skeleton Jungle (Hall, Sutton) RIV tape 2514 A

SIDNEY BECHET with THE ALL STAR STOMPERS (This is Jazz
1947): with Wild Bill Davison % or Spanier # tpt; Nicholas or Hall
cl; Brunies or Archey trom; Barker gui; Foster bs; Dodds or Moore
dms; Joe Sullivan or James P. Johnson or Ralph Sutton p.
NY-187 Wild Cat Blues (Bechet and James P. Johnson) (1:57)
                                                RIV tape 149 A
NY-188 Sugar (4:20) % (Archey, Nicholas, Sullivan) RIV tape 149
A
NY-189 Love For Sale (3:18) % (Archey, Nicholas, Sullivan)   "
NY-190 St. Louis Blues (2:43) % (Archey, Hall, Sutton)   "
NY-191 Sweet Lorraine (4:03) % (Archey, Hall, Sutton)   "
NY-192 Black and Blue (4:02) # (Brunies, Nicholas, Johnson) "
NY-193 Dear Old Southland (3:47) % (Archey, Nicholas,
Sullivan) "
NY-194 Charleston (3:46) # (Brunies, Nicholas, Johnson)   "
NY-195 Sensation (3:12) # (Brunies, Nicholas, Johnson)   "

NY-196   Ain't Misbehavin' (1:42) % (Brunies, Nicholas, Johnson)
"

NY-197   Blue Turning Grey Over You (3:24) %   "
"

NY-198   Summertime (2:51) # (Brunies, Nicholas, Johnson)
"

JAMES P. JOHNSON p solos 1947 (This is Jazz)
*NY-199 Capice Rag   Queens College tape
*NY-200 Carolina Shout Queens College tape

DONALD LAMBERT p with Howard Kadison dms. March 1, 1961
*NY-201 Continuous performance: a: If You've Never Been
Vamped By a Brownskin You've Never Been Vamped At All; b:
Tea For Two; c. Sunday (total 6:40)   CI tape
*NY-202 Continuous performance: a Hallelujah; b. Carolina
Shout; c. I Know That You Know c. Sleepy Lagoon f. Autumn
        Leaves (total 12:22)   CI tape
*NY-203   Moolight Sonata (3:35)   CI tape
*NY-204 Tea For Two (4:25)   CI tape
*NY-205 The Lady's In Love With You CI tape
*NY-206 Gate You're Bringing Me Down(Lambert) (4:33) CI tape
*NY-207 Handful of Keys (Waller) (2:16)   CI tape
NY-208   Liza (4:00) LP SA/502 M MO   CI tape
*NY-209   How Can You Face Me (Waller) (3:04)   CI tape
*NY-210   Golden Wedding (3:38)   CI tape
*NY-211 I'm Just Wild About Harry (Eubie Blake) (3:01) CI tape
NY-212   When Your Lover Has Gone (3:50) LP SA/502 M MO "
*NY-213   Hold Your Temper (The Lion) (2:44)   CI tape
*NY-214   Pork and Beans (Luckey Roberts) (2:50)   CI tape
NY-215   Continuous performance: a. Swinging Down the Lane;
b. My Sweetie Went Away (4:07) LP SA/502 M MO   CI tape
NY-216 People Will Say We're In Love (2:30) LP SA/502 M MO "
*NY-217A Overnight (1:39) faulty   CI tape
*NY-217B Overnight (2:56) issuable   CI tape
*NY-217C Overnight (3:36) issuable (perhaps cross edit
                        [w/NY 218])
NY-218   If I Could Be With You One Hour Tonight (2:55) LP
                        SA/ 501 M MO CI tape
*NY-219   Sweet Lorraine (2:34) faulty probably erased CI tape
*NY-220   Bells of St. Mary's (2:32)   CI tape
NY-221   I'm Putting All My Eggs In One Basket (3:03) LP SA/
                        501 M MO CI tape
NY-222   Trolley Song (2:45)   LP SA/ 501 M MO CI tape
NY-223   Misty (Erroll Garner) (2:16) LP SA/ 501 M MO CI tape

NY-224 Rose Of the Rio Grande (2:25) LP SA/ 501 M MO CI tape
NY-225   Sophisticated Lady (3:20)   LP SA/ 501 M MO CI tape
*NY-226 Anitra's Dance   CI tape
NY-227   There'll Never Be Another You (3:25) LP SA/ 501 M
                                        MO CI tape
*NY-228 Lullaby Of the Leaves   CI tape
NY-229   Spain (2:07)   LP SA/ 501 M MO CI tape
NY-230   Linger Awhile (2:45)   LP SA/ 501 M MO CI tape
*NY-231 If You've Never Been Vamped By a Brownskin You've
            Never Been Vamped At All (James P. Johnson) (3:16)
                            prob. better than NY-210 CI tape
*NY-232   Golden Wedding   CI tape

DONALD LAMBERT p solos -- earlier session   probably 1949
                            [from another source?]
*NY-233   Golden Earrings   CL/1 M MO
*NY-234   Overnight   CL/1 M MO
*NY-235   Blue Waltz (Valse Bluette)   CL/1 M MO
*NY-236   Harlem Strut (James P. Johnson) CL/1 M MO
*NY-237   Tea For Two   CL/1 M MO
*NY-238   Russian Lullaby (Irving Berlin)   CL/1 M MO
*NY-239   Rocking In Rhythm   CL/1 M MO
*NY-240   Liza   CL/1 M MO
EUBIE BLAKE p solos (see also NY-281/282)
From Jamming At Rudi's Session No. 1, January 7, 1951
*NY-241   Maryland, My Maryland   CI tape
NY-242   Maple Leaf Rag   CL27/28 M MO

EUBIE BLAKE p solos May 20, 1951 (see also NY-281/282)
*NY-243   Maryland, My Maryland   AC tape
*NY-244   Blake original to be identified   AC tape
*NY-245   Dicties On Parade   AC tape
*NY-246   Charleston Rag (1899) (take 2 has corrections AC tape
*NY-247   Troublesome Ivories (1914)   AC tape
*NY-248   identify   AC tape
*NY-249   Lovie Joe (w/ Blake v)   AC tape
*NY-250 Rufus Rastus Johnson Brown (w/ Blake v) AC tape
*NY-251   Mr. Johnson (Harney)   AC tape
*NY-252   The Dream (Jess Pickett)   AC tape
*NY-253   Sugar Babe   AC tape
*NY-254   Ida Sweet AS Apple Cider (w/ Blake v) AC tape
  no #   Add: I Wonder Who's Kissing Her Now

SIDNEY BECHET with Muggsy Spanier (This Is Jazz 1947):

NY-255   Baby Won't You Please Come Home (Brunies v)
(Foster,
          James P. Johnson)   CI tape RIV tape 12-138 A
NY-256   Blues Improvisation (w/ Nicholas) same personnel
                                CI tape RIV tape 12-138 A

SIDNEY BECHET with Wild Bill Davison (This Is Jazz 1947):
NY-257   Dardanella (Archey, Nicholas, Sutton) CI tape RIV
                                        pressing CL/29
NY-258   I Never Knew "   "   " RIV virgin press
12-138B

SIDNEY BECHET with Spanier; Nicholas; Foster; James P.
Johnson; Barker; Foster; Dodds (This is Jazz 1947)
*NY-259   I Know That You Know   CI AC tape
Bechet out; Luckey Roberts for Johnson; Cy St. Clair tuba for
                                                Foster:
*NY-260 Up a Lazy River   CI AC tape
Joe Sullivan in for Luckey; Soot Grant v:
*NY-261   Squeeze Me   CI AC tape
*NY-262   Sweet Lorraine (no v) (2:51)   CI AC tape
*NY-263 Love Is Just Around the Corner (no v) (3:43) CI AC tape
Bechet in, Art Hodes in for Joe Sullivan:
*NY-264   Farewell Blues   CI AC tape
Bechet with Davison, Bob Wilber (This Is Jazz 1947):
*NY-265   Polka Dot Stomp   CI AC
*NY-266   Kansas City Man Blues   CI AC
Wilber out:
*NY-267   Laura   CI AC

BERTHA CHIPPIE HILL with Davison, Brunies (This is Jazz
1947):
*NY-268   Don't Leave Me Daddy   CI AC

 MARY LOU AT MIDNIGHT: Mary Lou Williams, p solo; two
segments of continuous improvisation. 1951
*NY-269   Yesterdays   CL/55 M MO
*NY-270   It Ain't Necessarily So   CL/55 M MO
*NY-271   Why Evade the Truth?   CL/55 M MO
*NY-272   Mary's Waltz   CL/55 M MO
*NY-273   It's the Talk Of the Town CL/55 M MO
*NY-274   Stompin' At the Savoy   CL/55 M MO
*NY-275   Caravan   CL/55 M MO
*NY-276   Crazy Rhythm   CL/55 M MO

*NY-277   Scorpio   CL/55 M MO
*NY-278   The Man I Love   CL/55 M MO
*NY-279   People Will Say We're In Love   CL/55 M MO
*NY-280   For You   CL/55 M MO
Note: above tracks cannot be separated as the playing is
continuous.

EUBIE BLAKE p solos   November 27, 1949
*NY-281   Spanish Venus   RB/AC
*NY-282   The Dream   RB/AC

[next nine recordings penciled in:]

Parenti, Hodes:
*NY-283   12th St. Rag
*NY-284   Eccentric
*NY-285   Blues By Two

Bechet, (Buster Bailey?) Wilbur de Paris, Sutton, Ch. Teagarden,
Geo. Wettling:
*NY-286   I Found a New Baby
*NY-287   H.T Blues
*NY-288   Dear Old Southland

All Star Stompers - Davison, Archey, Hall, Sutton, Barker, Foster,
Dodds:
*NY-289   On the Sunny Side of the Street (2:40)
*NY-290   How Deep Is the Ocean (3:24)
*NY-291   Tiger Rag (4:35

HOCIEL THOMAS v and p; Mutt Carey tpt August 30, 1946
SF-1A   Gambler's Dream   AC M
SF-2   Muddy Water Blues   AC M MO
SF-3   Go Down Sunshine   MO
SF-4   Advice Blues   M MO
SF-5   Barrelhouse Man   MO
SF-6   Tebo's Texas Boogie (p solo) MO
*SF-6A   "   "   "   "   AC M
*SF-7   Nobody Knows You When You're Down and Out AC M

LU WATTERS YERBA BUENA JAZZ BAND: Watters, Scobey,
tpts; Helm cl; Murphy trom; Harry Mordecai bjo; Lammi bs and
tuba; Dart dms [also Wally Rose p]:   August 16,
1947

SF-8	Cakewalking Babies From Home	RIV tape 12-213 A
SF-9	Antigua Blues	RIV tape 12-213 A
SF-10	Beale Street Blues (Murphy v)	RIV tape 12-213 A
SF-11	Chattanooga Stomp	RIV tape 12-213 A
SF-12	Jazzin' Babies Blues	RIV tape 12-213 A
SF-13	Snake Rag	RIV tape 12-213 A
*SF-14	Pineapple Rag (Rose w/ rhythm	tape

PLAYER PIANO ROLLS: recorded in 1949 on a Pianola from original rolls. (The six issued were only on 78 rpm pre-1953)

SL-1   Maple Leaf Rag (Scott Joplin 1899; played by the composer)
SL-2   Sunflower Slow Drag (Joplin - Scott Hayden 1901)
SL-3   Weeping Willow Rag (Joplin 1903)
SL-4   Hilarity Rag (James Scott 1910)
SL-5   Excelsior Rag (Joseph Lamb 1909)
SL-6   Incandescent Rag (George Botaford 1913)
SL-6A   "   "   "   "   "
SL-7   Quality Rag (James Scott 1911)
(more rolls follow begin w/ SL-15)

CHARLES THOMPSON p solos 1949

*SL-8	Buffet Flat Rag (Thompson)	AC tape
*SL-9	Deep Lawton (Thompson)	AC tape
*SL-10	Hop Alley Dream (Thompson)	AC tape
*SL-11	Mound City Walk-Around (Thompson)	AC tape
*SL-12	Ragtime Hummingbird (Thompson)	AC tape
*SL-12A	" " " " "	
*SL-13	I'm Livin' Easy (Irving Jones)	AC tape
*SL-14	The Dream (Jess Pickett)	AC tape

PLAYER PIANO ROLLS, cont.

*SL-15	Oh! You Devil Rag (Ford Dabney 1909)	AC
*SL-16	Meancholy Mose (1907 public domain)	AC
*SL-17	Monkey Rag (Wheatley Davis 1911)	AC
*SL-18	The Thriller (May Aufderheide 1909)	AC
*SL-19	The Bowery Buck (Tom Turpin 1899)	AC
*SL-19A	" " " " " " "	
*SL-20	St. Louis Tickle (Barney and Seymore 1904-05)	AC
*SL-21	Red Pepper -- Spicy Rag (Henry Lodge 1910)	AC
*SL-22	Wild Cherries--Characteristique Rag (Ted Snyder) AC	
*SL-23	Apple Jack (Some Rag) (Charles L. Johnson)	AC
*SL-23A	" " " " " " "	

*SL-24   Ragtime Engineer (Clay Smith 1912)   AC
*SL-25   Creole Belles--March Two-Step (J. Bodewalt Lampe
                                                                  1900) AC
*SL-26   That Rag! (Browne unknown date)   AC
*SL-27   Dixie Belle (Percy Wenrich)   AC
*SL-28   Ma Ragtime Baby (Fred S. Stone 1898)   AC
*SL-29   Rambling Mose (John F. Barth 1903)   AC
*SL-30   Original Rags (Scott Joplin 1899)   AC
*SL-30A   "   "   "   "   "   "
*SL-31   Magnetic Rag (Scott Joplin 1914)   AC
*SL-32   Jackass Blues (played by Teddy Weatherford)   AC
*SL-33   Jazz 'Em Up Tune (played by Paul Jones)   AC
*SL-34   Gladiolus Rag (Scott Joplin 1907)   AC
*SL-34A   "   "   "   "   "   "
*SL-35   Charleston (Composed and played by James P.
                                                  Johnson 1923) AC
*SL-36   At a Georgia Camp Meeting (Kerry Milles 1897) AC
*SL-37   Midnight Mama (composed and played by Jelly Roll
                                                        Morton) AC
*SL-38   Black Bottom   AC

KID ORY'S CREOLE JAZZ BAND: Andrew Blakeney tpt; ory
trom; Joe Darensbourg cl; Bud Scott gui and v; Ed Garland bs;
Buster Wilson p; Minor Ram Hall dms. (This is Jazz from
Hollywood)
August 9, 1947:
LA-1   Snag It (Scott v)   M MO RIV tape 12-119
LA-2   Savoy Blues   M MO RIV tape 12-119
LA-3   Down Among the Sheltering Palms M MO RIV tape 12-119
LA-4   Weary Blues   M MO RIV tape 12-119

BERTHA CHIPPIE HILL v, with Lee Collins tpt; John Lindsay bs;
Baby Dodds dms; Lovie Austin # and J.H. Shayne % pno. Feb.
1946:
C-1A   Trouble In Mind # AC MO RIV tape 1059
C-2A   Careless Love # AC MO RIV tape 1059
C-3A   Mr. Freddy's Rag (Shane p solo) % AC MO RIV tape 1059
C-4A   Charleston Blues % AC MO RIV tape 1059
C-5   How Long How Long % AC MO
C-6   Chestnut Street Boogie (Shayne p solo) AC M MO
C-7   Steady Roll (Around the Clock) % AC MO RIV tape 12-113 A
*C-8   Nobody Knows You When You're Down and Out # M MO
                                                        RIV tape 1059

CHIPPIE HILL, MONTANA TAYLOR (p on all) w Almond
Leonard washboard #   April 17, 1946
C-9   Worried Jailhouse Blues, Chippie # M MO RIV pulled
                                                tape/=1059
C-10   Black Market Blues # (covered)
*C-11B Lowdown Bugle (Montana Taylor p solo) M RIV tape RLP
                                                152A
C-11C   "   "   "   "   "   "   "   "   "   "
*C-12   Toot Your Whistle and Blow Your Horn (Taylor solo) M
C-13   Mistreatin' Mr. Dupre   Chippie # M MO RIV pulled
                                                tape=1059
*C-14   See Ulysses Thomas, seq
*C-15   "   "   "   "
C-16   Sweet Sue # M M MO
C-17   In the Bottom M RIV tape RLP 152 A
C-18   Rotten Break (Montana p and v) (covered) RIV tape
                                                RLP 152 A
C-19   I Can't Sleep   "   "   "   "   M RIV tape 152 A
*C-19B   "   "   "   "   "   "   "   AC

ULYSSES THOMAS, p solos, April 18, 1946
*C-14   Blues   AC
*C-15   Blues   AC
*C-20   Slow Blues   AC
*C-21   Fast Blues   AC
*C-22   Don't Keep All the Candy AC
*C-22A   "   "   "   "   "   AC
*C-23   Evening Road AC
*C-24   Fast Blues   AC

COW COW DAVENPORT and PEGGY MONTEZ v, with Montana
Taylor p, 4/18/46:
*C-25   Hang Crepe On My Door   AC
*C-26   Patrol Wagon Blues   AC
*C-27   Rabbit Blues   not located
*C-28   Come Home Blues AC
*C-29   Casey Jones Blues (Montez out) AC
*C-30   One More Gal For Me not located

MONTANA TAYLOR, p and v   April 19, 1946
*C-31   Montana's Fives   MO
*C-32   Memphis Four O'Clocks M
C-33   'Fo' Day Blues M MO
*C-34   Detroit Rocks   M

C-35   Indiana Avenue Stomp M MO RIV tape RLP 152 A
C-36   Montana's Blues (with v)   RIV tape RLP 152 A
*C-37   Rag Alley Drag   M

ORIGINAL ZENITH BRASS BAND: Avery Kid Howard, Peter
Bocage tpts; J. Robinson trom; Geo. Lewis cl; Isidore Barbarin
alto horn; Harrison Barnes baritone horn; Joe Howard tuba; L.
Marrero bs dm; Baby Dodds snare dms. February 26, 1946:
NO-1   Fidgety Feet AC AC AC M MO RIV tape 12-283 A vinyl
NO-2   Shake It And Break It AC AC AC M MO RIV tape 12-283 A
                                                            vinyl
NO-2A   "   "   "   "   " AC AC AC M
NO-3   Bugle Boy March AC AC AC M MO RIV tape 12-283 A
vinyl
NO-4   Salutation March AC
NO-4A   Salutation March AC AC AC M MO RIV tape 12-283 A
vinyl
NO-5   If I Ever Cease To Love (w/ Little Brown Jug) M M
NO-5A " "   "   "   "   "   "   "   "   " AC AC M M
                                                MO MO RIV 12-283
NO-6   'Taint't Nobody's Biz-ness If I Do AC AC M M MO MO
                                                RIV 12-283 A

ECLIPSE ALLEY FIVE: Lewis, Robinson, Marrero, Pavageau,
Dodds
GOSPEL FIVE: same personnel, w/ Berenice Phillips and Harold
Lewis # February 27, 1946:
NO-7A   I Couldn't Hear Nobody Pray # M MO MO RIV tape
                                                12-282 A
NO-8   Bill Bailey (Harold Lewis v) M MO MO RIV tape " "
NO-9   Royal Telephone # (Phillips, Lewis v) " " " " "   " "
NO-10   Far Away Blues M MO
*NO-11   Wade in the Water # (Phillips v) M
NO-12   I Just Can't Keep It To Myself Alone # (Lewis V) M MO
                                                MO RIV tape 12-283 B
NO-13   God Leads HIs Dear Children Along # (Phillips, Lewis v)
                                                M MO RIV tape 12-283 B
NO-14   Bucket's Got a Hole In It 78 CI shellac coverage
*NO-15   Angel's Got Two Wings # (Lewis v) M
NO-16   The Girls All Love the Way I Drive 78 CI shellac

BASIN STREET SIX: Bunny Franks dms; George Girard tpt; Pete
Fountain cl; Joe Rotis trom; Roy Zimmerman p; Charlie Duke bs.
August 28, 1950 # and November 30, 1950 %:

NO-17   Margie # M MO
NO-18   Farewell Blues # M MO
NO-19   That's a Plenty (Fountain ten sax) % M
NO-20   Up a Lazy River & M
NO-21   Jazz Me Blues # M
NO-22   I Am Going Home # M
NO-23   High Society % Virgin vinyl pressing
NO-24   South Rampart Street Parade % Virgin vinyl pressing
Notes: Above are the first records ever made of Fountain and the
late George Girard. There are two more Basin Street Six masters,
see NO-72/73 seq

PAUL BARBARIN and HIS NEW ORLEANS BAND: Ernie
Cagnolatti tpt; Albert Burbank cl; Edward Pierson trom; Richard
McLean bs; Lester Santiago p; Paul Barbarin dms. January 23,
1951 Add Johnny St. Cyr gui; May 8, 1951 #
NO-25   Eh La Bas! (Burbank v) # M MO tape CL 45/46 MO RIV
                                          tape 12-217 A
NO-26   Lily of the Valley # M CL/45/46 MO
NO-27   Walk Through the Streets of the City # M MO CL/45/46
                                          RIV tape 12-217 A
NO-28   Just a Closer Walk With Thee # M MO CL/45/46 MO
                                          RIV 12-217 A
NO-29   Panama MO CL/45/46 MO RIV tape 12-217 A
NO-30   Just a Little While To Stay Here MO CL/45/46 MO RIV
                                          12-217 A
NO-31   Clarinet Marmalade MO CL/45/46 MO RIV tape 12-217 A
NO-32   Fidgety Feet MO CL/45/46 MO RIV tape 12-217 A

ARMAND HUG p solos June 24, 1951 # and July 16, 1951
*NO-33A Cannonball Rag   CL/51 MO tape
NO-33B   "   "
*NO-34A Baby Won't You Please Come Home # CL/51 MO tape
NO-34B   "   "   "   "   "   "
*NO-35A Mr. Jelly Lord # tape
NO-35B   "   "   "   CL/52 MO
*NO-36A Blues For Paul # tape
NO-36B   "   "   "   CL 51 MO
*NO-37A Heliotrope Bouquet tape
NO-37B   "   "   CL/52 MO
*NO-38A   Eye Opener tape
 NO-38B   "   "   CL/52 MO
*NO-39A How I MIss You tape
NO-39B   How I Miss You CL/52 MO

*NO-40A   Milneberg Joys   tape
NO-40B   "   "   CL/51 MO

GEORGE LEWIS and HIS NEW ORLEANS ALL STARS: Henry
Red Allen tpt; Lewis cl; Jim Robinson trom; L. Marrero bjo; Slow
Drag Pavageau bs; L. Santiago p; Paul Barbarin dms. Probably
Aug 18, 1951:
*NO-41   Darktown Strutters Ball tape
*NO-41A   "   "   " tape
*NO-42   Hindustan   tape
*NO-42A   "   tape
*NO-43   St. James Infirmary (Allen V) tape
*NO-43A   "   "   "   "   " tape
NO-43B   "   "   "   "   " tape
*NO-44   After You're Gone   tape

GEORGE LEWIS and HIS NEW ORLEANS ALL STARS: same as
above except Alvin Alcorn in for REd Allen and Bill Matthew in
for Robinson. Probably August 19, 1951:
NO-45   Bill Bailey CL/60 M MO CI tape RIV tape 12-207 A
*NO-45A   "   "
NO-46   Dippermouth Blues CL/59 M MO RIV tape 12-207 A
NO-47   Tin Roof Blues CL/59 M MO RIV tape 12-207 A
NO-48   Long Way To Tipperary RIV tape 12-207 A
*NO-49   Bugle Call Rag   CL/60 M MO RIV tape 12-207
NO-49A   "   "   "   CI tape

GEORGE LEWIS and HIS NEW ORLEANS ALL STARS: same as
Aug. 19, above August 20, 1951:
*NO-50   Big Butter and Egg Man   CI tape
NO-50A   "   "   "   "   "   CL/59 M MO
*NO-51   Bourbon Street Parade CI tape
NO-51A   "   "   "   CL/59 M MO
*NO-52   Over the Waves (Sobre las Olas) CI tape
*NO-52A   "   "   "   "   "   CI tape
*NO-53   Who's Sorry Now CI tape
*NO-53A   "   "   "   CI tape
NO-54   Weary Blues CL/60 M MO RIV tape 12-207 A

SHARKEY and HIS KINGS OF DIXIELAND: Sharkey Bonano tpt;
Harry Shields cl; Julian Laine trom; Monk Hazel dms,
mellophone#; Chink Martin tuba, bs; Stanley Mendelson p.
October 26, 1951:
NO-55   Alice Blue Gown M (issued on 78 rpm only) MO

NO-56   Peculiar Rag RIV tape 12-217 B
*NO-57   Clarinet Marmalade orig CI tape
*NO-58   The World Is Waiting For the Sunrise orig CI tape
NO-59   She's Crying For Me RIV tape 12-217 B
NO-60   Missouri Waltz M MO RIV tape 12-217 B
NO-61   Land O' Dreams RIV tape 12-217 B
NO-62   Back Home in Indiana M MO RIV tape 12-217 B
Armand Hug in for Mendelson, same date:
NO-63   I Like Bananas Because They Have No Bones
                    (Sharkey v) (issued on 78 rpm only MO
NO-64   Sweet Georgia Brown M MO
NO-65   Put On Your Old Grey Bonnet to be located
NO-66   My Blue Heaven to be located

LIZZIE MILES v, with HER NEW ORLEANS BOYS: Fred
Neumann p; Joe Loyocano bs; Frank Federico gui. January 16,
1953 private issue on 78 rpm pre-1953 only:
NO-67   Careless Love   M
NO-68   I Cried For You   M MO
NO-69   Basin Street Blues (in English) M MO
NO-70   Basin Street Blues (in Creole patois) M MO
NO-71   Ace In The Hole M MO

BASIN STREET SIX, personnel as on NO-17/24, above:
*NO-72   Mahongany Hall Stomp AC
*NO-73   The World Is Waiting For the Sunrise AC

SOLO ART MASTERS, all 1938-39, New York and Chicago:

PETE JOHNSON, p solos:
R-121   Shuffle Boogie   M RIV pressing 1054
R-122   Lone Star Blues   RIV tape 12-114 A (CI MO)
*R-123   Untitled SA M CI MO
*R-124   Untitled SA M CI MO
R-125   B&O Blues CI MO RIV tape 12-106 B
R-126   How Long How Long CI M MO RIV pressing 1054
R-127   Climbing and Screaming CI M MO RIV tape 12-106 B
R-128   Buss Robinson Blues CI MO RIV pressing 1054
R-129   Pete's Blues No. 1 CI MO RIV pressing 1054
R-130   Let 'Em Jump CI MO RIV tape 12-106 B
R-3360   Pete's Blues #2 CI MO RIV tape 12-106 B
(for masters 3361/3362 see Lofton seq)

ALBERT AMMONS, p solos:

284

R-2090   St. Louis Blues M MO RIV tape 12-106 A
R-2091   Mecca Flat Blues M MO RIV tape 12-106 A
R-2092   Bass Goin' Crazy M MO RIV tape 12-106 A
R-2093   Monday Struggle M MO RIV tape 12-106 A
R-2094   Boogie Woogie CI M

MEADE LUX LEWIS, p solos:
R-2087   Messin' Around M MO RIV tape 12-106 A
R-2088   Deep Fives RIV tape 12-106 A
R-2089   Blues "De Lux" RIV tape 12-106 A
R-2095   Closin' Hour Blues RIV tape 12-106 A
R-2096   Far Ago Blues Pulled RIV tape from 12-114 A

JIMMY YANCEY, p solos:
R-2417   Jimmy's Stuff RIV tape 12-124 A
R-2417A   "   " take from original shellac
R-2418   The Fives CI M MO RIV tape 12-114 A
R-2419x   La Salle Street Breakdown RIV tape 12-124 B (CI AC)
R-2420x   Two O'Clock Blues RIV tape 12-124 B
R-2421x   Janie's Joys (CI AC) RIV tape 12-124 B
R-2422x   Lean Bacon (CI AC) RIV tape 12-124 B
R-2423x   Big Bear Train (CI AC) RIV tape 12-124 B
R-2424x   Lucile's Lament (CI AC) RIV tape 12-124 B
R-2425x   Beezum Blues (CI AC) RIV virgin pressing
R-2426x   Yancey Limited (CI AC) RIV virgin pressing
R-2427x   Rolling the Stone (CI AC) RIV tape 12-124 A
R-2428x   Steady Rock (CI AC) RIV tape 12-124 A
R-2428x   P.L.K. Special (CI AC) RIV tape 12-124 A
R-2428x   South Side Stuff (CI AC) RIV tape 12-124 A
R-2428x   Yancey's Getaway (CI AC) RIV tape 12-124 A
R-2432x   How Long No. 1 (CI AC) RIV tape RLP 1061
R-2433x   How Long No. 2 (CI AC) RIV tape RLP 1061

CRIPPLE CLARENCE LOFTON p solos:
On 78 r.p.m. only: (pre-1953)
R-2771   Had a Dream   M MO
R-2772   Streamline Train   M MO
R-3361   I Don't Know MO
R-3362   Pine Top's Boogie Woogie MO

R-2773x   More Motion CI AC RIV tape 1037
R-2774x   Sweet Tooth CI AC RIV tapes 1037 and 152
R-2775x   Sixes and Sevens CI AC RIV tapes 1037 and 152
R-2776x   Clarence's Blues CI AC RIV tapes 1037 and 152

R-2777x   Lofty Blues CI AC RIV tapes 1037 and 152
R-2778x   House Rent Struggle CI AC RIV tapes 1037 and 152
R-2779x   Juice Joint CI AC RIV tapes 1037 and 152
R-2780x   Salty Woman Blues CI AC RIV tape 1037
R-2781x   Blue Boogie CI AC RIV tape 12-114

ART HODES p solos:
R-2197   Rose Tavern Boogie (CI MO) (78 rpm issue only)
R-2198   South Side Shuffle RIV tape 12-114 A
R-2199   "   "   "   (CI M MO) 78 rpm issue only

The following unidentified masters are presumed to be unissued
Solo Art originals:
*R-9501   Unidentified and untitled   M
*R-9502   Unidentified and untitled   M
*R-9503   Unidentified and untitled   M
*R-9504   Unidentified and untitled   M

(end of Circle/Solo Art masters list)

notes:

This appears to be a recreated Circle Masters list put together by
Rudi, probably at least partly from memory, in 1964 when he was
dealing with the collapse of Riverside, the original Circle masters
list having been part of that Circle Records lot and presumably
lost. It's interesting how sections of earlier sessions crop up with
later numbers, as if to say: here's something I forgot.

Missing seem to be numbers for the Gospel recordings I know my
grandfather made in New York (except for NY 169/172). I
attended a couple of services with Rudi at the Abyssinian Baptist
Church in Harlem in the 1960s (to hear the music of course) and
he described some of that. He told me that in the early 1960s he
and Hansi had intended to create a label just for Gospel
recordings. More research (as always) still needed.

Although I did get to listen to a safety tape of the 1961 Lambert
session (unissued material - simply wonderful), I never saw any
evidence of the 1949 recordings Rudi describes. Perhaps these
were masters Donald Lambert did for another producer, acquired
by Circle at some point from the artist himself.

One more note on Donald Lambert: Rudi told me the inclusion of drummer Howard Kaddison at the 1961 sessions had been the pianist's idea, as Rudi said: "to get one of his friends a paying gig". I know I read some criticism of my grandfather somewhere for this additional rhythm element. Why would one of the greatest, perhaps the greatest Stride pianist of all time need any help keeping time? Perhaps Rudi was mindful of that gripe and was planting his defense in talking to me. Having grown up loving the Solo Art LP that came out of those sessions, obviously I'm not an impartial critic. Still I have to say that from my point of view, the addition of the Jazz drummer Kaddison working out with the brushes makes these breakneck/bravura recordings absolutely breathtaking. When Lambert gets going, it's intense. Personally, I've never heard anyone play so fast, with so many notes on so many levels--and with so much space and swing, not even Art Tatum. But that's just my own humble opinion.

Also interesting to see Dan Burley return to recording for Circle in 1951, actually in the apartment on 38 East 4th (Jamming At Rudi's). Even more fascinating how they returned to the Skiffle idea, this time even more explicitely (Skiffle Jam - the 1946 recordings had just been Dan Burley and His Skiffle Boys). Seems sales in England may have indicated a return to the theme. If Rudi had only known. Maybe it was the Skiffle session I broke up with my one year old vocalisations. Trying to get in on it early I might be tempted to say.

Appendix #5

Principles/Initiatives of the New York Greens (1987 edition)

Introduction:

The New York Greens have undergone successive transformations since we had our original meetings in 1984. It is our feeling that the changes in personel or "rotations" were mostly the result of our continuing desire to remain independent and avoid domination by any existing organization or group. We continue to be a potent local ecological force, an effective cooperative alternative based on mutual trust rather than rigid hierarchy.

Last years original initiatives papter represented a rather utopian agenda, a proposal to advance the causes of recycling, bicycling, feminism for women and men, liberations struggles local and global, squat homesteading, urban ecological gardening and a nuclear free future for NYC. These projects, or initiatives, came out of the inspiration we shared in discussing our six principles which had themselves been derived through consensus by the group-at-large. These principles or values we defined as: Ecology/Earth Ethic, Social Responsibility/Liberation, Grassroots Democracy/Consensus, Peace/Non-violence, Community Economics/Bio-Regionalism, and Supportive Human Relations/ Inclusive Feminism.

The Initiatives Groups which formed around the various issues were empowered by the group-at-large to excercise their creative energies to implement positive changes based on the values we had set forth. Each working group is expected to report on their activities at the monthly meetings. In this way groups acting in the name of the New York Greens are held accountable for their actions without being limited by the dreaded "central committee."

The consensus process compels us to discuss our differences and learn to recognise the ethic we hold in common. When all must basically agree there is no need to fall into winners/losers political power play strategies. Instead we learn to rely on trust. Consensus serves us well also as a means of implementing our basic process mechanism: rotation. All group functions (mailing, publications, treasury, outreach, regional and inter-regional representation) are subject to change of personel based on the

288

feelings and decisions of the group-at-large represented at the open monthly meeting.

The last initiatives paper began with the Ecology Committee's recycling and bicycling initiatives. It was in these efforts to ecologize the urban environment that we found our first success as New York Greens.

RECYCLING

The NY Greens continue to run the bulk of the operations for the Village Green Recycling Team at 4th Street and 6th Avenue. In the last two years, with our efforts, the VGRT has become the largest, and most successful independent non-commercial recycling operation in Manhattan. We have expanded the operations by taking in new materials (cardboard, magazines, consumer metals, batteries and plastics) and by creating new pick up locations in Soho, Chelsea and the Lower East Side. We have worked to get Community Board Support and a location on East 11th Street for a new larger recycling center to service all of lower Manhattan.

We last reported our intentions to support the city's curbside recycling program, set to begin in Community Board #2 (Greenwich Village) in mid-July. Little did we know what this would entail. The day before the program was to begin it was announced by the mayor's office that it was being cancelled indefinitely because the union refused to agree to a one-man (or woman?) truck run. Sensing intended saboutage, our reaction as Greens was to take the program over, organizing volunteer truck runs for 16 consecutive all-night Wednesday pick-ups in the district. To put pressure on the Department of Sanitation we testified at City Council hearings and talked with Ruth Messinger and the Controllers Office. By taking the initiative we were able to force the city to resume the program which they are now running successfully.

In addition to running the volunteer programs at the VGRT, Green energy has been able to provide part-time jobs doing recycling marketing with our truck coop. Through this small beginning (a few of us earning a modest living off the wastestream) we intend to eventually build a Greens jobs program - employment through ecological transformation.

As the Cooperative Recycling Council of NYC we have taken on the task of keeping New York's other voluntary recycling centers and independent agency programs going. This had involved making pick ups and trucking recyclables to market when the price per ton won't support private hauling.

Our educational work in the area of recycling has included slide and field trip programs for children as well as regular consultant work with the Department of Sanitation.

BICYCLING

In bicycling as in recycling we found we could be most effective by consolidating our energies within an existing organization. The New York Greens Bicycling Initiatives Group decided our best chance to be effective would by joining Transportation Alternatives, New York's only real bicycle/pedestrian interest group. At this time members of original Green group occupy the positions of President and Executive director of TA.

The revitalization of TA has brought new energy to the NYC cycling scene, long burdened with failure of bikelanes and a bike messenger / pedestrian safety crisis. The City Cyclist, TA's newsletter has begun to address the vital issues of road use, pedestrian safety and the appropriateness of high speed motor traffic in NYC.

In the meantime, as TA, we have started the difficult process of organizing the unruly independent NYC cyclist. In conjunction with the Independent Couriers Association we put on a demonstration at City Hall on behalf of bike messengers being harassed during the city's recent crackdown.

In another action we attended an anti-bicycling event sponsored by Pedestrians First. We were successful in getting across to the media and politicians present the message that cyclists who have some rights on the road are more likely to respect the rights of others. While we in no way condone dangerous riding, the characterization of all city cyclists as "killers" demanded a response. A similar message was presented by our group and broadcast on WINS in resoponse to the anti-cycling editorial they had aired.

As spokespeople for city cycling we have taken the opportunity to speak out on related issues at appropriate forums such as at the Mayorial hearings on pollution reduction in NYC where we testified effectively on the need to reduce motor vehicle traffic in the city.

Members of TA and the New York Greens also met as representatives from the NYC bicycling community in a November meeint with Ross Sandler - Commissioner of Transportation, members of his staff, Captain Campisi - head of traffic enforcement (and bike crackdowns) for Manhattan and various other city officials concerned with safe sewer grate procurement and other bicycle issues. During our discussion with the Department of Transportation we were able to suggest several so-called utopian solutions to the NYC traffic/pedestrian safety dilemma - 1. Slowing down the traffic lights to safe cycling speed (15 mph) - 2. Elimination of automobiles from sections of the city - 3. Bike safety education for cyclists, drivers and pedestrians instead of police repression.

At the present time the TA/NY Greeens Bike Initiatives Group iw working to promote a meaningful safety code among messengers and other city cyclists. We have secured financing from the DOT to construct a prototype of a neighborhood bicycle shelter and are looking for money to conduct an office building access and parking survey.

WOMENS/MENS GROUPS

Originally part of the Supportive Human Relations Green Group, the Women's and Men's groups now function as independent cooperative initiatives circles. The functions of the original SHR group are now incorporated into our supportive and rotational process and continue to be monitored by the women's/men's groups.

The Women's Group took on the household ecology issue as their first project. Using street theatre to educate they demonstrated against food irradiation in front of supermarkets dressed in oversized vegetable and fruit costumes. They printed the ecological tipsheet - "How To Make Less Garbage" on recycled paper with a hand driven mimeograph press. The Green Women are continuing their consumer education efforts, researching plastics for a future tipsheet and preparing a newsletter - "Green

Women Reports" which will concentrate on consumer issues, herbal healing and other issues. They also plan to initiate a sicker campaign designed to educate consumers on packaging materials.

Another extremely successful New York Green Women sponsored project was the Women in Politics forum presented in conjunction with the Learning Alliance in October. Speaking on women's role in political change were Ruth Messinger - New York City Councilwoman, Ynestra King - eco-feminist and Fran Farmer - president, Crossroads Africa. Representatives from this group, women leaders from Africa and the Caribbean were also in attendence, some listening and speaking through a French interpreter. The success of this event was that while it removed the illusions our so-called progressive society holds regarding women in America it reaffirmed the bond all women world-wide hold in common, the strength of their own brilliance.

The Green Women also plan to help organize a series of discussion workshops, open to all women, on Feminism and the Ecology Movement later in the Springtime.

The Green Men's Group, after having sponsored a series of conciousness raising meetings for men and planning a still awaited Men's Conference, did manage to pull off one event, a slide show and discussion focusing on women and art. The lively exchange of ideas and opinions on the subject of feminism, separatism and the role of men helped open up new avenues of communication and understanding for some of us.

LIBERATION

Efforts by the Liberation Green Group have been divided between supporting anti-apartheid, native rights and anti-interventionist groups/events and helping local liberation struggles: homelessness, exploitation and racism.

Green organized "War Chest Tours" to the NYC offices and outlets of US imperialist institutions (Selective Service, McDonalds, South African Airways, LaRouche, etc.)have opened these sources of dis-enlightenment to momentary public scrutiny. Greens have been involved with promoting and have participated in recent major demonstrations - Elinor Bumpers in the Village and the march at Howard Beach.

Other local liberation issues such as homelessness were covered in conjunction with the Habitat Green Group and are reported in the next section.

The Liberation Green Group has a long way to go in terms of reaching out to the dispossessed population with its message of social justice. Barriers of race, perception, age and class are all designed to keep us from organizing together. The Green effort will continue to promote and ecological/feminist alternative to the traditional power politics in the search for liberations.

HABITAT

Initially concerned with preventing the destruction of the Garden of Eden and the B 6 Garden, the Habitat Green Group soon expanded its focus to include local housing, homesteading and squatting issues.

A few weeks before the first initiatives paper was written, the 12 year old experimental ecological Earthwork known as the Garden of Eden was bulldozed by the city. The devastation of this peaceful place brought together the various creative energies of those who had enjoyed it. With support from the Greens, the Friends of the Garden of Eden have redoubled their efforts to keep the ecological spirit alive and recreate the Earthly place.

Although they have been claimed by groups as various as the junk sculptors on Rivington Street and even NYU itself, the purple footprints were actually laid down by an intrepid friend of the garden to lead to the Eldridge Street site. The circle of artists involved with preserving the spirit of the garden also created the animal/plant stencils which shared the sidewalk with the footprints. These all-species images bore witness to the other forms of life which also inhabit our island.

The Friends of the GOE have also sponsored a yearly Spring Equinox parade and/or ceremony at the garden site. Last year's event commemorated everyone's favorite species in a circle ritual and then set up the launching of a giant Earthworm ....into the ground! In January of this year, the Friends of the GOE staged a street theatre demonstration at city hall. In the human powered spirit of the garden the super-realistic bulldozer which plowed into the human garden in this reenactment was actually a bicycle covered with recycled cardboard and wood.

The ecological experiences shared by urban Earthfolk found expression in the themes and practices of this garden. Its circularity created an alternative concentric inclusivity to replace the masculist square-grid system we now experience. The garden's reliance on human power - muscles, bicycles, ingenuity - struck a deliberate counterpoint to modern mechanistic construction/destruction. Organic cultivation, the use of found materials and, most radical of all, the recycling of vegetarian human waste into soil all pointed to the possibility of a sustainable future for our kind.

Other Lower East Side community gardens have survived for now although it was learned recently that the Green Guerrilla Garden on the corner of Houston Street and the Bowery is listed as a "vacant lot" and is threatened with "development" by Cooper Square.

While gardens are being threatened and bulldozed in the name of housing, thousands of units lie empty, abandoned, warehoused, unimproved by a city deliberately running its housing stock down to force the poor out. Faced with an army of homeless souls, the Greens have responded by helping squat homesteads in the Lower East Side. We have publicized and participated in actions and programs initiated by the Valentine's Day Coalition, the Eviction Watch and the Coalition of the Homeless.

In the face of the incredible harassment from the city government - child welfare investigations, fire department break ins, police threats, water department shut-offs, urban homesteaders persevere. The New York Greens intend to continue to be part of their effort, the underlying principle being that no one should be denied the basic animal right to habitat (food, shelter, work and access to the Earth)

ANIMAL RIGHTS

Although no intitiatives were listed under this category the last time around, our group has always had strong inclinations in this direction.

Even though many of us are vegetarians and understand that such a diet could even end world hunger, we have not come out with a position or initiative to promote meatless eating as yet. This stems largely from our common feeling that it is a matter of personal choice and therefore not a particularly appropriate subject for political discussion.

The same could not be said for our feelings about fur coats and those who wear them. NYC is a mecca for these stone age fashion types so we have taken the opportunity this winter to engage them in creative dialogue. We are also working on street theatre to raise ecological conciousness on this subject. Using an all-species animal mask and a real fur coat we will reenact the life and death of one of our fellow creatures for the benefit of some of our other fellow creatures. Through simple peer pressure we hope to be part of the elimination of the concept that a dead animal coat is a high status object.

HEALTH AND HERBAL

The New York Greens have come out strongly in favor of proven, traditional herbal and homeopathic medicine and for an individual's right to treat her/himself accordingly. Greens mailings have included information on the dangerous radioactivity found in cigarettes, the connections between National Security Council gun running operations and our local crack (cocaine) epidemic, and a paper on AIDS and hard drugs.

Greens intitiatives in the area of health have included a mobile soup kitchen in the Lower East Side, pancake breakfasts and discussions on health and sanitation at waterless homesteads, two healers from the Rainbow Family living in residence for a few months and our efforts in helping to start a new Green Market on Mercer Street.

An additional idea, to start a cooperative breakfast and lunch club was superceded by the opening of new relatively low cost cafes in our locality.

NO NUKES

The No Nukes Green Group started out strong by presenting Dr. Ernest Sternglass as our guest speaker and subsequently publishing his theories on the connections between low level radiation, acid rain and immune system defects in a paper "Dr. Sternglass Talks With The New York Greens." Our next publication was the pamphlet " Chernobyl on the Hudson" which publicized the dangers and defects of the Indian Point nuclear reactors (actually closer to NYC than Chernobyl is to Kiev.)

In the meantime the group also participated in the Candlelight Vigil for a Nuclear Free Harbor in June. At this event we held a large "Freedom From Nuclear Madness" banner and handed out hundreds of "Nuclear Free Zone" posters we had manufactured to look like "no parking" signs.

The No Nukes group did tabling on behalf of their initiatives and for the Greens adding new support. As the year began we behan meeting twice a month in coalition with other local anti-nuclear groups to prepare for the Chernobyl on the Hudson Conference. This forum on the future of Indian Point was held at the Walden School in February. Speakers included Charlie Komanoff, Michio Kaku and Dr. Ernest Sternglass.

The No Nukes Green Group forsees a nuclear free future. We look forward to shutting down Indian Point, abandoning Shoreham, closing NY harbor to nuclear weaponry and learning to live better without them.

OUTREACH

It has been the perception of many that the New York Greens have not been adequately or accurately represented outside of the NY area. the reason for this is simply that we are almost all dyed-in-the-wool local activists preferring to pursue our local inititatives. Acting locally (while thinking globally) is considered a Green principleand those who try to skip that step by jumping up to regional and national leels may missing the whole point of what we're about.

None-the-less the New York Greens have participated in regional conferences in Philadelphia and Baltimore where workshops on Green concerns were given and a democratically derived "Programatic Concerns" paper was prepared. Because we believe in diversity we continure to support all other Green groups in our region. Recently we met with some of these other groups to set up regional representation to the Committees of Correspondence, a national Green clearinghouse.

296

We have also played host to several members of the German Greens and have presented a public discussion with Benny Haerlin, a publisher and Green elected official from Berlin.

DREAMS

Our plans for the future are utopian out of necessity. We dream because creating the alternative involves imagining it first. Our first initiatives paper, printed a year ago, reported on the work of our small community of ecological dreamers/planners. We amazed ourselves by managing to pull off almost all our plans, experiencing many constructive surprises along the way. All we can do now is redouble our dreaming and hope to imagine more ways to express and actualize the ecological ethic we know we all share.

The New York Greens intend to work hard to make 50-60% recycling a reality in our eco-system city. We intend to be as creative as we have to to make New York a pedestrian and cyclist city, liberated from the danger and pollution of the motoring madness. We would like to see grassroots consumer pressure rid the world, or at least our state, of excess plastic products and packaging. Green men and women want to do what it takes to fashion an alternative to traditional patriarchal process. We will outreach to schools and jobsites to find new supporters of the nuclear free future. We foresee a world/community where race, gender, age or sexual preference do not predetermine one's status in society. We'll continue to encourage homeless people to homestead abandoned buildings and stand up for their rights as human beings. We will someday set up a storefront to sell things directly from Third World cooperatives. Someday soon we really will have our men's conference and a children's conference as well, where concerned young people can set their own agenda for change. We see empty lots and rooftops turning into gardens growing food. We envision a world with clean water where humans do not feel the need to dominate and over-populate, leaving room to share with other forms of life. These are but a few of the dreams shared by the Greens. We hope you imagine things like these and will feel inspired to join us in their realization.

Principles or Values of the New York Greens:

Green values overlap. Green values are inter-related. Green values restate a common ethic from different points of view.

Green values are more like windows than pillars. Green values are universal. Green values are intensely personal. Green values are spiritual. Green values are r(apid)evolutionary. Green values are different for everybody.

Ecology/Earth/Earth Ethic - The science of balancing human activities to bring them into harmony with the Natural World. The wisdom that comes from Nature. A reverential attitude towards the planet and her processes. Stewardship. The seven generations. Borrowing the Earth from our children. Wholeness within the Earth household.

Social Responsibility/Liberation - A sincere committment to community. Solidarity with and support for all oppressed, exploited and dominated population groups, races and women. Thinking globally, acting locally. Confronting American militarism and imperialism. Essential activism.

Grassroots Democracy/Consensus - Political interaction where all voices are heard. The slow, sometimes painful but ultimately very solid process of building real agreement. The town meeting. Women (soft voices) speak; men (loud voices) listen. Deprograming needlessly competitive and hierarchical tendencies. Exploring the possibilities for organizing in circles rather than pyramids. Discovering the group genius in the spaces between the personalities.

Peace/Non-violence - An absence of violence in all situations. A constant effort towards peacefulness in politics. In inter-personal dealings and in our own mindspaces. Although the right to self defense is a personal choice, we reject pre-emptive definitions of such actions. Rejection of the glorification of armed struggle, even in struggles of liberation. Civil disobedience. Passive resistance. Satyagraha.

Community Economics/Bio-Regionalism - Decentralized, community controlled, ecologically responsible human economic enterprises. No more grandiose centralized masterplan solutions (capitalist, communist, socialist, etc.). The creation of locally based independence and awareness to take back control of essential economies from absentee stockholders, landlords, banks and bureaucrats. Not left, not right - forward! Empowerment.

298

<u>Supportive Human Relations/Inclusive Feminism</u> - An inter-
personal process which is cooperative. Men and women dealing
honestly with balanced contributions of both energies. Getting
beyond male dominant (patriarchal) behavior patterns. Specific
committments to women's minority, gay, children's, elder's and
handicapped rights. A new way of going about our group
business. A non-exclusive feminism with new male role models.

(sample of my 1980s eco-propaganda)

animal cemetery

after he shot the poor bird
w/ his brand new birthday 22
rudi buried that wretched rifle
the kid knew what he had to do

with his friends up on old boot hill
he fenced off a special reservation
and for every beloved deceased pet
their full funeral service consecration

mercy is mercy - that's what they say
rudi was right as usual against the grain
sometimes you can't have it any other way
animal rights - long before the campaign

at your disposal

the more I seek out mediocrity
the more life catches up w/ me
that attempt at pure simplicity
-all ways of trash and poetry

for your approval

program where you get to decide
what to show and what to hide
the best idea anybody has
turns into - this is jazz!

ragtime

held the place for an idea
took some time getting here
from the dreamers hear the call
black rhythms in the concert hall
a black professor wrote that song
the one we now love to sing along

yes but complete the ragtime story
take his music to the conservatory

78s

old mono recordings
black and white music
black and white people
they could never refuse it

the dancing and then praying
and then dancing some more
southern sharecropper revivals
from before the second world war

urban jazz babies - harlem pilgrims
hipflasks refilled at the old drugstore
unbroken shellac - still unscratched
forbidden but unforgotten - folklore

slapsticklers

speechless species
instantly inform us still
what it is in nature's will
at the juncture of the joke
(sight gag before we spoke)
where all come to see the show
in silent movies we used to know

through eden's gates

if I could only go
through eden's gates

(that's where I want to go)
(that's where I'm going to go)

I'm going to cakewalk right
through eden's gates

(know all there is to know)
(what the angels have to show)

you can join me high steppin'
through eden's gates

(but don't you walk too slow)
(or get caught there down below)

they say some people aren't allowed
through eden's gates

(don't you believe a word)
(that's sure not what I heard)

I'm going now
through eden's gates

(so for the good of all)
(rejoin the ragtime ball)

parading through eden's gates
through eden's gates

(for Bill Bolcom)

graceful ghost

so here comes that graceful ghost
she who's been imagined the most
ever radiant at the mixed race ball
now presented in the concert hall!

she who once worked here domestically
downstairs and upstairs until she was free
and then just disappeared so mysteriously
for years and years we never could see

but now she's back the graceful ghost
one once reknown from coast to coast
returned recycled and refurbished anew
scott free - but to the essence still true

she was once known as an octaroon
and gave readings based on the moon
then a courtesan or whatever they were
but could any of those - really be her?

here again haunting our graceful ghost
she always knew much more than most
a gentle genius from a mixed race mind
american ragtime - the best you will find

(for Bill Bolcom)

bert's blues

a hundred years ago he sang his last
ragtime humor soon a thing of the past
the original pre/post racial hipster dude
all round master of modernist attitude
blackface star of the ziegfeld follies
dispensed wit along with the jollies
see the negro (laugh) have no fear
stand up comedy starts right here

empty porches

oh those empty porches
in the summer heat when
the sun just scorches

a long time coming
a long time gone
empty porches
still hanging on

oh those empty porches
lost and lonely today
everyone searches

for some sweet place
out in the shade
empty porches
ready made

oh those empty porches
on rotten timbers with
a floor that lurches

a long time forgotten
in need of repair
empty porches
still sitting there

(for Donald Ashwander)

lost lady

well you told me this
so I said that
but we couldn't agree
so we left it flat
if you still loved me
we would have worked it out
but we didn't so we live in doubt

well you slammed the door
so I closed my eyes
looked out the window
when will I realize
that you don't love me
like you used to do
and I guess
I don't love you

lost lady and I
we pout and scream
when will we admit
we're living in a dream
who will be the first
to set the other free

my lost lady or me

(for Bill Bolcom)

the ragtime pest (song)

at being a bother
I'm the best

if I could catch
that ragtime dog
I'd take him off
behind the log

make him work
in the woodpile
for a while
until he lost
that stupid smile

did I intrude
or in some way molest

pleasant charming
and all the rest
nothing stops
the ragtime pest

nothing stops
the ragtime pest (2x)

another writ
we have to contest

I wish this guy
would give it a rest
captured and tortured
but never confessed

nothing stops
the ragtime pest (2x)

brass knuckles

you don't want me
to have to get out

the brass knuckles

after they're used
nobody chuckles

just a poor piano
so far out of tune

another promoter
paid way too soon

you don't want me
to have to get out

the brass knuckles

the jaw bone pops
the knee buckles

you say the money
there it was mislaid

so ragtime performers
will have to go unpaid

you don't want me
to have to get out

the brass knuckles

(for Bill Bolcom and William Albright)

sweet sixteenths

we never forget
our sweet sixteenths

if you know what I mean

those dresses of satin
on perfect prom queens
like some far off distant
golden thing that gleams

I mean just what I mean
drifting off into daydreams

not too far off in between
just a first secret sixteenth

still not every thing
was then as it seems
like strict curfews
and acne creams

just the ultra keenest
thing we've ever seen

that we'll never live down
somedays sweet sixteenth

(for William Albright)

the golden hours

yes those were golden hours
when we knocked down ivory towers
raised black jazzmen up to the sky
ragtime music now you know why

yes there now and then a complication
finding originators crisscrossing the nation
but somehow we managed to persevere
it was never hard when you were still here

if you ever have golden hours
press them like dried flowers
close to your heart and then
time to open that book again

yes those were our golden days
in so many memories in so many ways
working hard often day and night
just doing what we thought right

yes now and then a disagreement
worked out we knew what we meant
but still looking back now all I can see
these golden hours shining back at me

now those were the golden hours
only gifted from the higher powers
told the story straight and so it goes
what every ragtime composer knows

(for Max Morath and Harriet Janis)

news (2010)

we never used to watch the news
rudi would never have a stupid tv
folks who called to tell him he was on
got an earful of invective take it from me

the music he'd fought so hard to preserve
his faith in the power of words and the song
after he left - I fell into these dirty main streets
hauling newspapers to divide right from wrong

trying to herd the stray left footed cats
riding big city bicycles as few had done
into green gardener's circles understanding
still nothing new shaking under the sun

green in a movement - for a moment
news for a minute - and after a while
recalled the old slum goddess to the garden
faded back - as she suddenly lost her smile

in academia's odd basket case bower blunted
like grandfather - in the modern jazz crunch
flaked away years spinning on the turntable
buying/sampling old records by the bunch

that spirit once lifted our country's races
as we now re-invoke that old sweet jazz
these things we read - online in the news
solo in words the old ragtime razzamatazz

rudi on johnny carson (2010)

my grandfather was once on the tonight show
to promote his book on buster keaton
I got special permission to stay up late at school
and there was rudi next to ed mcmahon seatin'

my buddies at the academy were impressed
as rudi retold silent film star buster's history
telling johnny the footage was extremely rare
while they watched rudi spotted a mystery

I told you not to cut the film!
he lectured johnny on the air
then went mum so they cut to a commercial
and when they returned rudi blesh wasn't there

nor at the closing either when all rejoin
he'd left the studio in a huff
so this was television he thought to himself
his standards were just too tough

silent heroes

shown on screen downtown
every week another attraction
see iconic comic movie clowns
unbelievable stunts and action

charlie chaplin harold lloyd buster keaton
often knocked down but never beaten

somehow they speak without a word
and we know just how they're feeling
the next absurd thing that just occurred
and still the plot they're not revealing

charlie chaplin buster keaton harold lloyd
the pantomime sound movies destroyed

folkflorist

anthropologist went native
studying the old wild tribes
nothing in the ethno books
his experience describes

so the folk club was packed
and the critic heard the song
supposed to be impartial
but he loudly sang along

and the writer at the table
listening to his heroic jazz
with his own sax in his chair
playing along like a spazz

an authority's point of view
the intellectual distance joke
maybe if they're really lucky
lonely critics can join the folk

the village

suddenly it was the scene
washington square guitars
for a rock and roll has been
buddy holly or bobby darin
dion's robert johnson thing
but still a little too early man
wait/see what the 60s bring

fred neil was working in the brill building
while paul simon studied with rudi blesh
so carol king dropped out to get married
folk rock was coming it could matter less
fred held down half of old bleecker street
the other half belonged to dave van ronk
trad jazz vs the folkie songwriter rockers
then the world became their honky tonk

grandfather jazz (2009)

though his taste
in sound and art
was the greatest of the hips
and he searched out
and celebrated
all the proud originators
on his jazz and ragtime research trips

his culture was too perfect
too monumentally just his

so right on robert johnson
leadbelly - louis - elvis - bunk
jellyroll morton - bert williams
buster keaton - eubie - joplin
jimi - cream too frantic

unerringly daunting pedantic

commercial music is full of tricks

it thrives on selling
the soul of the land
voice of the people
a child's first song
the cry of the slave
ancient traditions straight
from immigrants lips

rudi called for
a folk music to be free
forever socialist
but because it was right
it could never be

for like the visionary cursed cassandra
everything he touched became eclipsed

radio-jive

all poetry all the time
more power in every line
sells your product its insane
but only from the astral plane
and a cure for the human soul
sure if your thing is rock and roll
ragtime jazz in a horse and buggy
and skiffle behind a boogie woogie
folk music madness call it the blues
about me and you -- all stories true
songs remorse should know better
tune in often keep sending letters

dump radio

the truth is you wouldn't if you knew
can you believe - the garbage we spew
scattered possessions if you don't mind
but from the store our lives were defined
now it is we who must pick it all through
and recycle our future if only you knew
listen to gossip with wisdom entwined
take home anything you might find

melody

this body is an instrument
upon which a musician plays
flesh disappears the player quits
and yet the music somehow stays
where ancestors are respected
in our memories all our days
the song they loved to sing
comes back again always

hit parade

first they killed the music
then they murdered the radio
without the voice of soul
where is a kid to go
to the ego (as an echo)
of our future human pride
metal hurts ringing hollow
(emerging species suicide)

so punky beatnik slackers
endgame always outside tragic
a holding place for the heartbeat
until the airwaves refill with magic
then we reclaim ancient nameless
self unknown secret of existence
from material male death vision
a being reborn in the resistance

come to hear the edgey echoes of
hearts and ourselves as we once are
reverberations of death engines end
once we hitch our wagon to a star
the sound of our own laughter
even before the joke is told
answer is as ever always
moldy oldy solid gold

jazzcritic

champion of the unsung
how could it be any more
ironic you are now among

so for all the things for me
I owe you that you've done
let these words (be just one)

-

epilogue: <u>The Revenge of Zip Coon</u>

Sometime I feel I should apologise for writing about myself, certain habits and the sub-culture I fell into in the 1960s. For years all this was hidden, and today still it's a big secret, even though Jazz, Rock and Roll and our literature are all full of it. Even though it borders on the mainstream on a daily basis in America we still can't mention it's name. Shhhh.....

(Jazz medicine)

Herb is like Trad Hot Jazz - a perennial forbidden fruit. Like the unfiltered Blues, the true story of Ragtime and the real roots of Rock and Roll. Like the secret behind The Beatles and their "jazz cigarettes" (first provided by Bob Dylan) that changed the world.

But please, don't talk about it. For like the vegetarian whose very existence disproves the hunter's necessity, the creative marijuana artist demolishes the whole essence of the drunk tank mentality of the self pity art establishment. Like my father, artist John Hultberg used to tell me, people like Jack Kerouac were fun to be around until they started smoking marijuana. Then they started turning inward, becoming self-reflective, something my father never tried. Who needs introspection when you're always right?

Are you always right? Are the women around you impressed by the guy who is always right? If so, I feel for you. Back in the Black community once affectionately and respectfully known as Negro, the women held great sway, both in the matrifocal families and in the Black church, still the center of the community. What Black women admired in men was nuanced feeling, receptivity, ability with vulnerability... something known as Soul. Even more puzzling than Rag, or Hot (or Cool) Jazz, or Swing, or Boogie Woogie, or Blues... all the concepts White trendsetters worked so hard to adopt, starting in the 1900s with the cool intellect of Bert Williams, even more stupifying than all that hip culture was the essence of <u>Soul</u>. To look at it, to see it, was to find it hard not to understand it. It was hyper-attractive. The essence of sex where women had a good time. The reason the Beatles existed and girls screamed. And in the end Soul had to be exterminated. By Rap.

But back in the 60s when Soul was still a mighty flowering culture phenomenon we did all we could to try to understand its essence. How did the Negro play that guitar? How did they sing? Dance?

317

How did he or she feel? What were his love secrets? Can I admit I also have a weakness, am in awe of women, or that I have the Blues? Can I humble myself to become a better woman or man?

(and what was that stuff the musicians liked to smoke?)

From Ben Harney and Bert Williams on the Bowery. Bessie Smith, Louis Armstrong, Fats Waller, Huddie Ledbetter, Robert Johnson, Josh White, Muddy Waters, Howlin' Wolf, Chuck Berry, Bo Diddley, Jimi Hendrix, Bob Marley... we are intoxicated by the lifeforce in the Black blooded entertainer. And also, by the abilities of certain talented White imitators. No this isn't racism, really. It's a form of reverence, the willingness to alter one's life to be more like another. Some follow Jesus, or Mohammed. Some follow Bert Williams, Louis Armstrong, Bessie Smith, Leadbelly, Robert Johnson, Muddy, Chuck Berry, Jimi, Bob Marley...

The minstrel show was and is our way of evolving, of becoming more like each other. The vaudeville stage, the Jazz bandstand, the Rhythm and Blues, Rock and Roll or underground comedy club are where we learned to be multi-racial, multi-cultural, often from White imitators, but most authentically from mixed race entertainers. We might have come in to mock but we left with the ability to mimic the slang, the slurred beats and notes, and most of all the attitude. Laid back Rastus or the dapper Zip Coon. The Negro mentality as represented by Amos and Andy. Dan Burley's Handbook of Authentic Harlem Jive. Lonnie Donegan, Bill Haley and his Comets, Elvis Presley. The Beatle's honest Soul...
and real tough American R&B as played by the Rolling Stones.

(from Rastus to Rastas)

The Hipster ethos is so internalized by now, kids in Japan grow up emulating Robert Johnson or Jimi Hendrix. Our technology has allowed us to create a common world language in music, based on the minstrel show and a few surviving authentic African artifacts that fled Mississippi after the floods of 1927. This slang, jive language(s) we inherited from multi-racial cowboys, Blues/ Jazz people, from Bert, from Louis, from Chuck, from Jimi, Bob and the Rastas are now all basic forms of Amerian expression.

The medicine bundle of practices we received from those African heritage or Africanized griots, minstrels, Blues and Jazz women and men is basically the same set of life practices we now consider

318

essential to human existence. Music, liquor, dancing, swearing, free love making, race mixing were all considered immoral or were actually illegal not that long ago in America. Of the whole counter-cultural package, only marijuana remains a criminal enterprise, from its cultivation to its consumption.

(harmless - but extremely dangerous)

Because in many ways marijuana is the most persuasively Negro element of all. Sourced from North Africa the weed is a diffuser, a balm for the sick, portal into poetry, blast furnace for the Blues, the plant for trance enducing Sufi dervish derived Trad/Free Jazz improvisations, the matriarchal essence of laidback beatnik hippy rasta spirituality and a window into the world as seen by the holy medicinal female organism. And so also a threat to the entire male dominant world - the alcoholism, egotism, depression, sexism, racism, industrial pollution, warfare...

and weed came from Jazz. Originally from Mexicans, Black cowboys, Blues people, but mostly from the hot but humble players of sweet swinging mixed race <u>Traditional</u> Jazz.

(message from the Mezz: Peace and Love.)

So my apologies to friends and neighbors who still see it as a scourge. For most people and the young it is probably a waste, a squandering of their hard work, time and talents, but for some, a cure-all, and for still others - the artistic, poetic, transcendental and/or otherwise blocked, attention deficit disordered Ragtime Jazz Blues expressionists, it can be one of nature's greatest ritual/ tools for artistic creativity and studied self realization.

As Buddy Holly explained to his mother in 1957: "But Mom, we're all Negroes now!" In this the elemental dance of the opposites, also another part of the irrepressible irony -- the exquisite inevitability of all this strangeness that is America. As in:

1. The man who tried to stop Bop is also the guy who brought you Skiffle, Ragtime and the word about Robert Johnson.

2. The musicians who had you all Foxtrotting after the War also turned your kids on to the Morroccan hashish trance.

Strange but true.

Acknowledgements:

I mention Jim Larkin in the Preface, mostly because like me he's a dump guy. But just as important are quite a few other folks in Danbury, NH. I wouldn't have gotten far with this project without the encouragement and insights offered by local music lovers Tom Curren and Kathy Neustadt. And others, Jim's sons Michael, Ben Larkin, Tom & Judy Brewer, Cal Opitz, Dale & Twyla Cook, the Danbury Community Center and the folks at the South Danbury Church. It was my talk there in February of 2013 that became the radio show Radio Free Ragtime. I should also mention the two stores now in our town, the legendary Dick's store (adjacent to NH's Hippy Hill) and the Danbury Country Store, each unique in their own way. The power of a community.

Also need to acknowledge my mother who probably would rather I'd left all this for someone else to do. But in the absence of that, this and a hope for healing is what I came up with.

Some of the most legendary figures in the Ragtime world have been just wonderful. Terry Waldo, John Edward Hasse, William Bolcom... encouragement along the way. Sure is nice to have a little family pull. Thanks to Max Morath for focusing me on the subject originally in 1998, interviewing me for his article about Rudi in the Mississippi Rag. And for scholarly advice along the way. Donald Ashwander's sister Judy Moore and her daughter Sharon, for their memories and help with important details. The top notch intern staff at the Institute for Jazz Studies at Rutgers, the Boston Public Library, musician/historian Lars Edegran at Jazzology Records in New Orleans and Archeophone Records for their terrific Edison Cylinder transfers and CD compilations.

Friends in NYC, all the members of the New York Greens, gardeners, bicycle activists, recycling volunteers... Bill Weinberg for putting our Ragtime Society collected recorded ethnographic music research on the radio, Charlie Komanoff for working together for bicyclists at Transportation Alternatives, Auto-Free New York. Both for helping me with my writing. Ticia Melvin for being artistic (and supportive). George Bliss and Laraine Goodman - simply inspirational. Pedicabs and Tap Dancing will now always go together. My critical mass...

Many others. Anyone who wrote honestly about my grandfather... thanks for your courage.

Bibliography:

This is Jazz, Rudi Blesh 1943
Shining Trumpets, Rudi Blesh 1946
They All Played Ragtime, Rudi Blesh and Harriet Janis 1950
Modern Art USA, Rudi Blesh 1956
DeKooning, Rudi Blesh and Harriet Janis 1960
Stuart Davis, Rudi Blesh 1960
Collage, Harriet Janis and Rudi Blesh 1962
Keaton, Rudi Blesh 1965
Combo USA, Rudi Blesh 1971

Nobody, Ann Charters

Reminiscing With Sissle and Blake, Robert Kimball / Bill Bolcom

Robert Johnson, Peter Guralnik

This Is Jazz, CD reissues on Jazzology: notes

In Search of the Blues, Mary Beth Hamilton

52nd Street, Arnold Shaw

Jazz Dance, Marshall Stearns

Skiffle, Brian Bird

Man on the Flying Trapese, Simon Louvish

Douglas MacAgy and the Foundations of Modern Art Curatorship,
David Beasley

Baby Let Me Follow You Down, Eric Von Schmidt / Jim Rooney

Bert Williams CDs, on Archeophone Records: notes, various CD/
LP sources, liner notes, radio shows, interview with Rudi done by
John Hasse (1978), stories, conversations remembered, rumors,
hearsay, ideas taken from Max Morath performances...

Photos: Skippy Adelman, Bob Campbell, Harriet/Conrad Janis,
Joan Morris, Rudi, others, me.

Index (does not include appendices):

322